Farther Along

Farther Along

TRANSFORMING DICHOTOMIES IN RHETORIC AND COMPOSITION

Edited by

Kate Ronald
University of Nebraska—Lincoln

and

Hephzibah Roskelly
University of North Carolina—Greensboro

BOYNTON/COOK PUBLISHERS
HEINEMANN
PORTSMOUTH, N.H.

Boynton/Cook Publishers
A Division of
Heinemann Educational Books, Inc.
70 Court Street, Portsmouth, NH 03801
Offices and agents throughout the world

We wish to thank the following for permission to reprint previously published material:

Pages 64–65: From *Late Night Thoughts While Listening to Mahler's Ninth Symphony* by Lewis Thomas. Copyright © 1980, 1981, 1982, 1983 by Lewis Thomas. All rights reserved. Reprinted by permission of Viking Penguin, a division of Penguin Books USA, Inc.

Library of Congress Cataloging-in-Publication Data

Farther along : transforming dichotomies in rhetoric and composition /
   edited by Kate Ronald and Hephzibah Roskelly.
      p. cm.
Bibliography: p.
ISBN 0-86709-249-1
1. English language—Rhetoric—Study and teaching. 2. Rhetoric.
I. Ronald, Kate. II. Roskelly, Hephzibah.
PE1404.F37   1990
808'.042'07—dc20   89-15440
                                           CIP

Designed by Vic Schwarz
Printed in the United States of America
90 91 92 93 94   9 8 7 6 5 4 3 2 1

To Our Mothers

Margaret Walsh Ronald
Hephzibah Perkins Crawford

Contents

Preface   ix

Introduction
You're Either on the Bus . . . Or off the Bus   1

One
Killer Dichotomies: Reading In/Reading Out   12
ANN E. BERTHOFF

Two
Personal and Public Authority in Discourse: Beyond
    Subjective/Objective Dichotomies   25
KATE RONALD

Three
The Convergence of Dichotomies in the Personal Journal   40
KEN AUTREY

Four
The Literacies of Science and Humanities: The Monologic
    and Dialogic Traditions   52
JOSEPH J. COMPRONE

Five
Professional Writing Meets Rhetoric and Composition   71
JOHN BRERETON

Six
Concepts of Culture: Cultural Literacy/Cultural Politics   86
KATHRYN T. FLANNERY

Seven
Between the Trenches and the Ivory Towers:
   Divisions Between University Professors and High
   School Teachers   101
JOY RITCHIE

Eight
Tenure, Status, and the Teaching of Writing   122
WANDA MARTIN

Nine
A Marriage of Convenience: Reading and Writing in School   137
HEPHZIBAH ROSKELLY

Ten
Content(ious) Forms: Trope and the Study of Composition   149
PHILLIP K. ARRINGTON

Eleven
Rewriting Composition as a Postmodern Discipline:
   Transforming the Research/Teaching Dichotomy   168
JAMES THOMAS ZEBROSKI

Twelve
The Demons of Old and New Rhetoric   183
DOROTHY C. BROADDUS

Bibliography of Works That Transform Dichotomies   197

Notes on Contributors   207

Preface

This collection began on a two-lane highway in southern Indiana. The two of us were on our way to say goodbye to a friend from graduate school, who was headed west for a job in composition. We had been home visiting in Louisville, Kentucky, having left there several years before for composition jobs that took us in opposite directions. We were a little nostalgic and more than a little frustrated as we drove along, remembering how much easier it had seemed to grapple with problems in our teaching and writing as graduate students, where we talked them over with one another around a table in the basement of the Humanities building. Like in the kids' car game of counting silos, we began to count up the ways we felt isolated as compositionists, and those ways turned into a group of what Ann Berthoff calls "killer dichotomies" in this profession.

By the time we hit Santa Claus, Indiana, we had a list of about twenty killers, those dichotomies that keep teachers at odds with researchers, reading isolated from writing, form from content, and theory from practice, to cite just a few examples. We also had an idea: to find ways around and through those dichotomies by confronting them, and perhaps transforming them into something useful. We decided to invite a group of our colleagues, some of whom had talked around that basement table years before, to participate in the project by writing about mediating principles that could put dichotomies into relationship rather than into battle. Thinking in thirds, as C. S. Peirce taught us to, became our speculative instrument, our way of transcending the either/or mentality that kept us isolated and frustrated. And it became our way to reestablish community, gathering around a metaphorical table—this book—to talk and listen, to influence and be influenced, to speculate and move a little farther along in our thinking about our thinking.

Many of the people who have encouraged us to move beyond dichotomies are cited in the bibliographies and notes to the essays that follow. But we'd like to thank several "triadic" thinkers who've directly contributed to this book. Bob Boynton gave wise advice, sound editing, and most importantly, an unwavering sense of humor to the project. He never let us forget we were having fun. Joe Comprone began our thinking in thirds by challenging us in our courses and our dissertations always to think of theory and practice together. Ann Berthoff has been both example and counselor throughout the process of creating this collection. We are grateful for her work, which illustrates how productive opposition can become when opposing forces are placed in dialectic rather than hierarchy. We are even more grateful for her friendship, which has enspirited our professional lives and enriched our personal ones.

Farther Along

INTRODUCTION

"You're Either on the Bus . . . Or off the Bus"

KATE RONALD • HEPHZIBAH ROSKELLY

> "There are going to be times," says Kesey, "when we can't wait for somebody. Now, you're either on the bus or off the bus. If you're on the bus, and you get left behind, then you'll find it again. If you're off the bus in the first place—then it won't make a damn."
> —Tom Wolfe
> *Electric Kool-Aid Acid Test*

As Tom Wolfe describes them, Ken Kesey's sixties band of Merry Pranksters believed they could identify every person or group according to predictable, unassailable categories. Everyone else not literally along on the cross-country adventure was labeled "not on the bus," but soon the bus became a metaphor for maintaining membership and position within the group itself. The labeling was rigid and simple: "Nobody had to have it spelled out for them. Everything was becoming allegorical, understood by the group mind, and especially this: you're either on the bus . . . or off the bus" (74). Like the Merry Pranksters, the "group mind" of rhetoric and composition began in the early sixties as a reaction against everyone who was not participating in the new adventure of composition studies. And like the Pranksters, who ended up competing within their group for status and "being at the center" of the group mind, composition continues to define itself by sep-

1

arating its work into competing identities and categories of opposition.

Some of the most influential books and articles of the mid-1980s have been those that attempt to organize the research in composition over the last twenty-five years into categories based on methodology, epistemology, or sphere of influence. The desire to categorize is understandable in a profession whose knowledge is proliferating at such a tremendous rate. Categories seem to organize and make sense of the confusing, often contradictory theories about what happens as writers compose. But categories tend to harden, to become exclusionary rather than revisionary. This collection of essays shows how ways of seeing can become ways of not seeing, and it argues that the categories composition has embraced as it seeks to understand itself may have become more divisive than useful.

Patricia Bizzell's division of writing theory into "inner-directed" and "outer-directed" views of learning was among the first attempts to classify approaches to writing theory and practice. Inner-directed theorists, she says, explore only what happens within individual writers' minds, while outer-directed theorists look at the contexts in which writers compose. Bizzell argues that "both . . . theoretical schools will have to contribute to a synthesis capable of providing a comprehensive new agenda for composition studies" (234–235). But her clear either/or scheme invited compositionists to place themselves, their students, and the theorists they read on one side or the other. Four years later, in "Competing Theories of Process," Lester Faigley designed a taxonomy to classify theories of the composing process according to their cognitive, social, or expressive emphasis. Despite his insistence that the "competing theories" must be synthesized into a "broader conception of writing, one that understands writing processes are historically dynamic" (537), his categories, like Bizzell's, easily translated into rigid stances and exclusive loyalties. James Berlin's taxonomies have been perhaps the most influential of these attempts at categorization. In *Writing Instruction in Nineteenth-Century American Colleges*, Berlin divides rhetorical pedagogy into classical, romantic, and epistemic systems, basing his categories on the relationship of the "knower" to the "known" and the role of language within that framework. Berlin sees these categories as "closed systems," historically determined and mutually exclusive. Through time, romantic rhetoric replaced the classical world view, and epistemic rhetoric subsumed romantic rhetorical approaches. In *Rhetoric and Reality*, Berlin refines this classification system by expanding it and changing the terms to make twentieth-century rhetorical theory fit into objective, subjective, and transactional categories. Unlike Berlin's nineteenth-century categories, these groups exist simultaneously but compete with one another for dominance. Most recently, Berlin's "Rhetoric and Ideology in the Writing Class" translates theoretical categories into current composition practice according to pedagogical emphasis on ideology as cognitive, expressionist, or social-epistemic. In this article, Berlin admits that these categories are slippery: "it should be noted that ideology is always pluralistic, a given historical moment displaying a variety of competing ideologies and a given individual reflecting one or another permutation of these conflicts . . . " (479). But he does not seem to realize that the very attempt to categorize in the first place undermines the concept of "pluralistic ideology." Nor does he seem to recognize the danger inherent when a profusion of slippery theoretical categories can too easily become rigid labels.

Stephen North does appear to understand the harm that comes from dividing a profession into competing ideologies. His taxonomy of the profession in *The Making of Knowledge in Composition*, which divides compositionists according to their methodologies, ends with a warning that "Composition-as-field has pulled itself apart with the majority Practitioners at the bottom of a hierarchy governed by an increasingly divisive minority of Scholars and Researchers" (370). North predicts that composition will remain trapped on the fringes of English studies unless the field can create "the grounds for an inter-methodological coherence," which would bring together these competing camps. Yet North's detailed overview finally falls into exactly the trap it warns against: the very act of labeling solidifies rather than dissolves the separations it explores.

All these taxonomies are useful insofar as they organize the impressive amount of writing that's been done in the years since composition has become Composition, as North has characterized the profession's growth. However, we want to argue that this impulse to categorize reveals the either/or mentality that has defined the field since its renaissance in the 1960s. We don't assume that people like Faigley and Berlin deliberately set out to pigeonhole their readership; their overviews clearly were intended to organize and assess varying perspectives on the work we all share. But once these perspectives are named, they tend to evolve into positions that require defending or attacking. Theorists situated in one category or another could easily fall into other categories as well. Does Emerson belong in Berlin's romantic category or the epistemic? Is Berthoff a Philosopher or is she a Practitioner? Arguments could be advanced on either side, of course, but the point is that taxonomies don't permit argument, aren't designed for dialectic, despite assurances from all the taxonomists about the flexibility of the categories or their interdependence. Just as restrictive and more destructive to dialectic is the way taxonomies create hierarchies as they position methods and theories. Any hierarchy invites, maybe even necessitates, a power struggle.

Composition began its own power struggle by vigorously attacking worn-out, product-centered instruction in writing with new process approaches. Perhaps it is because of that contentious beginning that it continues to identify itself in terms of opposing loyalties. Small stories illustrate. At a job interview this year, a candidate from Carnegie-Mellon complains that when people see her convention badge at national conferences, they say (some with glee and others accusingly), "Oh, you're from Carnegie-Mellon: you're a cognitivist." People who identify her this way feel that they know her work and can predict her perspectives on research and teaching; the category gives them a way to assign her to a particular group with a particular worldview. In graduate school, Kate was told by a professor of American literature that, being a composition specialist, obviously she "wouldn't like literature." His remark captures a philosophy of teaching that separates reading from writing, and assigns status to teachers of those subjects. While she was student teaching, Hephzibah's principal walked into her eleventh-grade classroom during group work to observe, then excused himself saying, "I'll come back when you're teaching." The principal's comment reveals the pervasive division between teaching and learning that centralizes authority to promote "objective" standards. All of these vignettes symbolize the either/or mentality that permeates work in composition and literary studies. For many professionals in English, you're either on the bus . . . or you're off the bus.

"If Composition is working its way toward becoming a discipline, it is taking the long way around," North says (324). Composition is struggling in its attempt to make knowledge, and for North, it's the constricted, unequal relationship between Composition and its much more powerful partner, literary studies, that is at the heart of much of the problem. The growing tendency among composition professionals to fragment themselves into isolated methodological fields is in part a reaction to their suspicion that to become a "knowledge-making field" in the existing system, they must take their cue from literary studies, whose knowledge is made apart from teaching and without demands for "practical" results. The dichotomies that result from the categorization of composition's work limit both teaching and scholarship. Defining itself in reaction to a position or in defense of one, composition is not able to create a philosophical system. Although the profession has always been defensive about this lack, it is the insistence on opposition that prevents philosophy from developing. Categories are useful and necessary, as philosophers since Plato have recognized, for separation helps define concepts and creates territories to explore. But this collection of essays suggests that division, embedded in and created by the taxonomy, has failed as a heuristic for productive work in the theory and teaching of writing. Composition's self-definition, created in reaction to a New Critical literary model dominant in English departments until the early sixties, has not progressed beyond its reactive mode very effectively, and compositionists, having finally achieved hard-won status in English departments, often find themselves aboard the same bus they were throwing rocks at twenty-five years ago.

The signs of this entrenchment in polarity are obvious in scholarship, teaching, presentations at national conferences. When James Britton wrote *Language and Learning* eighteen years ago, expressive writing became a teaching strategy and a theoretical position for scores of composition professionals. Look at articles in issues of *College English* and *CCC* a decade ago and you'll see Britton's work cited, discussed, implemented in issue after issue. But the reactive mode took hold quickly. In a growing passion for credibility and political respectability in departments, composition embraced the trappings of the scientific method, and expressive discourse gave way to discussions of assessment; T-units and computer metaphors replaced conversations about the role of the imagination in composing. Now, in a kind of uneasy negotiation with provocative work in literary study and sociology, work in composition increasingly is dominated by descriptions of the social and cultural influences on individual thought. The conference buzz words of "process" and "personal knowledge" have been replaced by "social constructionism" and "dialogism." But whatever the terms, compositionists remain stuck in the same arguments that keep them from seeing imagination and science, personal and social views, subjectivity and objectivity in relationship rather than in battle. And so they feel compelled to deny Britton in order to embrace Bakhtin.

Any division of theories and methods, in our view, is primarily useful to philosophy for its ability to initiate dialectic, which is defined not primarily by the oppositions it provokes but by the relationships it uncovers. Unlike traditional argument, dialectic insists on a search for the underlying principle that makes the conversation between two ideas possible and dynamic. Unfortunately, some theorists have seen dialectic as either conflict or compromise, mistakenly linked with classical and Rogerian argument, where competing sides do win or cede power in order to dominate or agree. But dialectic involves what Plato called a "search in common" for new positions, a search that includes more than defending or abandoning present ones. In defining novelistic discourse, Mikhail Bakhtin explains this sort of dialectic: "In almost every utterance there is an intense interaction and struggle between one's own and another's word. In this process they oppose or interanimate one another" (346). For Bakhtin, as for I. A. Richards, interanimation results in interpretive power; it is a process that moves beyond opposition toward a consciousness of the double-voicedness of opposing words. Like metaphor, dialectic works when tenor and vehicle—two unlike, or opposing, elements—are brought into relationship through a third factor that acknowledges division and combination in the service of new thought.

A hundred years ago, C. S. Peirce set the terms for a philosophical system based on this kind of recognition of how to move beyond action and reaction. For Peirce, ideas are all essentially three-pronged, and philosophy develops most effectively when all three—action, reaction, principle—are brought to bear on systems of inquiry. His new term, "thirdness," is no compromise doctrine, no détente that calms opposing sides by offering each a bit of power and a bit of compromise. Peirce does not seek to mix opposing ideas but to expose deeper ideas embedded in division. "The third," he says, "does not so much demand that special ideas shall surrender their particular arbitrariness and caprice entirely. It only requires that each shall influence and be influenced by one another" (*Chance*, 237). His work explores the relationships that allow individual and social, science and art, word and meaning to transcend their either/or distinctions as philosophers in any field become conscious of the reasons for division and combat. Peirce's recognition of the power that results from collaboration between apparently opposing ideas can help teachers and scholars see how composition is kept in a trap of conflict by dichotomies that are never transcended.

The metaphors of war, of winning and losing, of domination and control, permeate the taxonomies we described earlier, as well as the theories debated in journals and at conferences. The advocates of cultural literacy fight illiteracy with weapons that look like lists. The social constructionists define a battleground between dispossessed and privileged cultures. One of the reasons that the issue of how and why to teach grammar will not disappear in conversations about the teaching of English at all levels is that teachers have not moved beyond the form/content split to find the relationship of grammar to meaning. You either teach standards or you don't. English departments hire, assign course loads, grant tenure and promotion according to the admitted conflict between teaching and research. A hierarchical power struggle, arising from rigid categorization, lies at the center of each of these dyadic conflicts. Either power is seized, with inevitable violence done to the lesser force that has power stripped or power is granted, with the inevitable condescension that accompanies the act. Thinking in dichotomies, or what Peirce would call "seconds," forces composition into just such positions of attack and defense. These battles not only keep the conflicting sides separate; they keep individuals defensive and frustrated in attempts to think about their thinking and define their work in integrated rather than fragmented ways.

This collection attempts to move beyond the battles between concepts in composition by looking beneath the surface of apparently conflicting ideas to discover oppositions transformed—not merely synthesized—into new conceptions. Each author in this book addresses specific forms that dichotomous thinking takes in the profession and searches for ways around or through these oppositions toward a concept of "thirdness" that might transcend the limitations of any one perspective. One overarching opposition that permeates every one of these essays is the dichotomy between personal ways of knowing and impersonal knowledge, between subjective and objective views, between the individual and the community. This powerful separation confronts each author as he or she strives for the transcendent, "third" idea which will put self and other in negotiation rather than in conflict.

Another dichotomy, perhaps at once deeper and more obvious, is the division between male and female ways of knowing, a division implicitly operating in almost every essay here. The issue of gender is a difficult one to discuss, in part because there is so much disagreement among feminist scholars about whether or not a division between male and female *ought* to be transcended. There is no chapter in *Farther Along* that specifically addresses the dichotomy between men and women in English classrooms and departments, or between masculine and feminine epistemologies. The entire collection suggests that to argue for multiple perspectives is to argue for feminist agendas in composition research and teaching. Patrocino Schweickart describes feminist theories of reading this way: "the problematic is defined by the drive 'to connect' rather than that which is implicit in the mainstream preoccupation with partition and control" (55). That same impulse drives this collection. The politics of departments need to change, the approaches to pedagogy need to change, and perspectives on scholarship need to change to accommodate voices that have been muted by academic chauvinism. Those voices are of course not limited to women. We saw a chapter on male/female dichotomies as somehow reductive and potentially dangerous, especially in a collection seeking to get beyond the dichotomies that keep compositionists isolated as individuals and as a profession. The role of gender in writing instruction is far too large an issue to confront in any one essay, though it informs many of the essays in this collection. The essay on tenured and part-time instruction, for example, exposes the sexual politics in institutional decisions; the essay on high school and college teaching, and the one on science and humanities discourse, discuss philosophical issues that converge with feminist perspectives on knowledge and teaching. The essays on public and private writing also compel readers to consider the implications of gender for granting authority to kinds of discourse. We invite readers to see the transformation of the male/female dichotomy in the premise of each essay in *Farther Along*.

The collection begins with Ann Berthoff on "Killer Dichotomies." Berthoff argues, first, that dichotomizing is a conscious act of mind, not a natural phenomenon. She insists that other acts of mind—what she calls a "triadic semiotics"—must replace thinking in dichotomies. Berthoff replaces "reading in" and "reading out" with the act of "identification," in Burke's sense of the term, where the writer or reader comes to realize that she is both a part of and separate from the text she creates. For Berthoff, that activity represents composing, a reclaiming of the imagination.

The next two essays deal explicitly with one of the killer dichotomies Berthoff wants to slay. Kate Ronald's "Personal and Public Authority in Discourse" argues that composition has deliberately privileged objectivity, both in professional scholarship and student writing. She shows how a dialectic of personal and public discourse can change concepts of "authority" or "power" in writing. Ken Autrey examines a type of writing seen as exclusively personal—the journal—and finds a "convergence" of private and public language. He argues for seeing the journal in the writing class as a way to help students and teachers realize the necessary tension between individual and communal voices.

One of the most obvious dichotomies in composition courses is the division of writing into disciplinary categories. The next two essays discuss the separation of professional writing and scientific writing from writing in the humanities. Joseph Comprone argues in "The Literacies of Science and Humanities" that monologic views of literacy (where one kind of reading and writing is taught to the "masses" and another to the "elite") must be replaced with dialogic views of reading and writing, no matter what the context.

John Brereton sees the gap between professional writing and composition as deriving in part from their shared history as low-status subjects in English departments. He suggests that professional writing and composition can learn from one another and locates "some of the most exciting thinking about prose" in the intersection of these disciplines.

Both Brereton and Comprone acknowledge the political contexts in which these divisions occur. The next group of writers directly confronts political issues in composition scholarship and teaching. Kathryn Flannery offers a cultural materialist's critique of cultural literacy. Using the work of recent ethnographies of literacy, she suggests that you "cannot develop new enabling competencies without cultural change." Joy Ritchie addresses one of the most long-standing and politically charged divisions in composition, the tendency for college and high school teachers to blame one another for the failures in their classrooms. And Wanda Martin argues that the tenured/untenured organization of English departments is symptomatic of a larger theoretical division between the creation and the consumption of discourse. All three of these writers explore some of the most tangled divisions embedded in the assumptions about the work of composition and rhetoric. They each offer new definitions of what it means to be literate and to teach literacy.

Hephzibah Roskelly also examines assumptions about literacy as she investigates the dichotomy between reading and writing texts, a division resulting from internal versus external thinking. She argues that the link between reading and writing in schools is spurious and convenient, and she advocates a new view of literacy as imaginative interpretation of one's own and others' texts. Phillip Arrington takes on the traditional split between form and content in "Content(ious) Forms." He uses the study of tropes to make the link between what one knows and how one knows it, in both professional discourse and student writing.

James Zebroski and Dorothy Broaddus bring this collection full circle, back to collapsing divisions between objectivity and subjectivity. In "Rewriting Composition as a Postmodern Discipline," Zebroski challenges the academic community to see these two roles as interdependent; only when teachers invite their students to join them in research, and only when researchers connect their work to their teaching, will anything like progress be made. His essay argues that "the action is where one of the pair changes into the other or into something else entirely." Like Zebroski's, Broaddus's essay collapses distinctions between personal reading and writing and impersonal scholarship. Her "demons of old and new rhetoric" are very much her own, but she encourages readers to examine their own "demons" as they continue to read, write, and teach in worlds that operate along oppositional lines.

Tom Wolfe, the reporter who exposed the either/or mentality of the Merry Pranksters, challenged that perspective recently in an interview with the *Boston Globe:*

> I grew up thinking I had a self inside my skull like a brass crucible. And you could do anything to me, put me through the worst sort of ordeal—but you could never get at my self. I really think the self *is* our ties to other people. (And of course for a writer that's a terrible thing to think) (51).

Wolfe has learned that self and other aren't either/or distinctions; you're not either on the bus or off it; you get at self through others. Twenty years after the Pranksters parked the bus, Wolfe finds a way to escape the dichotomy of personal and social by recognizing that an insistence on defining perspectives according to unassailable categories can be worse than unproductive. "We blew it," the Pranksters lament at the close of the novel. This collection—this conversation—tries to answer the warnings of North and others with a call for negotiation. Peirce says that people are not "whole" as long as they are "single." They are only "possible members of society." He reminds each writer, reader, and teacher that "it is not my experience but our experience that has to be thought of; and this 'us' has definite possibilities" (*Selected Writings*, xx). Only through recognition of common cause and common possibility can we transform the oppositions that separate and limit our work. Then we can get farther along.

Works Cited

Bakhtin, Mikhail. *The Dialogic Imagination*. Austin: U of Texas P, 1981.
Berlin, James. *Writing Instruction in Nineteenth-Century American Colleges*. Carbondale: Southern Illinois UP, 1984.
———. *Rhetoric and Reality: Writing Instruction in American Colleges, 1900–1985*. Carbondale: Southern Illinois UP, 1987.
———. "Rhetoric and Ideology in the Writing Class." *College English* 5 (1988): 477–95.
Bizzell, Patricia. "Cognition, Convention, and Certainty: What We Need to Know About Writing." *Pre/Text* 3 (1982): 213–43.
Faigley, Lester. "Competing Theories of Process: A Critique and a Proposal." *College English* 6 (1986): 527–41.

North, Stephen. *The Making of Knowledge in Composition: Portrait of an Emerging Field*. Portsmouth, NH: Boynton/Cook, 1986.

Peirce, Charles Sanders. *Chance, Love, and Logic*. Ed. Morris Cohen. New York: Barnes and Noble, 1923. Rpt. Harcourt Brace, 1968.

———. *Selected Writings*. Ed. Philip P. Wiener. New York: Dover, 1966.

Schweickart, Patrocino P. "Reading Ourselves: Toward a Feminist Theory of Reading." *Gender and Reading*. Eds. Elizabeth A. Flynn and Patrocino P. Schweickart. Baltimore: Johns Hopkins, 1986. 31–63.

Wolfe, Tom. *Electric Kool-Aid Acid Test*. New York: Bantam, 1969.

———. "Vanities and the Novel." *Boston Globe*. 13 Nov. 1987: 51–52.

ONE

Killer Dichotomies
Reading In/Reading Out

ANN E. BERTHOFF

In the *Phaedrus*, Socrates makes the following declaration:

> I am myself a great lover of these processes of division and
> generalization; they help me to speak and think. And if I find
> any man who is able to see a One and Many in Nature, him
> I follow, and walk in his footsteps as if he were a god. And
> those who have this art, I have hitherto been in the habit of
> calling dialecticians; but God knows whether the name is right
> or not (265).

In this, Benjamin Jowett's, translation Socrates sounds a bit like
E. M. Forster defining the novel: "Oh dear, yes I suppose we do
have to concern ourselves with the character of dialectic, though I
certainly don't think that defining it will get us very far!" But
Socrates needn't have worried; if you'll remember, it was the definition of rhetoric that really exercised the philosophers that
afternoon.

On those occasions when dialectic has been praised and hon-
ored, it becomes synonymous with system and rationality itself.
But of course so fundamental a skill is easily corrupted, with the
result that *dialectic* is just as ambiguous a term as *rhetoric* and has
developed just as questionable a reputation. Logic-choppers and
question-beggers are skillful dialecticians; the dialectical skill of
dividing, for which lawyers and theologians are celebrated, is called

casuistry, and it is generally not held in high regard. Mark Twain speaks of casuistry as "the Spiral Twist" and then tells us:

> That is a technicality—that phrase. I got it off an uncle of mine. He had once studied in a theological cemetery, he said, and he called the Department of Biblical Exegesis the Spiral Twist for short. He said it was always difficult to drive a straight text through an unaccommodating cork, but that if you twisted it it would go. He had kept bar in his less poetical days.

Casuistry is, nevertheless, socially and morally useful. Martin Luther King, Jr. broke the law in Birmingham, and he called the subsequent turmoil not "civil disorder" but "creative tension." His casuistry was subversive of hypocrisy in the style of a famous answer: "Render therefore unto Caesar the things which be Caesar's and unto God the things which be God's."

Casuistry—the art of stretching words and manipulating categories—is one servant of dialectic; dichotomy is another. A dichotomy is a pair of mutually exclusive categories; it divides by cutting. Susanne K. Langer explains the function of dichotomy this way: "Whenever we form a class within any universe of discourse, then every individual in that universe must either belong to the class or not belong to it." Classifying, that is to say, entails differentiating A and Not-A, but that is not to make a claim about the character of reality. It is not because they are two-valued that dichotomies are dangerous; it is because the categories they establish can so easily be confused with reality. That point completely escaped the General Semanticists who, in their railing against Aristotelian logic, never understood the function of dichotomy. Korzybski and his followers tirelessly explained that words are not the things they stand for. Indeed, their conception of language as a map for the territory of reality required this insistence, for if you claim that the only role of language is to correspond to reality and if you know there are no dichotomies in reality, then you will find no justification, theoretically, for dichotomies in language. However, dichotomy is not a linguistic but a logical concept: many linguists and many semioticians confuse language and logic. What we need to remember is that dichotomies can forestall critical analysis if they are taken to correspond in a point-to-point way with the real world. If their logical function is misconceived, they become Killer Dichotomies, hazardous to both our theory and practice as writing teachers.

There are no dichotomies in reality: dichotomizing is an act of mind, not of Nature. We may say "as different as night and day" and know what we mean, but that dichotomy is tenuous in the real world, as I discovered afresh a few years ago in traveling first to Kenya and then to Scotland. Out on the great plains of Africa, I suddenly understood what Kipling meant when he wrote "And the dawn comes up like thunder." But that is not to say that there is a single point in real time at which even equatorial Africans can cry, "It's day!" And in the Hebrides, ten degrees below the Arctic Circle, it is folly to try to fix nightfall in June; you just begin to find that it's become a little hard to read around 11:00 P.M. But what about sea and land? Surely one is really, actually wet and the other is really, actually dry. Well yes, wet and dry constitute a dichotomy and so do sea and land, as abstract—or mythical—categories, but where does one end and the other begin, at the shore? There is no line in nature that establishes that difference. The fact is, rather, that land and sea constitute a dialectic, which is now happily called The Coastal Zone. (The fact that it can aid in understanding interdependencies like sea and land is precisely what makes the new field of ecology so useful to composition teachers as a source of metaphors.) In the British Isles, which have quite a lot of coast line, there is an intricate dichotomy—a trichotomy, really—that legally establishes ownership: that which lies between low-water mark and high tide belongs to the monarch (a beached whale is a Royal fish, as Melville says); whatever has lodged above high tide belongs to the property owner, to the laird; and whatever is in the sea belongs to whoever can catch it, within whatever limit has been set to protect local fishermen. All these lines are inventions, averaged out from local data. The twenty-mile limit is not a line in the ocean; it's on the charts, measured from some arbitrarily designated point on shore. I have watched a little boy in a Hebridean harbor, harvesting the Queen's own winkles without a care, but in other times, that would have been a criminal act. Often, the relationship of dichotomies to reality becomes a matter for the courts to decide. That is why good lawyers must be good casuists.

But casuistry alone is not enough, nor is dichotomy, when we want to form concepts. To say that that particular animal over there is a warthog is simultaneously to identify it as not a not-warthog. But note what happens when we move from such a formal classification to definition. A warthog is a warthog is a warthog because it is not a bongo, not a waterbuck, not an impala, etc. Whether or not a whale is a fish depends on our taxonomy: we must develop rather subtler criteria for definition because we are not just implicitly classifying but are forming a concept—and that is a dialectical act. Concept formation takes us way beyond dichotomy.

Criteria for definition are developed not by asking "Is it X or is it not?" but by asking "What does it mean to say that thus and so is X rather than Y?" And not asking it once but continually: that is why I. A. Richards called dialectic "the *continuing* audit of meaning." We can't carry out that audit just by naming. The real danger of jargon is not that we are inundated by hideous new words—though we are and they are—but that specialized language is often deployed to mask the problematic, to reify the tenuous and abstract, to override the ambiguities that should, rather, serve as "the hinges of thought." By the same token, dichotomies such as binary opposition can be useful, precisely because they do not allow for ambiguity. But binary oppositions—dashes and dots, the 0/1 of computer language, the botanist's key, semaphore flags—all these either/or's are elements of signal codes: they can in no way help us interpret the messages they signal. The radical confusion of signal and message is so widespread, so befuddling, that I want to consider this Killer Conflation before turning to the Killer Dichotomies.

What's between the encoder and the decoder in Jakobson's famous wiring diagram of "the communication situation" is labeled *message*, but that is an error. The message is encoded, but what is sent, what the decoder receives, is a signal. Here is Richards' comment:

> Messages are generated by Contexts; they are conveyed by signals. Messages are living. They are animated instances of meaning, determinations from the context field; the signals which convey them are dead. . . . It is essential to a Message that what forms in the Addressee (or other recipient) should be of the same order of being with what has formed in the Addresser. He may get it wrong (and often does) but there is an IT. The two apparitions are both meanings. But a sound track and a system of meanings are not things of a sort, able to agree or disagree. The distinction between Message and signal . . . is indeed a *pons asinorum* in linguistics.

The Killer Conflation of message and signal is really only a variant of the perennial confusion of "information" as it's used in information theory and what it means, say, to dial "Information." As a term in cybernetics, *information* has nothing to do with wanting, getting, reporting, or relaying facts; it means "absence of noise in the channel"—both "noise" and "channel" having special meanings. As Max Black puts it, in information theory it is irrelevant whether the message is "Max Black is white" or "Max White is black." Given the fundamental ambiguity of the term *information*, how many researchers know what they're talking about when they talk about "human information processing"?

The view of language modeled by information theory is precisely that of meaning as a dyadic relationship, as in the Saussurian signifier and signified. The dyadic conception of the sign—which is of course what we have in all versions of structuralism, including most so-called post-structuralist critical theory—encourages the proliferation of killer dichotomies. I believe that until and unless we base our pedagogy on a triadic semiotics, all dichotomies will be hazardous and we will find ourselves defenseless against divisions like critical/creative, subjective/objective, cognitive/affective, and reading in/reading out. I want to focus on this last-named dichotomy and to consider how triadicity can slay it.

We don't want our students to "read in," we say, meaning we don't want them to disregard "the words on the page," to relate to the poem or the novel or the essay only in their own terms. Of all the misconceptions Richards identified and cataloged in *Practical Criticism*, his analysis of the responses recorded in his experiment, the one we all find the most tiresome is "mnemonic irrelevance." We don't want our students to tell us what it makes them think of until they have figured out what it says: we want them to read out before they read in.

I mean this "we" to refer to those who are the legatees of a debased New Criticism, but it may be that this population is in rapid decline. It may be that a new majority of teachers subscribe to the idea that neither author nor text can be determined; that a pervasive "indeterminacy" makes it impossible to establish any reading, but since all reading is misreading, establishing any reading is no longer a priority. There have been some comic moments in this new era; one, especially, is instructive.

A British motor car company recently advertised its product with a soft-focus photograph of the front seat, on which was superimposed the text of the second stanza of Marvell's "The Garden," which opens thus:

> Fair quiet, have I found thee here,
> And Innocence, thy Sister dear!

The poem ends with a reference to "this delicious Solitude." There were some changes in the ad. The opening lines went like this:

> Fair quiet have I found thee here
> And comfort, thy companion dear?

And it closed with a salutation to "this luxurious solitude." A lady in New Jersey wrote to say there'd been a mistake, but some scholars were unperturbed. Professor Geoffrey Hartman thought it was not a "very grave infringement of morality." The comment of the scholar who heads something called The Society for Textual Scholarship included the following:

> [Reception theory, he tells us, holds that] authorial intention has no particular precedence. It is just one interpretation of many. . . . Many famous texts have been changed in the transmission in order to give more meaning to the original lines.

Intention is conflated with interpretation and both are taken to mean the text, in the old-fashioned sense of "the words on the page." This scholar has confused the two senses of "text"; he then goes on to confuse a manipulation with "transmission" errors and editings. There is no evidence that Marvell wrote *luxurious* rather than *delicious*. If I had had this statement on an exam, together with the faulty text, I would have noted that the student had badly confused "The Garden" and "The Mower Against Gardens." There is plenty of evidence (from the rest of the poem) that Marvell did not "intend" *luxurious*, which did not refer to leather seats in the Renaissance. This is not a variant text, not a variant reading; it is not even a misreading, in the usual meaning of that term: it is a deliberate mangling, what we expect in parody.[1]

The ad itself is not worth our time; the comment of the textual scholar is emblematic of the perverse practices that now pass for critical theory. If interpretation is taken to mean changing the words of the text to fit our needs, whether commercial or sentimental, as in Nahum Tate's version of *King Lear;* if interpretation legitimizes constructions with neither authority nor argument, then *reading in* is all there is. There will be no warrant for establishing one text rather than another, much less for determining an appropriate reading of it.

This is not the place to argue the case, but let me simply state it: many English teachers are in thrall to critical theories that are not only wrongheaded and perverse but also are almost entirely irrelevant to the concerns we should have about illiteracy in the United States. This is not xenophobia, as J. Hillis Miller seems to call any attempt to point out that European intellectual crises, and what they have spawned, are not necessarily pertinent to our academic concerns. "Semioclasm" (the denial and destruction of the very idea of signification, an idea sponsored by Barthes) has risen from a peculiar set of circumstances, including the tardy recognition of the gulag and the consequent collapse of Marxist critical positions, which needed thus to be supplanted. If we are to counter the know-nothing academics who are so successful in peddling the pedagogy of exhortation—I mean Diane Ravitch, William Bennett, Allan Bloom, E. D. Hirsch, Jr., inter alios—we find no aid or comfort in the works of Derrida or de Man or Foucault.

The attitudes I have been excoriating are mirror images of one another: a mouldy faux-New Criticism and a faddish deconstruction are antithetical versions of a single attitude, which is an incapacity to tolerate mediation. If we don't want our students to read in, *or* if we believe that that is all they can do; if we believe that there is only one appropriate reading, *or* if we believe that there is nothing but misreading; if we believe that we always know what's the right reading, *or* if we believe that some specious "interpretive community" will decide if it's all right to print "luxurious solitude"—in either case, we teachers have lost a conception of reading as the making of meaning and of meaning as subject to interpretations, which *must* be subject to interpretation as part of the semiotic process.

If we are to reclaim reading as a matter of interpretation, we will have to convert the killer dichotomy of reading in/reading out to a dialectical opposition. That enterprise will require of us the following:

1. We will have to be able to account *for* meaning in order to give an account *of* meanings.
2. We will need to conceive of interpretation in logical, not psychological, terms.
3. We will need to know how to relate construing and constructing.
4. We must be able to theoretically differentiate variant readings from misreading.

Since I have written extensively on the making of meaning and on triadicity, I will focus here on the third and fourth points listed above, especially as they are illuminated by the theory and practice of I. A. Richards.[2]

If we are to provide opportunities for students to see how construing a text entails constructing meaning, we will need to return to what Richards considered the focus of any practical criticism, namely, the relationship of what is written or said and what is meant. All reading, that is to say, is like translating from one language to another. Translation, as Richards realized, provides an excellent model for the reading process because it is never a matter of substituting one word for another; it always requires what he came to call "comparison fields"—overlapping contexts, grounds for analogies and metaphors, linguistic or experiential commonalities. The extraordinary thing about Richards's ideas of how translation works is that he developed them pedagogically. As readers explore the range of meaning of the words of the text and the kinds of divisions and differentiation definition requires, they are letting the process of construing guide and direct the process of constructing, and vice versa: the meanings we are making become the means of reviewing the meanings we have made. Richards was fond of noting that the semiotic process provides not only feedback but *feedforward* as well.

Writing teachers are in an excellent position to know how to make this process heuristic. The best description Richards provides comes, interestingly enough, in the following comment on composition:

> Composition is the supplying at the right time and place of whatever the developing meaning then and there requires. It is the cooperation with the rest in preparing for what is to come and completing what has preceded. It is more than this, though; it is the exploration of what is to come and of how it should be prepared for, and it is the further examination of what has preceded and of how it may be amended and completed.[3]

I believe that there will be a revolution in the teaching of English when the realization is won (it will not dawn) that reading can best be taught as we teach writing, meaning both at the same time and in the same enlightened ways.

Our students nowadays seldom come to us with any experience of translation from or into a foreign language. Whatever instruction in grammar they have had has been, generally speaking, detached from any discursive purpose; few have had practice in rewriting, where attention is focused on how changes in sentence structure change the way a text reads. A debased New Critical approach has made paraphrase taboo. Diagraming, which can be very valuable in helping students attend to the interdependence of words in a sentence, has been universally scorned—on the left, because it has seemed merely mechanical; on the right, because it is not mechanical enough. The result of these deficiencies is that the experience of observing meaning emerge as one attends to grammatical construction is uncommon.

We could begin to remedy this state of affairs by inventing quasi-translation exercises. The best one I know of is Phyllis Brooks's "persona paraphrase" in which students try to sound like an author by imitating his or her syntactical structures, with different subject matter.[4] This exercise makes construing as compelling as any other aspect of interpretation by challenging students to attend to purposes. They read as prospective writers and are thus interested in the author's problems and solutions. I think we have a lot to learn from teachers of music composition and painting. Imitating the rhythmic structure of a motet, while changing the melodic and harmonic structure; transcribing an orchestral score for two pianos; changing the color values but not the figural composition of an El Greco: these are all ways of learning the interdependence of construing and constructing. The techniques of "creative" writing instruction await adaptation in the "critical" writing class. Kenneth Burke's criticism offers dozens of points of departure for "translating," changing registers, developing perspectives by incongruity; even his dramatistic metaphor has yet to be put to work in the way it was meant to serve.

Richards first developed his theory of translation in considering the problems of making Chinese wisdom accessible to Westerners. He continued to believe that "translation" of English texts into Basic English offered the best opportunity for students to practice interpretive paraphrase and multiple definition.[5] His other techniques are familiar because they are commonly used in ESL instruction. He was convinced that two "channels" were better than one; he urged that students should attend to a written text as it's being read aloud. Dictation is another useful technique: every student of English, native speaker or not, should have the opportunity of hearing an excellent English sentence read aloud every day—like taking a vitamin pill. Learning to listen is learning to anticipate, a skill that must be exercised in conjunction with judgment.

The poor quality of our students' note taking is only the converse of poor critical reading: they often do not know how to record and listen simultaneously because they have not learned to imagine what's coming. Without practice in anticipation, the alternative is guessing. (Richards is seldom sardonic, but guessing promoted as a technique of learning makes him apoplectic.) To learn to anticipate is to become an active learner; as Coleridge observed, "To know is in its essence a verb active." And the active mind must tolerate ambiguity. The challenge to all English teachers

is to see to it that ambiguities are allowed to serve as "the very hinges of all thought," as Richards put it. Anything learned about note taking will be helpful in learning to read critically, in maintaining the dialectic of construing and constructing.

Multiple definition, interpretive paraphrase, persona paraphrase, parody, glossing, and all other techniques of what has been called "vertical translation" can aid students in distinguishing variant readings from misreading. It is not a matter of developing foolproof validation techniques or mystical powers of intuition but of accounting for what has been said/written in as many contexts as are found useful.[6] Learning how texts and contexts answer to one another; how feedback and feedforward work together; how words work interdependently with other words—such practical criticism will gradually help students abandon the idea that an opinion about what is being read needn't be argued, that gut reactions are the only authentic form of appreciation. Learning to support their interpretations will teach students that while all knowledge is mediated, it does not follow that any opinion or interpretation is as good as another. "Relativism" has gotten a bad name because of a failure to establish the principle that "fallibilism"—Peirce's word for acknowledging that since we do not see face to face, we can never know for sure—does not mean "anything goes."

At the conference on style that occasioned Jakobson's famous "closing statement" in which he set forth his definition of poetry in terms of syntagmatic and paradigmatic axes, I. A. Richards read two papers, "Poetic Process and Literary Analysis" and "Variant Readings and Misreading."[7] He has some very amusing things to say about the "reckless disregard of all the means by which language defends itself" and some important things to say about how the risk of error might be controlled and how misreading is connected to the way reading is taught. His observations about the limitations imposed by the linguistic system on any one component are based, typically, on the metaphor of discourse as a state that must be organized, controlled, and protected. I quote from the closing paragraphs:

> A linguistics that is properly aware of the processes through which language grows in the individual and of the effects that his attitudes to language can have upon its health in him must be concerned with pedagogy and with what sorts of assumptions are spread in the school. . . . For the purposes outlined above and on the appropriate occasions, may *misreading* mean the taking of a sentence in such a way that the equivalence

relations of one or more of its parts to the rest of the language lapse and thereby, if such taking were to continue, harm would be done to language—due regard, however, being given in applying this criterion to the necessity for change in language activity with change in the situation to be met, and, in general, to the health of the language.

For all that he believed in the centrality of purpose, which necessitates an awareness of situation, and despite the fact that he was deeply aware that all language acts are social, Richards focused his practical criticism and his pedagogy on the reader/writer and a text. We will not find in his educational designs more than a fleeting mention of social contexts, of such procedures as, say, students reading their interpretive paraphrases aloud to one another. The metaphor of the state is reserved for discourse and does not function in his discussion of the classroom, which he saw as a "philosophic laboratory" for the study of meaning and meanings. Richards is a thoughtful, provocative, cheerful, inventive, encouraging guide to all who engage in practical criticism, but if we want to consider the pedagogical consequences of his conviction that literacy is essential to the very survival of the planet, we will need to supplement our reading of Richards with the study of those who have thought carefully about the social contexts of the making of meaning. The two most important are, I believe, Paulo Freire and Louise Rosenblatt.

Freire's "pedagogy of knowing" takes as its point of departure the idea that the mind is self-intelligible; that consciousness is always "consciousness of consciousness, intent upon the world"; that reflection is a necessary dimension of human acts and is made possible by the power of language. Conscientization is thus not a dizzying *self*-consciousness, as it would be in the positivist perspective, but a model for the act of choosing, on which liberation depends. Freire's pedagogy of the oppressed—which is the same as the pedagogy of knowing, a fact which Marxists often neglect—entails the conception of a community of learners who, by "problematizing the existential," by representing and interpreting all their recognitions, come to "know their knowledge," in Coleridge's phrase. Of course there are differences between Richards's "design for escape"—which is what he called literacy education, an escape from global catastrophe—and Freire's education for "critical consciousness," but the parallels are instructive. Both great teachers understand the dialectic of reading in and reading out and both know how to follow out the consequences in pedagogical terms. Paulo Freire's "generative words" are, I believe, analogous to Richards's "speculative instruments": they are names for the ideas, the differences, the distinctions by means of which we make meaning.

And Louise Rosenblatt, a student of John Dewey's and a careful reader of his masters, William James and C. S. Peirce, is a trustworthy guide to an understanding of the pedagogical consequences of triadicity. For half a century, she has lucidly explained how we do indeed make meaning in a process she calls *transaction*, in contradistinction to *interaction*, which, as Dewey warned, is consonant with the stimulus-response model of the behaviorists. Rosenblatt talks shamelessly of *beauty* (she has written in the field of aesthetics), and in reminding us of the reason for distinguishing reading for the sake of information and reading for pleasure (which has its own profit), she helps to reclaim the study of literature from indeterminists and authorial intentionists alike. Furthermore, Louise Rosenblatt's analysis of kinds of reading helps us to consider more carefully the kinds of writing. Her efferent/aesthetic differentiation functions as a continuum, allowing her to describe the dialectic of private and public aspects of reading, and it serves as a speculative instrument for the study of reading and writing as "transactions [that] are at once intensely individual and intensely social activities."[8] In the course of considering current interest in "ethnicity," she turns to Walt Whitman, finding that his "intense individualism seems... both to support affirmation of the importance of ethnic roots and to qualify it."[9] Whitman, she writes,

> shows us the man and the woman accepting themselves in all their uniqueness, honoring their own roots, but free to reach out in all directions to their fellow humans.

She salutes the uniqueness of great writers but believes that

> their greatest value lies in their permitting us to transcend our limitations of time and place and ancestry, and to participate in the common life of humanity.

Perhaps the chief reason for wanting to slay the killer dichotomy of reading in/reading out is that doing so is propaedeutic for an understanding of the relationship of the individual and society, which is where all discussions of literacy must begin and end.

Richards, Rosenblatt, and Freire are all pragmatists, which means that they ask not "Does it work?" or "Can we afford it?" but "What difference would it make to our practice if we proceeded from these principles?" But it is equally true that they are all alert to what Rosenblatt calls "the common life of humanity"; to what Richards, citing Coleridge, calls "the all-in-each of human nature"; to what Freire recognizes in Man's character as a creature not only of Nature but of History. We read Richards, Rosenblatt, and Freire not because they are "reading specialists" but because their passionately held convictions can guide us in reclaiming the imagination, understood as the power of the active mind. Against that power, no killer dichotomy has a chance.

Notes

1. An account of this affair is given in *The Wall Street Journal*, 29 April 1988. I have enjoyed discussing this matter with my friend Clare Finley McCord, who provided the report from The Society for Textual Scholarship in the *Journal*.

2. See my *The Making of Meaning: Metaphors, Models and Maxims for Writing Teachers* (Portsmouth, NH: Boynton/Cook, 1981) 42–44, for an explanation of the triadic sign. In introducing the selections from *Reclaiming the Imagination* (Portsmouth, NH: Boynton/Cook, 1984), I have tried to develop contexts for an understanding of the interdependence of hermeneutics (the general theory of interpretation) and semiotics (the science of signs).

3. I. A. Richards, From "Meanings Anew," in *So Much Nearer* (New York: Harcourt Brace, 1968).

4. See Phyllis Brooks, "Mimesis: Grammar and the Echoing Voice," *College English* 35 (1973): 161–68.

5. The Basic English Word List may be found in I. A. Richards's *Design for Escape* (New York: Harcourt Brace 1968, 70–71) and in his *Techniques for Language Control* (Rowley, MA: Newbury, 1974). *Basic English and Its Uses* (1943) considers the need for an international "second" language and various pedagogical procedures, especially the use of audiovisual aids.

6. Psycholinguists, in discussing orality and literacy, have taken up the term *decontextualization* to name the fact of abstraction from one or another actual situation—as if only utterance but not texts have contexts! This mischievous terminology must not distract us from teaching the importance of *contexts* to *texts*.

7. The proceedings were published as *Style in Language*, edited by Thomas A. Sebeok (1960).

8. "Writing and Reading: The Transactional Theory," Technical Report No. 416, Center for the Study of Reading, University of Illinois at Champaign (1988). Forthcoming in *Reading and Writing Connections*, ed. J. Mason (Boston: Allyn and Bacon).

9. "Whitman's Democratic Vistas," *Yale Review* (Winter 1978).

TWO

Personal and Public Authority in Discourse

Beyond Subjective/ Objective Dichotomies

KATE RONALD

> "It's not personal; it's just business."
> —Mario Puzo
> *The Godfather*

Recently my department met to consider and vote on this motion: "Professorial faculty shall participate regularly in the first-year composition program." On the face of it, it seemed an innocuous enough idea; voting against participation in the first-year writing program would be analogous to voting against clean air or reduced teaching loads. But as I walked into the room and looked around at my colleagues, I knew the meeting would soon become less than collegial. I was right. There were many arguments against the motion—some of them pragmatic (who will cover the upper-level courses?), some emotional (I'm afraid my student evaluations will suffer!). What surfaced was the clear assumption that teaching beginning students was somehow beneath many of the senior professors' dignity and a waste of their valuable research time; and in a brilliant rhetorical move, they argued that it was something they were not trained to do in the first place. The left-handed compliments about how much better the junior faculty and adjuncts were at running composition courses seduced many around the room. After the meeting (the motion was tabled), I was complaining to a colleague in creative writing that the objection was not to freshmen and women but to composition. She tried to soothe me by saying, "You know, you really shouldn't take people's notions about composition so *personally*." But I *do*. And I think I should. It's my business.

Composition's business should remain personal. The array of self-studies and self-exploration going on in professional journals these days attests to the field's rather desperate need to understand itself, examine its conscience, and take its place among the disciplines. It's clear that composition takes its newcomer, outsider stance very personally. And that's good. When composition is at its best as a discipline, the healthy paradox between subjective and objective views of discourse is clear. When composition tries to privilege objectivity and mask its subjectivity, as it historically persists in doing, it becomes a fragmented field criticized for not being either theoretically rigorous enough or practically useful to its clients.

This essay explores the dichotomy between personal and public senses of discourse, both in scholarship and pedagogy, that leads composition to this fragmentation. George Mead's concepts of self and other may help frame the discussion. Mead says that individuals develop two distinct senses of self that are always and necessarily in conflict. The first—the "socialized me"—is a structure or reflection of attitudes learned from others; the "duty one must perform" (173–178). The second—the "subjective I"—reacts to the demands and requests the "socialized me" faces. Mead says that both the "I" and "me" are "essential to the self in its fullest expression" (199). This tension between the private and the public selves leads to learning and commitment. Roy Baumeister also argues that the development of a mature sense of self comes from being forced, first, to make choices privately, then to explain those choices and justify intentions publicly. In its attempt to define and defend its own identity as a discipline, I think that composition needs to reclaim this dual sense of itself, which fueled its recent emergence in the first place. It must continually react to demands from outside the academy, from other departments, from students, many of whom hold notions contrary to the theoretical knowledge accumulated over the last twenty-five years. The "subjective composition" reacts to those demands and takes responsibility for the ways it tries to meet them, often ways that won't be popular with outsiders' expectations. In this way, composition has developed its sense of authority and autonomy as a discipline. Too often, however, composition's sense of authority gets confused when subjective, personal ways of establishing authority are subsumed under objective stances. The necessary tension is lost, and along with it the resulting growth and commitment.

Mikhail Bakhtin's concepts of discourse as applied to the novel might also help explain the tension I am describing. Bakhtin says that the "ideological becoming of a human being... is the process of selectively assimilating the words of others" (341). In school, this process is taught in two ways: "reciting by heart" and "retelling in one's own words," two language acts Bakhtin terms "authoritative discourse" and "internally persuasive discourse" (342). Authoritative discourse "demands our unconditional allegiance.... It enters our verbal consciousness as a compact and indivisible mass; one must either affirm it or totally reject it. It is indissolubly fused with its authority—with political power, an institution, a person— and it stands and falls together with that authority" (343). Where authoritative discourse remains distant and static, internally persuasive discourse is personal and dynamic. Bakhtin describes this language as "one's own word... half-ours and half-someone else's. Its creativity and productiveness consist precisely in the fact that such a word awakens new and independent words, that it organizes masses of our words from within, and does not remain in an isolated and static condition" (343).

Internally persuasive discourse, for Bakhtin, plays a crucial role in the evolution of individual consciousness: "consciousness awakens to an independent ideological life precisely in the world of alien discourses surrounding it" (345). The interplay between the two types of discourses causes "ideological becoming":

> Both the authority of discourse and its internal persuasiveness may be united in a single word—one that is *simultaneously* authoritative and internally persuasive—despite the profound differences between these two categories of alien discourse. But such unity is rarely a given—it happens more frequently that an individual's becoming, an ideological process, is characterized precisely by a sharp gap between these two categories: in one, the authoritative word (religious, political, moral; the word of a father, of adults, of teachers, etc.) that does not know internal peruasiveness, in the other, the internally persuasive word that is denied all privilege, backed up by no authority at all, and is frequently not even acknowledged in society (not by public opinion, nor by scholarly

norms, nor by criticism, not even in the legal code). The struggle and dialogic interrelationship of these categories as ideological discourse are what usually determine the history of an individual ideological consciousness (342).

Yet composition tends to forget this paradox too often as it continually separates personal and public senses of language, both in its theory and resulting practice. We react to the demands to become socialized into the academy and run the risk of forgetting our subjective identity, buying into dichotomies between writing and reading, teaching and research, form and content, male and female, to name just a few examples. One could read the entire collection in *Farther Along* as an attempt to move beyond and transform the oppositions between subjective and objective views. In an effort to become a discipline, composition has ignored the subjective sense of "I" in favor of the socialized "me"; it continually rejects the personal in order to embrace the publicly authoritative. In order to analyze its own ideological consciousness, composition needs to remember this necessary tension between subjectivity and objectivity, between authoritative and internally persuasive discourse, where the source of its authority lies. More importantly, in order to maintain that tension, composition as a discipline needs to place the subjective sense of itself in the foreground much more than it currently does.

Rhetoric and composition began its renaissance in the 1960s with a reaction against the objectivity and the public nature of writing instruction—what we now call the "current-traditional paradigm." Under that model, it was assumed that there were forms and rules "out there" somewhere, and a writing teacher's job was to show students how to fit their ideas into those forms. Yet composition's reaction to the objective authority of the current-traditional paradigm in theory was not to replace it with a new sense of subjectivity but with a new kind of objectivity. In many ways, the "new rhetoric" of the last twenty years has worked to bring the subjective, the personal, the individual back into writing classrooms. In its research, however, composition's recent history has been a heroic attempt to move from subjective knowledge to objective description. During this time, composition has challenged itself as a discipline to become more objective—to verify its subjective knowledge about writing and student writers through quantifiable and theoretically rigorous research. While the whole concept of a "writing process" has been based on personal strategies of composing, such as the studies by Janet Emig and Linda Flower that generalized from individuals working at writing to theories about how process operates, that concept of a "composing process" has become more and more objectified. In methodology as well as in spirit, objectivity reigns in research. Justifying the validity of one's approach to studying writing takes precedence over conclusions or implications for individual authors and student writers. In Mary Belenky's terms, composition's knowledge is often procedural rather than subjective.

Thus, despite composition's beginnings in reaction to objective forms, this discipline continues to value the impersonal over the personal, the objectively verifiable over the subjectively suspect theory. Stephen North makes this point repeatedly in *The Making of Knowledge in Composition*. His division of composition into Practitioners, Scholars, and Researchers operates according to subjective/objective dichotomies. He makes it quite clear that the "lore" of practitioner knowledge is devalued, suspicious, not quantifiable or valid precisely because it is subjective knowledge. "Each Practitioner's version of lore will have," says North, "a unique experiential structure" (28). The idiosyncratic ways of individual teachers, their "mythic self-image," their "experience-based testimony," all testify to the subjective stance of the Practitioner. North describes Practitioner knowledge as "private," as opposed to Researcher or Scholarly inquiry in composition, "where the greatest authority over what constitutes knowledge resides with the community—lies, in effect, with *public* knowledge" (28).

North dates the beginning of modern composition by the publication of Braddock's *Research on Written Composition* in 1963, which insisted that the discipline would never be more than a collection of personal lore until it undertook systematic, objective investigation into its subject—writing. The report, answering NCTE's call for an investigation into the State of Knowledge about Composition, described a field "laced with dreams, prejudices, and makeshift operations" (5). Braddock and his coauthors argued instead for a model of inquiry based on scientific, objective research, with experimentation, replication of studies, and appeals to certain knowledge.

In the twenty-five years since Braddock's report, composition has tried hard to imitate that kind of objective inquiry. There are many places where such a history has been documented, North's work among them, and this essay will not attempt such a review. Case studies like Janet Emig's *The Composing Processes of Twelfth Graders*, Linda Flower's and John Hayes's protocol analyses of experienced and novice writers, and the emergence of journals such as *Research in the Teaching of English* and *Written Communication* all testify to the move toward objectification of knowledge about writing and writers. These are the most obvious examples. Less obvious but perhaps more influential are the appeals to outside, more "objective" authorities that permeate the more "scholarly" or "philosophical" research in composition. Throughout the last fifteen years, Jean Piaget, Lev Vygotsky, Noam Chomsky, Thomas Kuhn, Paulo Freire, Mikhail Bakhtin, Erving Goffman, Michael Polanyi, among many others, have at one time or another been seen as holding some "objective" truth that composition could latch onto and thereby leave the subjective realm of dreams and prejudice. These voices have taken on the "authoritative" stance in our scholarly discourse that Bakhtin describes.

Yet in our practice in the last twenty-five years, our teacherly voices seem to be arguing from another kind of authority. The workshop models of Donald Murray, Donald Graves, James Moffett, Ken Macrorie, and Peter Elbow have diffused and scattered the idea of objective authority around our classrooms. During this time, teachers have worked to empower students by inviting them to abandon what Macrorie called "Engfish," or school writing, and to explore their own experiences in their own voices. Students' subjects become their own, instead of their teachers' or their institutions'. Janet Emig was among the first to argue for "reflexive writing" as opposed to "extensive" discourse. Yet her distinctions set the terms for the persistent dichotomy between personal and public authority in discourse:

> The reflexive mode . . . focuses upon the writer's thoughts and feelings concerning his experience; the chief audience is the writer . . . ; the domain explored is often the affective; the style is tentative, personal, and exploratory. The extensive mode . . . focuses upon the writer's conveying a message or a communication to another; the domain explored is usually the cognitive; the style is assured, impersonal and often reportorial (4).

Teachers recognized that their students' reflexive writing was often more powerful than their extensive writing for school. Emig encouraged teachers to invite their students to write in modes beyond the school-sponsored, and she urged teachers to write reflexively themselves. But the opposition between self and other inherent in her study, and the hierarchy apparent in that opposition, ensured that extensive writing and objective authority would remain the privileged discourse of the school and the academy.

In the last several years, as composition has been trying to make sense of itself, to take stock of its knowledge, Braddock's call for objectivity is still being answered. All the taxonomies of the field discussed in the introduction to this collection operate according to subjective and objective divisions, despite their stated themes of reconciling opposition through some dialectical or social scheme. James Berlin's latest taxonomy in the September 1988 issue of *College English* will serve as a representative example of the kind of public discourse that currently carries objective authority. In "Rhetoric and Ideology in the Writing Class," Berlin attempts to expose political ideologies inherent in varying rhetorical theories. He contrasts objective stances (cognitive rhetoric) with completely subjective ones (expressionist rhetoric), and then opposes them with the middle way—social-epistemic rhetoric. Cognitive rhetoric, he argues, ignores the ideological issue altogether, leaving out of its theory and practice questions about "what is good, possible, and how power ought to be distributed." Expressionist rhetoric means to provide a "critique of the ideology of corporate capitalism," but its "radical individualism" remains naive and can lead to "marginalizing" or "co-optation" of its practitioners and students. Berlin argues that the only responsible view is to highlight ideology through social-epistemic rhetoric, which "offers both a detailed analysis of dehumanizing social experience and a self-critical and overtly historicized alternative based on democratic practices in the economic, social, political, and cultural spheres" (492).

Berlin chooses representative authors to illustrate each of these rhetorics: Flower for the cognitive stance, Elbow and Murray as expressionists, and Ira Shor for the social-epistemic camp. Berlin clearly argues for the ideological stance inherent in Shor's pedagogy, but despite his admitted prejudice for the social-epistemic camp, his scheme remains clearly objective in the "socialized" sense of composition. Berlin uses the authoritative stance in his own discourse. There is no "telling in his own words"; he appeals to "ideology" as if it were something "out there," something that remains constant for the practitioners of expressionist rhetoric, for example—always the same for Peter Elbow as it is for Donald Murray as it is for the teachers who order their textbooks and the students who use them. Berlin argues that expressionist rhetorics "include a denunciation of economic, political, and social pressures to conform—to engage in various forms of corporate-sponsored thought, feeling, and behavior" (486). He equates Flower's problem-solving techniques for writing with "the pursuit of self-evident and unquestioned profit-making goals in the corporate marketplace" (483). In these kinds of sweeping statements, Berlin assumes that ideology is a constant, a static "indivisible mass," as Bakhtin would say, that one must either affirm or reject.

Berlin here seems to be answering Patricia Bizzell's call in "Cognition, Convention, and Certainty" for "politicizing" composition theory. In that essay, Bizzell urged composition not to bury ethical and political questions in seemingly neutral pedagogies, arguing that composition needs to inspect the hidden agendas behind its theories. But in Berlin's attempt to delineate ideologies inherent in competing theories, and in part as a result of his own categorization scheme, he reaches for the very "certainty" that Bizzell warns against. Bizzell admits that certainty appeals to composition specialists because it would "help us retaliate against the literary critics who dominate English studies" and help us to "survive the slide of humanistic disciplines into a low-status enclave." The strongest appeal of certainty, according to Bizzell, lies in its ability to make us accountable to others outside composition. But she warns that certainty will make us complacent:

> Invocation of certainty, then, performs the rhetorical function of invocation of the Deity. It guarantees the transcendent authority of values for which we do not need to argue but which we can now apply with the confidence of a "good cause" (236).

Berlin's "good cause" is the critique of culture in order to empower students. And it is a good cause, one that I cannot dismiss. But just as Berlin says that no pedagogies are "innocent," so I would argue there is no neutral, or objective, scholarship. Michael Polanyi celebrates this fact when he says:

> As I acknowledge, in reflecting on the process of discovery, the gap between the evidence and the conclusions which I draw from them, and account for them in terms of my personal responsibility, so also will I acknowledge that in childhood I have formed my most fundamental beliefs by exercising my native intelligence within the social milieu of a particular place and time. I shall submit to this fact as defining the conditions under which I am called upon to exercise my responsibility (*Personal Knowledge*, 322–323).

Yet I do not find that sense of responsibility in Berlin's latest work. He does not include the internally persuasive discourse that would allow us to see the connection between Linda Flower and corporate

America or Peter Elbow and protest politics. Despite his acknowledgment in the introduction to *Rhetoric and Reality* that any author, including himself, must be candid about her interpretive strategies and the effect of her "terministic screens" on the object of her attention, Berlin comes close here to exactly the kind of stance he objects to in Robert Connors: an authoritative description that "bring[s] discussion to a close" (*Rhetoric and Reality* 17). Because despite all of Berlin's caveats about his own subjectivity, he does not trace his thinking or explain its context. As readers, we experience what Belenky and her coauthors call "separate" rather than "connected" knowing (102). They describe two kinds of epistemologies, one where truth is established through self-extrication, and the other where truth is discovered in attachment. Without any sense of Berlin's subjective knowledge, but only his procedural voice, we are left to rely on James Berlin's "authority" to interpret the rhetorics we must choose among. And his voice clearly argues that we must choose.

What's frustrating about essays like Berlin's is that they are so seductive. It's difficult for me to argue with his conclusions, that ideology must become an overt part of teaching, inasmuch as it has always operated behind the scenes in education. I do believe that teaching is political. But I question his authority to translate other scholars' theories into pedagogy the way he does. And I question his categorization scheme in the first place. In a profession where we must continually rethink what it is we're doing in the classroom, it's tempting simply to buy into one theory or another and be done with it. To accept Berlin's authority, however, would mean closing down speculation and ceasing to look for connections between theory and practice.

Berlin's is simply one example of the kind of "authoritative discourse" that dominates our field. I choose him because he has the floor these days. His categorization of composition theory and his interpretation of pedagogical implications not only sets the terms for recent discussion, but it also excludes other voices that are less objective, less "certain." On the other side of Berlin's authoritative words are the internally persuasive voices of teachers and students in classrooms, voices that may not fall so neatly into categories. As North documents, these subjective voices of experience are often not heard. Donald Murray and Peter Elbow, today labeled (and dismissed) by Berlin and others as expressionist rhetoricians, have for years argued for the individual voice in writing, the personal search for meaning through composing. Both Murray and Elbow, for example, base their theories of composing, learning, and teaching on their own personal experiences as writers, students, and teachers. Elbow says quite frankly in *Embracing Contraries* that he is "really engaged in trying to work out a definition of good learning and teaching that doesn't exclude me" (xiv). Teachers throughout the country have relied on Elbow's and Murray's advice and become better teachers, perhaps because they have not only adopted pedagogical advice but reacted to the voices they hear in Elbow's and Murray's work—an *ethos* that does not separate the teacherly and the scholarly stances, that does not ignore personal discourse in a public forum. Yet "expressive" discourse, once considered a powerful resource for learning and thinking, has become the least privileged form of writing in the academy. Composition seems to have relegated "expressive" writing to diaries, personal memories, and reverie, while writing across the curriculum programs and the focus on social context or discourse community lead teachers away from attention to personal voice. Taxonomies like Berlin's push the subjective view out of composition's discourse community in favor of more objective stances. Thus, the tension that leads to productive inquiry and self-examination gets lost.

The temptation toward certainty and objectivity that pervades professional journals also translates into the classroom. Louise Phelps says that "the link between knowledge and action, theoria and praxis, distinguishes composition from other language-related academic fields by making the teaching act itself a primary topic of scholarly inquiries" (187). Yet there seems to be less and less attention to the teaching act in recent scholarship, less attachment between scholarship and pedagogy. Even the embracing of current critical literary theory, with its emphasis on "subjective" readings of texts, becomes objectified when it is used as pure theory and never translated into practice. The consequences are real for our students. When composition attempts to objectify its knowledge, "personal" writing is relegated to the beginnings of textbooks, the beginnings of courses and course sequences, something to get "past" before students can move on to more rigorous, more objective exposition or argument.

Two recent treatments of personal and public writing reflect this tendency to privilege the objective view over the subjective. Both argue that rhetoric has moved dangerously close to purely subjective views and warn that teachers must return to more "public" writing in their classrooms. Robert Connors, in his 1987 *CCC* essay "Personal Writing Assignments," maintains that the classical tradition taught "relentlessly" impersonal writing up through the end of the nineteenth century, when romantic individualism led to more attention to the individual writer's unique experience. In a 1982 article in *Pre/Text*, S. Michael Halloran describes "the decline of public discourse" during this same period. Classical rhetoric, he maintains, emphasized analysis and communication of "public problems that arise from our life in a political community" (246). However, by the end of the nineteenth century, because of changes in education's perception of mission and subject, Halloran says, this "rhetoric of citizenship" was replaced by a pedagogy concentrating on students' personal, intellectual, or professional identity, and the earlier rhetoric has been in a "severe eclipse" ever since. Halloran sees the emphasis on writing from personal experience as evidence that our culture/educational system has come to value the individual's advancement over the society's need for leadership and public, political debate.

Connors, too, sees the use of personal writing assignments as a mirror of philosophy. He acknowledges that many teachers are "uncomfortable" with the question of personal writing, worrying whether writing from personal memory, for example, is serving the needs of audiences outside the classroom—other departments, employers, the community. Connors says: "The continuing debate [between "honest personal writing" and "writing that gets the world's work done"], tacit and sub-channel though it may be, indicates that we as a profession have not yet come to an agreement about the larger purposes of writing in this culture" (181).

In other words, we have not been able to find the internally persuasive discourse that will allow us to combine personal and public, subjective and objective senses of language, either in our own or our students' discourse. There's a difference operating here that Berlin, Connors, and Halloran need to remember—that personal writing does not necessarily lead to personal investment on the part of the writer, that personal writing may not be "internally persuasive," in fact may be an imitation of "authoritative discourse." Public writing, on the other hand, need not exclude the internally persuasive language of "one's own words" in order to carry authority. Both Connors and Halloran define "personal" discourse as a narrowing of subject from public issues to private experience and a reduction of audience from public forums to an individual listener, usually the teacher or the writer herself. "Patriotism," for example is a public topic, while "How a Boy Can Be Patriotic" is a personal one. Yet I would argue that these differences are superficial. Students writing about their summer vacation or their last family gathering can take on the most public, objective tones of indifference and distance, as any teacher knows. And topics like the presidential debates or campus parking rules can invite students to tell personal stories, to connect their private language to the public forum. The topic does not matter; the writer's stance does. Writers who "take it personally" operate somewhere between certainty and speculation, and their authority resides in the tension between objectivity and subjectivity.

In practical terms, that tension resides in the kind of writing dismissed by Berlin and others as "expressive," writing that stays close to the contours of thought, as Britton says, but that makes connections between the private and public worlds. It is writing to figure things out with the kind of "connected knowing" Belenky describes. Yet that sense of writing is not valued in our institutions, or even in our own talk about discourse communities as clubs with set rules and regulations for discourse and thinking. When I ask my students in professional writing classes, for example, to explore the language of their disciplines, they experience the frustration that comes from realizing that they can find no connection between themselves and that discourse. And because they have been trained as "separate" knowers, they have trouble finding a way to make that discourse their own other than imitating it or memorizing it. Somehow the institution teaches them that they can "own" disciplinary knowledge and discourse by remaining apart from it. Like the Godfather, they believe business can't be personal. Alternatives, such as exploring a personal connection between knowledge and knower, are often seen as weak, soft, or unacademic. Even the "process" movement in composition becomes open to the attack of being navel-contemplating, or too concerned with how the writer feels rather than how she thinks or what she knows. And because as a discipline we have embraced objective stances, we increasingly find it difficult to defend such attacks.

We do not need to continue to live in this dichotomy between speculation and certainty, affective and cognitive, personal and public. Of course, objective and subjective views cannot be so neatly separated, as Connors admits at the end of his essay when he calls for "metapersonal" writing. Susanne Langer explains in *Mind: An Essay on Human Feeling* that subjectivity and objectivity are processes in constant tension, not attributes outside the thinker's mind or heart. She says that "the dialectic" that makes up a "life of the mind" is

> a real and constant cerebral process, the interplay between the two fundamental types of feeling, peripheral impact and autonomous action, or objective and subjective feeling. As fast as objective impingements strike our senses they become emotionally tinged and subjectified; and in a symbol-making brain like ours, every internal feeling tends to issue in a symbol

which gives it an objective status even if only transiently (Vol II: 342).

Langer suggests that the mind in its very operation "takes it personally." The way out of this dilemma is not, then, to label some thinking "objective" and some "subjective," or to privilege public discourse over personal. We cannot escape the personal dimension in our discourse, and we must not try.

Sam Watson, writing about Michael Polanyi, describes two trends in current rhetorical theory:

> Sooner or later, most rhetoricians begin assuming that their theory applies only to "other people"; they tacitly declare themselves exempt from their own rhetoric. Second, they demarcate rhetoric by contrasting it to an image of knowledge that is certain, and therefore, superior to rhetoric (9).

Although compositionists often invoke the name of Michael Polanyi in their work, they may not recognize the instances of tacit knowing in their own reporting of their knowledge. Polanyi says that all knowledge is personal—it comes about through an "indwelling" with the subject: "To know something by relying on our awareness of it for attending to something else is to have the same kind of knowledge of it that we have of our body by living in it" (*Meaning* 36). "You dwell in a theory as you dwell in your body," according to Polanyi, and one's knowledge of a theoretical, interpretive framework lies in the uncritical use of it. Watson argues that modern rhetoricians, in their quest for objective certainty, tend to ignore this tacit dimension of their knowledge.

Polanyi also insists on the personal responsibility one has for theory. His work attempts to mend the break between the ideal of objective science and our understanding of ourselves as responsible beings. Polanyi warns that "as long as science remains the ideal of knowledge and detachment the ideal of science," research will not be able to tell us anything "interesting" or anything "we need to know" (*Meaning* 28). So, Polanyi advises:

> Let us incorporate into our conception of scientific knowledge that part which we ourselves necessarily contribute in shaping such knowledge. Let us displace quite generally the current ideal of detached observation by a conception of personal knowledge (*Meaning* 29).

That conception includes the tension between objectivity and subjectivity that both Mead and Bakhtin describe. For Polanyi, Langer, and Bakhtin, authority in discourse arises from the interplay of voices that are one's own and another's, from acknowledging the personal nature of all public utterances. Yet current research and practice in composition continues to embrace the objective certainty that the academic culture believes lends authority to discourse. It embraces "separate" rather than "connected" knowing, even when our own classrooms and our own experiences as writers show us differently.

Composition, as a pedagogical discipline, needs to change its perspective—from an imitation of the scientist's objective stances toward an embracing of what we know to be true about language: that objective and subjective views are continually in flux, that "taking it personally" is our only choice. If, as Bakhtin says, "internally persuasive discourse" comes out of the tensions between words that are "half-ours, half-someone else's,'" then the half that's ours— or our students'—should carry equal authority. If my senior colleagues believed in that tension, they would not be afraid to return to the writing program, where personal stories carry as much authority as public texts, and where public discourse connects to personal business.

Works Cited

Bakhtin, Mikhail. *The Dialogic Imagination*. Trans. Caryl Emerson and Michael Holquist. Austin: U of Texas P, 1981.

Baumeister, Roy F. *Identity, Cultural Change, and the Struggle for Self*. New York: Oxford, 1987.

Berlin, James. "Rhetoric and Ideology in the Writing Class." *College English* 5 (1988): 477–495.

———. *Rhetoric and Reality: Writing Instruction in American Colleges 1900–1985*. Carbondale: Southern Illinois UP, 1987.

Belenky, Mary F., et al. *Women's Ways of Knowing: The Development of Self, Voice, and Mind*. New York: Basic Books, 1986.

Bizzell, Patricia. "Cognition, Convention, and Certainty: What We Need to Know about Writing." *PrefText* 3 (1982): 213–243.

Braddock, Richard, Richard Lloyd-Jones, and Lowell Schoer. *Research on Written Composition*. Champaign, IL: National Council of Teachers of English, 1963.

Connors, Robert. "Personal Writing Assignments." *College Composition and Communication* 38 (1987): 166–182.

Elbow, Peter. *Embracing Contraries: Explorations in Learning and Teaching*. New York: Oxford, 1986.

Emig, Janet. *The Composing Processes of Twelfth Graders*. Urbana, IL: National Council of Teachers of English, 1971.

Halloran, S. Michael. "Rhetoric in the American College Classroom: The Decline of Public Discourse." *PrefText* 3 (1982): 245–269.

Langer, Susanne. *Mind: An Essay on Human Feeling.* Volume II. Baltimore: Johns Hopkins UP, 1972.

Mead, George H. *Mind, Self, and Society.* U of Chicago P, 1934.

North, Stephen. *The Making of Knowledge in Composition: Portrait of an Emerging Field.* Portsmouth, NH: Boynton/Cook, 1986.

Phelps, Louise W. "The Domain of Composition." *Rhetoric Review* 4 (1986): 182–195.

Polanyi, Michael. *Personal Knowledge: Towards a Post-Critical Philosophy.* U of Chicago P, 1962.

———, and Harry Prosch. *Meaning.* U of Chicago P, 1975.

Watson, Sam. "Breakfast in the Tacit Tradition." *Pre/Text* 2 (1981): 9–33.

THREE

The Convergence of Dichotomies in the Personal Journal

KEN AUTREY

> ALGERNON: Do you really keep a diary? I'd give anything
> to look at it. May I?
> CECILY: Oh no. [Puts her hand over it.] You see, it is
> simply a very young girl's record of her own
> thoughts and impressions, and consequently meant
> for publication. When it appears in volume form I
> hope you will order a copy. . . .
>
> —Oscar Wilde
> *The Importance of Being Earnest*

With the exception of the expository essay, the journal must be the most common type of writing required in composition classes. Although often associated with what James Berlin calls the "expressionist" or "neo-platonist" school, journal keeping is required in composition classrooms covering the gamut of teaching philosophies. Most writing textbooks give some attention to this genre, usually presenting it as an aid to invention and practice. Its flexibility is its most attractive feature and explains its broad appeal. But for students, this flexibility can translate as confusion, an excess of options, some of them contradictory. As Cecily's response to

40

Algernon suggests, a diary has both private and public dimensions. Similarly, a journal may serve both expressive and transactional functions and constitute both process and product.

I want to examine these dichotomies (private/public, expressive/transactional, and process/product) as manifest in the student journal. I hope to show that these categories, which have contributed greatly to our understanding of writing in recent years, become unstable when applied to specific texts. My focus remains on the journal because it demonstrates particularly well the blurring of these polarities, but I believe that classification of other texts is similarly problematic.

Implicit in this examination of accepted categories is the notion that any classification scheme is suspect. This point has been made by C. H. Knoblauch, who argues that composition research has recently moved from "characterizing structural properties of texts to characterizing the personal and social processes that give rise to them . . . " (37). He is particularly critical of taxonomies that "assume the 'real' character of empirical evidence" and thus conceal the complexity of the phenomena under study (40).

A synthesis of potentially disruptive polarities should not eliminate the terms altogether but acknowledge their paradoxical entanglement. Furthermore, facing the interplay between dichotomous terms can enrich our students' use of the journal and their appreciation of the complex motives undergirding all discourse.

Private/Public

The journal as now used in composition courses is a product of conflicting impulses, one public and the other private. The journal combines the attributes of the commonplace book and the diary. As the former, it contains knowledge, observations, even quotations that may later prove useful in communicating with others. As a diary, the journal is a private realm where the writer's words are safe from public scrutiny. Commonplace books were used for centuries in rhetorical instruction; every aspiring scholar was expected to keep one. While diaries also have a long history, only since the increased emphasis on personal (as opposed to communal) insights in the Renaissance have diaries been widely used. The romantic era prompted increased attention to individual reflection, and the nineteenth century saw unprecedented growth in diary keeping.

The recent popularity of the journal in composition instruction is traceable to a renewed emphasis on invention and a search for specific strategies to help writers generate ideas. As prescribed in most composition textbooks, this tool may serve several functions, some private and others public. According to NCTE "Guidelines for Using Journals in School Settings" these functions are as follows:

> (1) to help students find personal connections to the material they are studying in class and textbook, (2) to provide a place for students to think about, learn, and understand course material, (3) to collect observations, responses, and data, and (4) to allow students to practice their writing before handing it in to be graded (6).

The guidelines go on to suggest that students be told journals "are neither 'diaries' nor 'class notebooks,' but borrow features from each" (7). This peculiar mix is not unprecedented; writers as dissimilar as Katherine Mansfield and James Dickey have kept journals combining details from their personal lives with plans for stories or poems, sometimes jumping abruptly from one to the other. But it is not surprising that students, so often told to sharpen the focus of their work, are confused by this protean genre.

While the history of the pedagogical journal reveals a tension between the diary and commonplace book, the matter of reader or audience for the journal points up in another way the instability of the private/public dichotomy. This instability is attributable to a curious paradox familiar to Oscar Wilde's Cecily: the more private our writing, the more public its appeal. Diaries are kept under lock and key for good reason. The explorer Sir Richard F. Burton shows an awareness of this paradox in introducing his account of a pilgrimage to Mecca:

> I have entitled this account of my summer's tour through Al-Hijaz, a Personal Narrative, and I have laboured to make its nature correspond with its name, simply because it is the personal that interests mankind. (4)

Burton's narrative is more a travelog than an intimate diary; he had every intention of publishing it, and he was fully aware of a potential audience. But Peter Elbow and Jennifer Clarke note that students often develop a stronger voice by ignoring audience in their journals. As they put it, "Ignoring audience may permit an overly self-conscious, mannered, or cute voice finally to run clear" (25). They relate this claim to Linda Flower's differentiation between writer-based and reader-based prose. In effect, they argue, "writer-based prose can be better than reader-based prose—even for readers" (26). In this connection, Elbow and Clarke quote the poet John Ashbery: "Very often people don't listen to you when you speak to them. It's only when you talk to yourself that they prick up their ears" (25).

In published journals sometimes the least coherent entries are the most appealing, like this passage from Sylvia Plath's journal:

> Keep a notebook of physical events. My visit to the tattoo shop and my job at the hospital supplied me with two good stories. So should my Boston experience. If only I can go deep enough. A party at Agatha's. Starbuck's wife. The gardens. Oh, God, how good to get it all. Slowly, slowly catch a monkey. Small doses of acceptance help (329).

This lacks the structure and direction that would characterize most published prose (or poetry), yet it seems far richer than many of Plath's more "reader-based" entries. If it were more polished, laced with transitions, would it really be more "reader-based?" Would it interest us more? I, for one, prefer reading my students' weekly entries when they try this more associative, spontaneous mode of expression. Ironically, they would probably take such a risk more often if they knew I would not read their work.

Complicating this scramble of private and public dimensions is the argument that writers—even in their most unguarded moments—cannot ignore audience. Thomas Mallon asserts that there is always a "you" to which journal entries are addressed. According to Mallon, "No one has ever kept a diary for just himself" (xvi). Walter J. Ong, in his widely cited article, "The Writer's Audience Is Always a Fiction," makes a similar point:

> What is easier, one might argue, than addressing oneself? As those who first begin a diary often find out, a great many things are easier. The reasons why are not hard to unearth. First of all, we do not normally talk to ourselves—certainly not in long, involved sentences and paragraphs. Second, the diarist pretending to be talking to himself has also, since he is writing, to pretend he is somehow not there (20).

And subsequently, Ong writes,

> The case of the diary, which at first blush would seem to fictionalize the reader least but in many ways probably fictionalizes him or her most, brings into full view the fundamental deep paradox of the activity we call writing, at least

when writing moves from its initial account-keeping purposes to other more elaborate concerns more directly and complexly involving human persons in their manifold dealings with one another (20).

Indeed many diary or journal writers explicitly fictionalize their readers. Katherine Mansfield thought of herself as writing to her dead brother. Anne Frank explains here why she always wrote to her imaginary friend, Kitty:

> Yes, there is no doubt that paper is patient and as I don't intend to show this cardboard-covered notebook, bearing the proud name of "diary," to anyone, unless I find a real friend, boy or girl, probably nobody cares. And now I come to the root of the matter, the reason for my starting a diary: it is that I have no such real friend (12).

Our students usually start their journals because of a course requirement, so in a sense the instructor remains the audience. But various entries—even those within one journal—often seem to evoke a number of different audiences. These audiences are seldom explicit, but the mix of voices within particular journals hints at this multiplicity, as seen in these final six entries in one student's journal:

> O.K. Let's write a few lines in the ol'journal. [November 11]
> Talked to Damon last night. Great conversation! [November 13]
> Looking back over my journal, I see that this semester I have had a one track mind. [November 16]
> We did it! We beat Navy. Now for Clemson! [November 17]
> I'm sitting here with candles lit, the radio on and not studying. [December 1]
> Well. This is it. You're last journal to be turned in. But you need to keep writing in it. [December 7]

In these diary-like entries, this young woman alternates among first person plural, first person singular, and second person, occasionally using fragments without subjects. She remains the actual subject, but her shifting perspective makes it impossible to designate these clearly as private or public.

Just as the terms "reader-based" and "writer-based" seem to blur in certain passages, the audience for some entries, whether self or other or both, appears indeterminate. If we assume along with many rhetoric textbooks that the journal is a private realm, we overlook its public appeal and its voices that seem to call forth an audience beyond the self.

Expressive/Transactional

The terms "expressive" and "transactional" are now established in the composition lexicon as a means of differentiating texts by aim or purpose. James Kinneavy's *A Theory of Discourse* is the most exhaustive theoretical treatment of rhetorical aims. His elaborate taxonomy is based upon the communicative system (encoder, decoder, reality, and signal), particularly the aims (expressive, referential, literary, and persuasive) he associates with the system's elements. Kinneavy comments on the neglect by textbooks "of the aims to which discourses are oriented." Yet, he argues, "purpose in discourse is all important. The aim of a discourse determines everything else in the process of discourse" (48). For him the aim is "embodied in the text itself," rather than in encoder or decoder (49). Among examples of expressive discourse he lists journals and diaries, placing conversation, gripe sessions, and prayer under the same heading.

While Kinneavy's taxonomy of aims grows out of his work in philosophy and semantics, the "function categories" formulated by James Britton and his colleagues are based upon research in English secondary schools. Whereas Kinneavy assumes that there are four aims of discourse, Britton and his research team claim that writing begins with an expressive urge ("the tentative first drafts of new ideas") and then develops into one of three basic functions: transactional, expressive, or poetic (82–83). Transactional writing encompasses, roughly, Kinneavy's persuasive and referential categories, and Britton's other two categories—poetic and expressive—are comparable to Kinneavy's literary and expressive divisions. Like Kinneavy, Britton mentions the diary as a type of expressive writing (89).

Other researchers have adopted similar constructs, sometimes altering the key terms. Janet Emig, for example, prefers the words "reflexive" and "extensive" to Britton's "poetic" and "transactional," although she keeps the term, "expressive," to describe the writer's initial motivation. According to Emig, "the notions that all student writings emanate from an expressive impulse and that they then bifurcate into two major modes is useful and accurate" (37). Now it is commonly assumed that expressive or preliminary writing often precedes more polished work and that finished writing may be broadly categorized as either expressive (poetic, reflexive) or transactional (communicative, extensive).

Certainly these efforts to classify writing by aim have added much to our understanding of the composing process, particularly as they helped shift the pedagogical focus away from the traditional four modes. Yet, when applied to specific texts, these descriptive terms seem problematic. If we take journal writing by definition to be expressive, then of course everything we find in student journals matches that aim. But if such labels are at all meaningful, they must apply to identifiable textual features apart from the context. Yet, individual journal entries seldom lend themselves to such neat differentiation.

Britton and his colleagues characterize expressive writing as "close to the self," less explicit than transactional writing, and relatively unstructured (90). But the following student journal entry—not an atypical passage—seems directed to an audience, explicit, and structured:

> I had a dream that was interesting in the respect that it was in the third person point of view, and I wasn't even in it or even involved in it at all. Two girls were walking in a mall and noticed a gathering of people in black robes and hoods. They were chanting some mysterious songs that seemed to be in another language. In the dream, you never could see the faces of the people in the group. The group then went into a movie theater in the mall and the two girls followed them. A film came on showing accounts of torture, various accounts of decapitations. The weird group of people sat and watched the movie—like a bunch of zombies. Girl A thought the movie was revolting and wanted to leave, but Girl B enjoyed the film and wanted to stay until the end. Sometime during the night they go home, and you can see Girl A sleeping in her bed. A pink cartoon cat's face comes out of the wall and glides into the wall above the girl's head. End of dream.

This dream account does not fit Britton's definition of expressive writing nearly as well as it fits "reporting," a subcategory of transactional writing, which he defines as follows:

> In report, the writer takes up a retrospective stance (a stance which gives him a basis of selection denied to the writer in the previous category). . . . he may write as one who by some means or another knows about the past . . . and is a reliable informant (95).

Dreams are notoriously associative and loosely structured, the most personal of events. Yet in the dream journal entry, the student imposes an order retrospectively, reporting selectively and chronologically. Of course, some imposition of order would be inevitable in any account of a dream, even if the aim were unquestionably expressive. This is precisely the point: although this entry may serve an expressive aim, its features would make it suitable for transaction, a clear explanation for others of the writer's experience.

Here is another student's journal entry that seems not to match the "expressive" category as Britton defines it:

> Studying all night for an exam can have some devastating effects on the human body. Beady red eyes are the first give away from an all nighter. People begin to prop open their eyelids with toothpicks.
>
> Coffee cups can often be seen filled with coffee stemming or sometimes running over, dripping down the sides. Occasionally when its warm a Coke can will replace the coffee cup.
>
> Dark circles under the eyes are another sign of a late night cram. It often resembles a raccoon.

What stands out here is not the student's "expression" of her thoughts or feelings about this experience but her movement beyond narrative to generalization as she enumerates the typical effects of all-night study. This entry seems to fit one of Britton's transactional subcategories, a form of writing he calls "analogic, low level of generalization." This type of writing, according to Britton, has "cast off the link with the organizing principle of narrative/description which is retained in generalized narrative" (96).

Related to the expressive/transactional dichotomy is Janet Emig's distinction between self-sponsored and school-sponsored writing, to which she refers in her study of the composing processes of twelfth graders. At first glance Emig's terms, now widely used, appear easily differentiated: work required by school is one thing, work initiated by the individual is another. But in the student journal the terms seem to converge. The journal as a whole is school-sponsored in the sense that the teacher requires it. But it's self-sponsored in that the student determines exactly what goes into it. More provocatively, some entries seem to have so many characteristics of standard school-sponsored assignments that they could pass for expository essays. Students frequently use school-sponsored forms for their self-sponsored composing. Take this argument for baseball's designated hitter rule:

> This week's first subject is the problem that has been blown out of proportion in major leage baseball. This "problem" is that of the designated hitter. It has been said that it takes something out of the game. It is true that the manager of the team is reduced to the capacity of spectator and the stadgedy the game is reduced. However, there are advantages it adds to the game that many people seem to be missing. My first example I'd like to cite is this year's World Series. This year the DH was not used, so fans were forced to suffer through 29 instances where the pitcher came to batt. The result was enough outs to account for one entire nine inning game.

This is only half of a long and articulate entry. This student's approach would be appropriate for a much more public forum than the journal. In fact, more than most students, he seems consciously to be working with ideas that could be used in other assignments, something we encourage students to do in their journals. This passage, then, is both self-sponsored and school-sponsored.

The segments of student writing quoted above, like most other journal entries, cannot be pigeonholed as public, private, expressive, transactional, self-sponsored, or school-sponsored. They seem to embody some of each, and this mix makes them effective. Similarly, we are perhaps most drawn to transactional discourse that also serves an expressive function. For this reason, politicians personalize their messages with references to their families and communities. And it explains why Don Murray draws on his own writing as he comments on focus in writing:

> I had published an earlier version of this chapter, and I had drafted a new version, and the readers hadn't liked it. I snarled back at the readers' comments, but decided they were right. I kept making false starts, guesses at what I might say. I was trying to focus on focus. None of them worked. And then I had the idea. . . . (88)

Murray, like the best rhetoricians, knows that the personal revelation is often inextricable from the public message.

The research of Britton, Kinneavy, Emig, and others has heightened our understanding of textual functions and writers' aims, taking us beyond the musty categories of current-traditionalism. But their work serves best as a provocative heuristic rather than a firm classification scheme. We and our students should notice how texts of all kinds display a rich interplay between the elements in these dichotomies. These bifurcated categories are useful in broadly describing textual prerogatives but collapse when applied to isolated passages.

Process/Product

Like the elusive terms mentioned above, the words "process" and "product" become unstable when applied to the student journal. We require journal keeping for invention and practice, elements of the writing process. We encourage students to draw on their journals as idea books for further writing. Yet most students have difficulty with this, as I do with my own journal. This is not surprising when we consider that many writers keep diaries or journals that show little or no connection with their other work. Virginia Woolf kept copious diaries but seldom drew on them for her novels and essays. James Gould Cozzens kept notebooks, of which only traces are evident in his fiction.

We tend to assume that assigned journals at least indirectly improve other student work. Even if students don't draw on journal entries for essays, letters, and reports, we hope they will benefit from the added practice. However, a passage from Anaïs Nin's diary presents a contrary view:

> Conflict with diary-writing. While I write in the diary I cannot write a book. I try to flow in a dual manner, to keep recording and to invent at the same time, to transform. The two activities are antithetical (II, 110).

Interestingly, Nin thinks of diary keeping as "recording," whereas writing a book requires her to "invent." This makes sense yet seems reversed if we see the journal only as a technique for invention. More provocatively, Nin suggests that the diary siphons off energy that could be devoted to other work. This view is not unique to her. May Sarton writes, "It has been next to impossible to keep at this journal lately because I am writing poems and they take the marrow of my energy" (44). Perhaps our students' similar complaints are not unfounded.

Whether or not they use them for inventing ideas, writers occasionally publish their diaries, journals, and notebooks as if they were finished products. Usually this only occurs following recognition in another genre or in another sphere of public life. In a strangely circular process, the publication of the journal may be the end product of the work it contributed to in the first place. The line between process and product disappears.

Literature specialists are likely to view the journal as a product, while those in composition think of it as a component in the writing process. A process-oriented myopia may lead us to ignore the journal's status as a product, for many students the longest piece of writing—and the closest thing to a book—they will ever create. Thinking of the journal only as an imperfect early stage in writing may lead us to dismiss it as a set of rough jottings to be gleaned and cast aside. In the case of the journal, the opposition between literature and composition begins to break down along with the artificial split between process and product.

In the classroom we can confront the dichotomies outlined above by showing students how writers such as Thoreau have produced journals that are both idea books and texts worthy of study on their own merits. We can encourage our students to experiment and gather ideas in their journals. But later, we should have them examine their work as a whole, drawing conclusions about what they find. Students can benefit from reading their journals analytically, looking for characteristic motifs and stylistic traits. They can be asked to reread their work in search of the controlling dichotomies and, ultimately, to apply their perceptions to texts of all kinds. The journal assignment should be more than a weekly pound of flesh. If used well, it can illustrate the rich mix of voices and motives that inhabit much of what we write.

In our teaching we should acknowledge that the journal has a public as well as a private dimension, that it is both an expressive and a transactional medium, and that it serves as both product and process. Students may understand these entanglements better than we, and we can increase our credibility by accepting the reflections of these juxtaposed terms within one another. We can thus transform the most pervasive dichotomy of all: student/teacher. We all become students again each time we write; our journals record a halting struggle with words. On the other hand, our students become our teachers each time we read their journals. We learn from them what the college experience is like and get from them a glimpse of the eighteen-year-old worldview. There is a teacher trapped within every student, expressive impulses within every transaction, and public purposes within every private gesture. Grappling with these paradoxes can enrich our teaching on all fronts and can make the journal a vital aspect of our writing courses.

Works Cited

Berlin, James A. "Contemporary Composition: The Major Pedagogical Theories." *College English* 44 (1982): 765–777.

Britton, James, et al. *The Development of Writing Abilities (11–18).* 1975. Urbana, IL: National Council of Teachers of English, 1979.

Burton, Sir Richard F. *Personal Narrative of a Pilgrimage to Al-Madinah and Meccah.* Vol. 1. Ed. Isabel Burton. 1913. New York: Dover, 1964.

Elbow, Peter, and Jennifer Clarke. "Desert Island Discourse: The Benefits of Ignoring Audience." *The Journal Book.* Ed. Toby Fulwiler. Portsmouth, NH: Boynton/Cook, 1987. 19–32.

Emig, Janet. *The Composing Processes of Twelfth Graders.* Urbana, IL: National Council of Teachers of English, 1971.

Flower, Linda. "Writer-Based Prose: A Cognitive Basis for Problems in Writing." *College English* 41 (1979): 19–37.

Frank, Anne. *The Diary of a Young Girl.* Trans. B. M. Mooyaart. Garden City, NY: Doubleday, 1952.

Kinneavy, James L. *A Theory of Discourse.* New York: Norton, 1971.

Knoblauch, C. H. "Modern Rhetorical Theory and Its Future Directions." *Perspectives on Research and Scholarship in Composition.* Ed. Ben W. McClelland and Timothy R. Donovan. New York: Modern Language Association, 1985. 26–44.

Mallon, Thomas. *A Book of One's Own: People and Their Diaries.* New York: Ticknor and Fields, 1984.

Mansfield, Katherine. *Journal of Katherine Mansfield.* Ed. J. Middleton Murry. New York: Ecco, 1983.

Murray, Donald M. *Write to Learn.* 2nd ed. New York: Holt, Rinehart and Winston, 1987.

Nin, Anaïs. *The Diary of Anaïs Nin: 1934–39.* Vol. 2. Ed. Gunther Stuhlmann. New York: Swallow and Harcourt, Brace, and World, 1967.

"NCTE Guidelines for Using Journals in School Settings." *The Journal Book.* Ed. Toby Fulwiler. Portsmouth, NH: Boynton/Cook, 1987. 5–8.

Ong, Walter J., S. J. "The Writer's Audience Is Always a Fiction." *PMLA* 90 (1975): 9–21.

Plath, Sylvia. *The Journals of Sylvia Plath.* Ed. Ted Hughes and Frances McCullough. New York: Ballantine, 1983.

Sarton, May. *Journal of a Solitude.* New York: W. W. Norton, 1973.

Wilde, Oscar. *The Importance of Being Earnest. The Complete Writings of Oscar Wilde.* Vol 2. 1899. New York: The Nottingham Society, 1908.

Woolf, Virginia. *The Diary of Virginia Woolf.* 5 vols. Vol. 1 ed. Anne Olivier Bell. New York: Harcourt Brace Jovanovich, 1977.

FOUR

The Literacies of Science and Humanities
The Monologic and Dialogic Traditions

JOSEPH J. COMPRONE

An Overview

About twenty years ago Richard Ohmann was at work on his classic political reading of the English profession, *English in America*. In that book Ohmann, with the help of Wallace Douglas, outlined the close but largely unrecognized connection between the economy of corporate America and English department approaches to literacy. Ohmann's book is essentially an argument for the politicizing of English departments and for a turning away from the dichotomizing split between those who taught literary consciousness to a smaller, more elite group of specially talented or advanced students and those who taught literacy to the masses, who were being fitted for management positions in business and industry.[1] In many, or even most, cases these two politically different professional roles were taken on by one professor, but not in an integrated way. In freshman English, the professor taught verbal manners to the masses; in advanced literature, the professor opened students to Arnoldian high culture and intellectual life (Ohmann 248).

For years now I have been influenced in my work as a director of composition and teacher of literature in several large, public universities by Ohmann's seminal, but still largely unappreciated, book. In this essay on science and humanities literacy, I wish, first, to use this book to describe an essential dichotomy between subjective and objective approaches to literacy, particularly in the academic professions. Then, I shall review some recent literary theory describing a dialogic approach to literacy that suggests a way the English profession might resolve this split. In the third and most important part of this essay, I will examine what I believe is a new type of modern writing, the contemporary science essay, from a dialogic, rhetorical perspective. This beginning step toward a new method of rhetorical analysis ought to suggest a more organic and synthetic theory of literacy, with both critical and pedagogical implications. It is this new theory of literacy that I believe can help English resolve this deadly dichotomy, as well as help English professors integrate their roles as teachers, researchers, and critics.

Richard Ohmann and the English "Problem"

Ohmann betrays a curious and honest mixed sense of purpose in *English in America*. It is that mixed purpose that brings me back to his book. He traces the modern English department's paradoxical motives back to what was then a new emphasis on specialization in literary studies in English from 1870–1900.[2] But, at the same time that Harvard's English department came into being with a new focus on literary studies, members of that same department (Barrett Wendell, Adams Sherman Hill) were writing textbooks that were to become dominant influences on the teaching of composition in America.[3] This complex change in the motive behind the modern English department evolved naturally enough, Ohmann asserts, from the teacher of literature and humanities' desire to become part of the general move toward professionalism, beginning in the latter part of the last century and progressing to the present (223). Specialization, of course, was the principal means of asserting one's professionalism. The need to specialize led, in turn, away from the more general language study and criticism course of study (with its broad concentrations in rhetoric, faculty psychology, and oral and written discourse) predominant in most American colleges before 1870.[4] English departments, by the 1890s, were coming to use specialization in two ways: they were using it to *serve* the need for functional literacy asserted by the larger, industrial society and other university departments at the lower levels (Ohmann, "Literacy" 675–679)—primarily through large freshman writing programs—while using a more literary sense of literacy to elevate the thinking of the academic and intellectual elect at the higher curricular levels.[5]

The result of this delicate and paradoxical balance between the service and high cultural aims of modern English departments was a kind of cultural schizophrenia concerning literacy. On one side, these departments financed themselves through large multisectioned service courses in which a mechanistic and functional notion of literacy prevailed. This functional literacy was marked by an emphasis on the surface forms of discourse—was it standard or correct, was it "readable," was it easy to follow (coherent), was it structured according to recognized patterns or modes of discourse (by 1930, almost always the expository mode; see Connors, and Berlin on Genung)—these were the kinds of questions considered important by those in English departments who taught freshman composition (often the part-time and graduate apprentice members of the profession). Their aims were to provide students with the language skills to communicate information clearly as they performed as middle-level managers and executives in business and industry and with the linguistic etiquette to handle verbal situations in an educated professional culture (Douglas, "Rhetoric" 125–127).[6] Mechanical and superficial perspectives on language served this efficiency model well, whereas approaches linked with the much longer and complex tradition of rhetoric and literary study, with their emphasis on organic relationships between thinking and writing, did *not* support this efficiency model.[7] In fact, the literary tradition complicated the issue of how to make students functionally literate for a capitalist-industrial society.

But English studies never, of course, focused entirely or exclusively on functional literacy. From 1870 on there was a consistent tendency to foster, at least in the largest and most prestigious departments, a second perspective as well, one that focused on the teaching of literature, creative writing, and advanced composition. Even Barrett Wendell at Harvard, often cited as an exemplar of functional approaches to freshman composition, wrote in a very different voice about his upper division courses, where he often deemphasized conventional forms, promoted discussion and collaboration over lecturing, and encouraged alternative modes of expression (Adams, 425–426). The English profession responded to the need to specialize, to become a *discipline*, by promoting one approach to literacy to pay its bills and another to educate its advanced students in ways that were more in line with the empowering and liberating goals of what Matthew Arnold would have called a Hellenistic education. The functional approach dominant in freshman English programs produced, when it succeeded, a more efficient student, one who was ready to take his or her part in the industrial process. The more liberal and critical approach, directed to a smaller number of self-selected students, produced, when it succeeded, a more thoughtful and critical student, one who was prepared to question the system, to respond critically to the assembly-line and production mentality.

There is another, complicating factor in this historical process, though. Ohmann suggests it in his assessment of the relationship between literary studies and science in this century (*English in America*, 16–17). Some of our best teachers and critics of literature have the scientist's sense of moral and ethical disinterestedness. Critics must stand back and objectively analyze literary works according to a systematic (scientific) body of critical principles. Some critics suggested that English could more effectively become a specialized field by making itself over into a positivistic science. After all, the whole notion of professional specialization had been greatly accelerated by the development of scientific disciplines. By becoming one of those disciplines, it was reasoned, English would ride into the twentieth century on the rising tide of professionalism.

But other critics and teachers of literature espoused the difference between literary studies, which were inextricably tied to questions of value, and modern science. Ohmann himself takes this perspective:

> Our activities of research and publication imitate those of the sciences, whose effort is toward the abstract and impersonal. The model is a bad one for us, since our inquiries point ultimately toward the concrete and personal. A critical book or article does not simply record a finding; it demands to be felt, argued, assimilated into the moral lives of its audience, and it admits of no guild limitations on that audience (*English*, 17).

Taken in full perspective, however, I would argue that this science/humanities dichotomy in English has created real problems in defining the purpose of the English curriculum. Seen as those who would scientize English would have us see it, the science/humanities relationship is one that promotes the objectification of all bodies of knowledge, one that reifies the positivistic relationship between the knower and the known in all serious (read, *scientific*) inquiries into reading and writing. Conversely, in adopting the view of those who, like Ohmann, would accentuate the difference between literary studies and science, the science/humanities relationship (at least when carried to its extreme) is one that promotes the essential subjectivity of all literary ways of knowing and asserts the impossibility of ever knowing anything definitely through literary experience. Both of these positions are extreme and have been questioned by recent epistemological work in both the sciences and humanities.[8]

This epistemological confusion in our professional lives is compounded in composition studies by the positivistic, pseudoscientific approach to discourse and its teaching that has been the staple of current-traditional rhetoric. Some English teachers teach freshman composition with positivistic and rule-governed methods, and then, probably sub- or semiconsciously, turn around and subvert those positivist conventions when they teach upper division creative writing or literature courses. As a profession or discipline, this certainly makes us seem unstable, often incoherent to the faculty, administrators, and public that inquire into our methods and philosophies. But, worse, it also makes us uncomfortable with our own methods of treating different courses and research projects.

Ohmann's definition of the English problem is a starting point in finding a solution to that problem. We must begin with a new, more integrated sense of what literacy is, and we must build on that new sense of literacy an equally new and integrated sense of what it means to connect the sciences and humanities. A good deal of recent theory in literary studies and rhetoric offers us a way out of this professionally schizophrenic situation. Beneath the surface of these professional ambivalences and contradictions lie considerations of monologic and dialogic theories of literacy, implied, consciously or subconsciously, by this complicated political surface. If we connect these implied theories to those being explicitly developed by Mikhail Bakhtin, E. D. Hirsch, Jr., and Paulo Freire, we develop a more balanced and synthetic theory of literacy; and in the process reconcile science and the humanities by countering the superficial tendency, at least as far as modern epistemological and social theory is concerned, to consider the sciences as objective and the humanities as subjective disciplines.

Dialogic and Monologic Theories of Literacy and the Teaching of English

Most commentators on literacy see Bakhtin and Hirsch as advocates of totally different ideological perspectives on literacy. But, as with all complex issues of language use in cultural contexts, there are both similarities and differences between Bakhtin and

Hirsch on literacy. It is important not to override these similarities as we consider the differences.

Both Bakhtin and Hirsch recognize that processes of literacy are contextually organized and defined and that meaning evolves from interactions among composer, text, and context. In fact, Hirsch, in the process of rejecting certain aspects of his earlier work (*The Philosophy of Composition*), revises his earlier positivistic framework on literacy, drawn from empirical psycholinguistics, and replaces it with the recognition that writers and readers build meaning out of a transaction between their prior knowledge of the subject of discourse and the knowledge transcribed in a particular text. Readers are not passive decoders of writers' meanings; rather, they actively participate in the making of meaning, drawing from their own previous experience and knowledge in order to create, as co-transactors with writers, the composite meaning of a textual utterance:

> The new picture that is emerging from language research . . . brings to the fore the highly active mind of the reader, who is now discovered to be not only a decoder of what is written down but also a supplier of much essential information that is not written down. . . . The explicit meanings of a piece of writing are the tip of an iceberg of meaning; the larger part lies below the surface of the text and is composed of the reader's own relevant knowledge (*Cultural Literacy* 33–34).[9]

This recognition by Hirsch that literacy does not depend on learning objective forms and conventions of language is, of course, a recognition shared by Bakhtin, with his emphasis on dialogic consciousness and literacy. Literate people, particularly those literate people who are experienced readers of literature, are able to hold two "objects" in attention at once; they are able, according to Bakhtin, to hear both the text they are reading at the moment and the voices of other texts that are not there. The modern novel has been at the forefront of developing this complex sense of dialogic consciousness in writers and readers.[10] Every novel contains in itself many voices—of authors, narrators, and characters, and of linguistic registers such as pieces from newspapers, popular songs, advertisements, and professional argots that are brought whole into the text of the novel. Every novel also contains imitations, parodies, and ironic references to voices of the culture that are not directly represented in the novel itself. Experienced readers of novels, thus, develop the ability to hear and synthesize these internal and external novelistic voices, and to turn the polyglot form of the novel into a unified, complex meaning—a total experience of linguistic culture:

> The novel orchestrates all its themes, the totality of the world of objects and ideas depicted and expressed in it, by means of the social diversity of speech types . . . and by the differing individual voices that flourish under such conditions. Authorial speech, the speeches of narrators, inserted genres, the speech of characters are merely those fundamental compositional unities with whose help heteroglossia . . . can enter the novel; each of them permits a multiplicity of social voices and a wide variety of their links and interrelationships (always more or less dialogized). These distinctive links are interrelationships between utterances [texts] and languages [in general], this movement of the theme through different languages and speech types, its dispersion into the rivulets and droplets of social heteroglossia, its dialogization—this is the basic distinguishing feature of the novel (Bakhtin 263).[11]

Bakhtin's concept of heteroglossia (see the definition of this term in note 11) is actually a more specific and organic rendering of what Hirsch means by context. But, it is here that the similarities between Hirsch and Bakhtin end.

Hirsch goes on in *Cultural Literacy* to posit a theory of literacy that is essentially *monologic*. For Hirsch, at least by suggestion, each act of literacy is separate from every other. Individual psychology and physiology and an *external* context of knowledge—that is, an objectified sense of cultural knowledge—come together for Hirsch in mechanistic ways every time a writer writes and readers read a text. It is as if a defined and systematic national effort has been made to fill individual heads with certain bits of cultural knowledge, and that individual readers and writers are programmed to use this cultural context as they build meaning out of individual textual utterances. This line of argument is especially apparent in Hirsch's analysis of how national/cultural identities are made and in his description of how these identities operate on individuals as they read and write (70–93). Each national culture formulates a national vocabulary that contains key pieces of cultural knowledge. These bits of cultural knowledge, embodied in a national vocabulary, serve as cues to readers and writers as they compose textual meanings, signaling certain key ideas in that culture. The process, then, is unitary and one-dimensional; static knowledge operates on individual consciousness through a static language (61).[12]

For Bakhtin, literacy is a far more dynamic and dialogic process. Readers and writers, as they become more and more literate, learn to hear and orchestrate many voices—voices represented both directly and indirectly in the texts at hand. Learning to hear multiple voices without losing one's bearings and without sacrificing the ability to produce coherent meanings is a central ability in a highly literate culture. What is at stake in these different perspectives on literacy is not simply who is right or wrong in describing a literate person, however. As Hirsch and radical theorists such as Paulo Friere recognize, our whole approach to education in and for literacy is at stake.[13] To clarify these high stakes, an extended consideration of Bakhtin's comparison of monologic and dialogic literacy is in order.

Bakhtin establishes his concept of the dialogic imagination through a contrasting analysis of epic and novel genres. To Bakhtin, the epic had become by the classical period a static genre, always set in the past, sure of its heroes and its perspectives on heroic action. Readers and hearers of epics received stories as past and finished action, as action emblematic of cultural values, but never as dynamic action, subject to the changing perspectives of readers and audience. The pastness of epic was itself reinforced by the stability and basic linearity of epic style—the oral formulas of Greek and Anglo-Saxon epic, the music and rhythm that accompanied those formulaic performances, and the formal occasions within which they occurred (feasts, banquets, "epic" occasions).

All these factors worked to make the epic a static cultural force. Individual consciousness in such an oral-epic context was not meant to be put into a shifting, dynamic relationship with cultural heritage and values; rather, language functioned as a means of enabling culture to permeate and control individual consciousness. In *The Dialogic Imagination*, Bakhtin summarizes the kind of consciousness epic modes of literacy produce:

> In general, the world of high literature in the classical era was a world projected into the past, on to the distanced plane of memory, but not into a real, relative past tied to the present by uninterrupted temporal transitions; it was projected rather into a valorized past of beginnings and peak times. This past is distanced, finished and closed like a circle (19).

Epic consciousness, then, provides its hearers/readers with a closed sense of culture, of cultural forms as given, as formally represented, by a linear and static rendering of past, heroic action. The original epic audience (if one ever existed) did *not* think about, or to use a popular current word, did not *internalize* the contents of epic stories, did not transform epic action into a personalized notion of abstract social values. Instead, they took representative action as directly expressive of commonly held social values. What Achilles did when he ran away from Hector was unquestionably cowardly, no matter how complex the conditions surrounding the action, and no matter how complex Achilles's inner response to the situation.

Later in *The Dialogic Imagination* Bakhtin turns toward the novel. The novel is, according to Bakhtin, a more open-ended and heterogeneous genre. Its roots in both folk and epic traditions provide it with potentials for the tragic and comic, for expressions of high- and low-life experience, character, and action. But far more significantly, the novel's multilayered language and more dynamic forms of narration and style provide it with a linguistic resonance and resiliency that, for Bakhtin, is unmatched by other genres. The novel mixes voices, dynamically representing the languages of all social registers and classes.

Novels have their roots in the underside of ancient literature: folklore and realistic and comic stories of everyday life; parodic and satiric classics such as Patronius's *Satyricon* and Apuleius's *The Golden Ass;* and in the catalogues of seasons in Hesiod's *Theogony.* In all these underlife sources, a cacophony of social voices were represented; hearers and readers heard the voices of culture speaking in dissarray—Lucius in *The Golden Ass*, metamorphosed into a jackass, hears the languages of thieves, servants, entrepreneurs, lawyers, patricians, priests, and the epic voices of Cupid and Psyche reformulated in more familiar, novelistic vernacular (*Dialogic Imagination*, 111–129).

Even this century's experimentation with interior and exterior narrative voices, Bakhtin tells us, has its roots in ancient folklore, satire, and realism. It is the novel's way of carrying on the heteroglossic tradition established in classical folklore, which was kept alive in Augustinian combinations of rhetoric and narrative in *The Confessions*, and slowly transformed by medieval romance, with its fusion of high, courtly, and low folk languages, into the modern novel from Cervantes and Rabelais on.

As teachers and theorists of literacy, we are not most interested in these generic, literary categorizations but in their implications for our conceptions of the functions and purposes of reading and writing. What Bakhtin is saying to us is that the novel has carried on for centuries the dialogic tradition. The novel has always fostered a kind of literacy in which the words of the text represent broad areas of culture and language, simultaneously. Within this dialogic context, readers cannot respond to the novel's heteroglossic structure and its clowning, comic parodic perspectives in monologic ways

(161). Readers of modern novels must learn to be receptive to many dialects and voices in the texts they read, must learn as well to hear one voice and interpret its meaning with another, must learn, ultimately, to turn the novel's "interanimation of languages," its "laughter," and its "polyglossia" into dialogic responses of their own (82). The reader's dialogic imagination, in actuality, becomes a new, more organic and dialectical form of literacy. What is in the text is always glossed by the reader's knowledge of context, by his or her sense of voices other than the ones immediately represented on the page. Readers complete texts by supplying the context that is implied by the words, by acknowledging realities that are dismissed or countered by the text itself.

This, of course, is a very different understanding of the type of consciousness produced by higher literacy than we find in Hirsch, whose sense of literacy seems more akin to epic than dialogic consciousness. But one must at this point recognize a possible explanation for Hirsch's more static and mechanistic approach to the knowledge-discourse relationship. Hirsch seems to suggest that the lower schools can inculcate cultural knowledge in a somewhat automatic, fact-driven way, but that later on those same fact-driven students might free themselves for critical thinking.

> A great deal is at stake in understanding and acting on this [the child's need for traditional information] essential perception as early as possible. The opportunity of acquiring cultural literacy, once lost in the early grades is usually lost for good. That is most likely to be true for children of parents who were not themselves taught the literate national culture (*Cultural Literacy* 31).

One must turn to the work of the South American Marxist Paulo Freire to develop a full perspective on Hirsch's position. Freire, in *Pedagogy of the Oppressed*, argues a theory of literacy with implications for curriculum diametrically opposed to Hirsch's. Working from his experience in teaching adult, illiterate peasants in Brazil, Freire asserts that learning literacy always, by definition, means expanding one's consciousness to include the social and political implications of language (67). Reading and writing cannot be taught or learned in mechanical, positivistic ways because people must carry out this learning in an environment that is saturated with the meanings and connotations of existing political and social structures. The relation of words written and read to objective or interpersonal reality are, in any cultural context, colored by existing sociopolitical structures. What Freire calls the "banking" approach to pedagogy assumes that literacy education is wholly informational: the learning of denotations of words, of syntactic rules governing the ordering of words, of idiomatic expressions, of the jargons and technical terms of particular fields or occupations (*Pedagogy*, 57–74). This approach ignores social context; it treats students as cogs in the wheels of industrial/corporate life, who require only the sets of appropriate linguistic skills that will enable them to fit efficiently into the functional roles industrial and high-technological cultures have laid out for them.

The similarities between Freire's notion of the functional "banking" approach to literacy pedagogy and Hirsch's concept of cultural literacy are striking. Educational bankers rely on teaching skills in so-called objective situations, as if learning to read and write can ever be separated from the homes, jobs, leisure activities, and civil lives of the learners. Hirsch acknowledges that reading and writing cannot be learned as sets of skills isolated from cultural contexts, but he then parallels the positivism of Freire's "bankers" by positing a literacy program that is based on an inert set of culturally approved facts and ideas.[14] It is, for Hirsch, as if—since he has learned from current psycholinguistic research in reading that fluent readers provide over half of the knowledge required to produce the meaning of a text—educators could replace a positivistic emphasis on skills with an equally positivistic and even more mechanical emphasis on cultural knowledge.

In *Education for Critical Consciousness*, Freire goes on to explain in more detail a pedagogy that he believes would result in the kind of literacy that combines skills and critical consciousness. The key word in Freire's approach, as in Bakhtin's, is *dialogic*. As young children or adult peasants learn to read and write, they must, from their first efforts at learning, come to see that words are functional, that they carry with them as they move from person to person and place to place, the social and political uses to which they have been put in the past. These past meanings combine with present uses to create dual, or dialogical, functions and meanings (43–47).[15] The voices of the manufacturer who will employ the peasant when he or she becomes literate are contained in the word *tractor*, just as the family connotations surrounding that word, as it is used to carry out the work of a small farm, are also contained in it. *Both* meanings, along with all the past spoken voices that have used the word in different contexts (the banker who finances the tractor, the mechanic who repairs it, the laborer who uses it, the landowner who possesses it, and the peasant who lives *in* it) are present in the word itself, resonating in it as it is used. Truly literate individuals, to Freire, are those who know and can use words in ways that build upon the essentially dialogic quality of words, and who can also expand their consciousness to include the many dialogic voices contained in everyday language (*Pedagogy*, 167–186; *Critical Consciousness*, 37–40).[16]

Just as Bakhtin describes the play of dialogic voices as they work in the novel, so Freire gives us a description of how the illiterate peasants of Brazil must, by becoming literate, learn to hear the voices and become part of the dialogue of cultural literacy. But, whereas Hirsch's emphasis on cultural literacy concentrates on fitting the learner to what the culture already knows, leaving the development of high critical consciousness to much later in the educational process, Freire describes a society in which even the basic learner comes to understand the sociopolitical implications of words.

The Dialogics Involved in Reading Lewis Thomas

The opposition between dialogic and monologic perspectives on literacy is often at the center of the academic profession's, and the modern English department's, dichotomous ways of treating the sciences and humanities. At least as far as teaching reading and writing is concerned, most academics foster only a monologic perspective based on understanding science texts as basically objective and positivistic instruments of knowing and on humanities texts as the result of essentially subjective ways of knowing. Science writing is taught as communication *after* the writer has applied scientific methods of induction or deduction to the object of study.[17] Language remains a neutral and transparent instrument for relaying objective information.

On the other side of this oversimplified way of looking at language, academic humanists, at least when they talk about writing, emphasize the subjectivity and ambiguity of literary or scholarly prose, and they often underline the dynamic and organic function of language in any epistemological endeavor. Humanists, these dichotomous thinkers say, can never remove language from the center of man's or woman's relationship with nature or society. As long as writing teachers allow this kind of dichotomous and monologic thinking to dominate the professional discourse about teaching writing, writing courses will never develop truly dialogic approaches to learning to write in the academy. And this failure of theory and methodology will, in turn, continue to contribute to the political divisions between those who teach literacy in a monologic way and those who teach literature in a dialogic way. Teachers of literacy (composition and reading) are then relegated to *serving* the masses with functional and admittedly oversimplified approaches to language, whereas teachers of literature are seen as *enlightening* a select few with more imaginative and aesthetic approaches.

I believe writing teachers can use textual analysis of a new genre of contemporary writing to overcome the false dichotomies now existing concerning science and humanities writing. The "science essay" is produced by professional scientists such as Stephen Jay Gould, Oliver Sacks, Richard Selzer, Loren Eiseley, and others who consciously mix forms and voices as they write about science for generally educated audiences.[18] These writers consciously produce dialogic texts in which different kinds of professional, literary, and conversational voices are represented, and in which these voices often parody and comment on each other. These types of essays represent what Bakhtin calls the "hybridization" of languages within one genre, and readers of this hybridized genre must be trained to hear and use these voices both as they interpret what they read and as they write essays and reports of their own (358–363).

Biologist and physician Lewis Thomas has penned National Book Award–winning essays that are a complex combination of scientific and literary voices. Compare these two passages from Thomas's essay "On Smell" (from *Late Night Thoughts on Listening to Mahler's Ninth Symphony*):

1

The act of smelling something, anything, is remarkably like the act of thinking itself. Immediately, at the very moment of perception, you can feel the mind going to work, sending the odor around from place to place, setting off complex repertoires throughout the brain, polling one center after another for signs of recognition, old memories, connections. This is as it should be, I suppose, since the cells that do the smelling are themselves proper brain cells, the only neurones whose axones carry information picked up at firsthand in the outside world. Instead of dendrites they have cilia, equipped with receptors for all sorts of chemical stimuli, and they are in some respects as mysterious as lymphocytes. There are reasons to believe that each of these neurones has its own specific class of receptors; like lymphocytes, each cell knows in advance what it is looking for; there are responder and nonresponder cells for different classes of odorant. And they are also the only brain neurones that replicate themselves; the olfactory receptor cells of mice turn over about once every twenty-eight days. There may be room for a modified version of the clonal-selection theory to explain olfactory learning and adaptation. The olfactory receptors of mice can smell the difference between self and nonself, a discriminating gift coded by the same H-2 gene locus governing homograft rejection. One wonders whether lymphocytes in the mucosa may be carrying along this kind of genetic information to donate to new generations of olfactory receptor cells as they emerge from basal cells (42).

2

If you are looking about for things to even out the disparity between the brains of ordinary animals and the great minds of ourselves, the superprimate humans, this apparatus is a good one to reflect on in humility. Compared to the common dog, or any rodent in the field, we are primitive, insensitive creatures, biological failures. Heaven knows how much of the world we are missing.

Here one finds, on the surface, two voices interacting to create one, unified scientific-literary whole. The first excerpt is marked by a mix of casual conversation and scientific/technical vocabulary. The stacking of nouns in series (the *something, anything* of line 1), the use of the more familiar second person pronoun (the *you* in line 3), the interjection of a first person narrator (the *I suppose* of line 7), the use of idiomatic and vernacular expressions (the *picked up at firsthand* in line 9), these are Thomas's devices for aligning his essay with the longstanding, literary tradition of the informal essay written by the person of letters—Montaigne, De Quincey, Lamb, and many others.[19] But, as the passage progresses, one notices the gradual transformation of this informal style, marked by a personal familiarity between author and reader, into a more scientific and technical style, marked by terms, drawn from biological science, such as *dendrites, cilia, receptors, chemical stimuli,* and *lymphocytes.* By the end of this passage Thomas has effected an even more complete switch to this scientific style—his change from the first and second person points of view early in this passage to the use of the impersonal *one* in line 23. Thus, in one paragraph, readers of Thomas's essay find two surface voices, marked by the styles of casual essayist and objective scientist, interacting with one another—in fact, even commenting on and responding to one another in an implied internal dialogue.

In the second passage cited, which appears a paragraph after the first, Thomas returns readers to the casual, literary style (note the "Heaven knows" in line 6 and the return to the familiar second person *you* throughout the paragraph). It is in this paragraph that

Thomas suggests his thesis for the essay: humans, who are efficient seers and hearers, can learn much about smell from animals. Here he implies a general point about the value of combined scientific (objective study of nature) and humanistic (subjective considerations of values and feelings) inquiry, about the value of a kind of reading and writing that I have called "dialogic literacy."[20] This sense of literacy makes the division of the languages of the sciences and the humanities into two separate categories a gross oversimplification of the way literate people actually communicate.

What are the implications behind this embracing of dialogic theories of literacy? For the profession of English teachers, it implies the conceptual unity of what, in this century, has been a painful and unproductive division between those who teach and develop theory about reading and writing (the "composition and reading" people) and those who teach and write about literary works and literary theory (the "literature" people). But, even more significantly, it suggests a way of teaching and writing about texts that will enable students and other readers and writers to hear the many voices in a world of plural texts, and to use those voices as students become part of that world.[21] Dialogism also brings subjectivity and objectivity into one, holistic process, including plural ways of knowing and expressing reality in one composing process. Such an integrated approach will eliminate many of our professional differences.

Notes

1. *English in America* has been out of print for some time. Those who have difficulty finding it in a library should consult "Literacy, Technology, and Monopoly Capital," Ohmann's excellent summary of capitalist influences on theories of functional literacy (see Works Cited).

2. Both Donald Stewart in "Two Model Teachers" and James Berlin in *Rhetoric and Reality* (8–9) describe Harvard's role in this literary movement in English departments.

3. See Berlin's essay on John Genung in his *Rhetoric and Reality* (36–43) for narrative accounts of these seemingly contrary developments; see also Robert Connors on the modes of discourse for a historical perspective on the dominance of what has come to be called "current-traditional" rhetoric in modern composition teaching. Wallace Douglas provides a description and cultural interpretation of Barrett Wendell's place in this paradoxical development of current-traditional rhetoric and literary studies in twentieth-century English departments (see "Barrett Wendell" in Works Cited).

4. Andrea Lunsford's *CCC* essay on Alexander Bain does a good

job of summarizing the influence of faculty psychology on Bain, who, in turn, became a major influence on current-traditional rhetoricians in the United States (see also Connors in Works Cited).

5. Katherine and John Adams, in "The Paradox Within," describe a pattern in the careers of Fred Newton Scott, Barrett Wendell, and Adams Sherman Hill, all of whom wrote freshman textbooks that were mechanistic and rule-governed but who taught upper division writing courses from a more organic and flexible perspective (421). Evidently some early English department leaders contained within their own professional roles a paradox that was shared by English teachers and curricula on a national, professional level.

6. Douglas describes the role played by President Charles William Eliot of Harvard in this move toward the teaching of literacy for the new industrial, corporate professionals, particularly management ("Meritocracy," 125–127).

7. I should point out here that there was a movement counter to the mechanistic approaches of current-traditional rhetoric from 1890–1930. That movement included teachers such as Gertrude Buck, Fred Newton Scott, and Sterling Leonard, whose work is described by Mulderig, Stewart, and Brereton in Works Cited.

8. Most of this new epistemological theory accentuates the interdependence of subject and object in the act of knowing. Both Kenneth Bruffee and David Bleich explain, argue, and describe the sources behind this new epistemology in both the sciences and the humanities (see Works Cited).

9. In this quotation Hirsch is belatedly recognizing what Frank Smith has been saying since the mid-1970s (see *Understanding Reading* in Works Cited).

10. Bakhtin's concepts of heteroglossic voices and the plastic form of the novel are best clarified in the fourth and final essay in *The Dialogic Imagination*, "Discourse in the Novel," 259–422.

11. The translators/editors of Bakhtin's *The Dialogic Imagination* define *heteroglossia* as "the base condition governing the operation of meaning in any utterance. At any given time, in any given place, there will be a set of conditions—social, historical, meteorological, physiological—that will insure that word uttered in that place and at that time will have a meaning different than it would have under any other conditions; all utterances [texts] are heteroglot in that they are functions of a matrix of forces practically impossible to recoup, and therefore impossible to resolve" (428).

12. Hirsch's chapter on *schema* in *Cultural Literacy* (33–69) is just as positivistic in its description of how cultural knowledge affects discourse as his earlier work (*The Philosophy of Composition*) was in its description of how a few simple higher cognitive skills (they were called "maxims") affected the ability to write.

13. Freire's idea that consciousness must expand along with growths in literacy is developed in several books, most notably *The Politics of Education, The Pedagogy of the Oppressed, and Education for Critical Con-*

sciousness (see Works Cited). In working with adult illiterates, Freire argues that words and linguistic structures are permeated with social and political connotations, and that their meanings are always tied in with those connotations. Therefore, a person cannot become literate unless he or she is also aware of and controls these sociopolitical connotations.

14. Hirsch presents a preliminary version of such a factual list in "What Literate Americans Know," an Appendix to *Cultural Literacy*. This appendix is coauthored by Joseph Kett and James Trefil.

15. Freire, in *Education for Critical Consciousness*, describes the illiterate peasant's growing sense of power *in* the world, achieved through a sense of dialogic literacy, as follows:

> From that point of departure [participation in dialogic literacy], the illiterate would begin to effect a change in his former attitudes, by discovering himself to be a maker of the world of culture, by discovering that he, as well as the literate person, has a creative and re-creative impulse. He would discover that culture is just as much a clay doll made by artists who are his peers as it is the work of a great sculptor, a great painter, a great mystic, or a great philosopher; that culture is the poetry of lettered poets and also the poetry of his own popular songs—that culture is all human creation (47).

16. The essays collected in Ira Shor's *Freire for the Classroom* (see Works Cited) describe particular exercises and writing sequences in college composition and ESL classrooms that are derived from Freire's notions of generation themes, problemization in immediate social context, and progressive interaction of writers and readers around such themes and problems. All classroom voices are dialogic in these Freirean contexts.

17. Robert Day demonstrates this position on science writing when he outlines the essentially objective format of the paradigmatic science report: introduction (definition of problem), methods, results, and interpretation. Day asserts that, when it comes to writing a report on a scientific experiment, the science writer ignores all epistemological relativisms or doubts and states findings in neutral, objective, and specialized language.

18. An essay of mine on Oliver Sacks and writing across the curriculum appeared in the Fall 1988 issue of the *Journal of Advanced Composition*, editor Gary Olson, University of South Florida. Abstracts describing several papers I have delivered on this subject at recent Modern Language Association and Conference on College Composition and Communication meetings will soon appear in *Resources in Education (RIE)*, published by the Clearinghouse on Reading and Communication Skills, Smith Research Center, Indiana University, Bloomington.

19. Wayne Booth relates the novel to this informal essay tradition in *The Rhetoric of Fiction* (128, 222, 226–228, 230, 237).

20. I should mention here two recent critical responses to Bakhtin's concept of dialogic imagination. Charles Schuster (see Works Cited) argues that Bakhtin's theories should suggest to rhetoricians that their Aristotelian concepts of the rhetorical triangle (speaker/subject/audience) should be revised into a circle, with subject, reader, and writer moving

around the circumference of the circle in an endlessly dialogic relationship (596). In "The Outer World and Inner Speech: Bakhtin, Vygotsky, and the Internalization of Language" (see Morson in Works Cited), Caryl Emerson argues that "the density of language," that is, its ability to contain many voices speaking simultaneously, will continue to pose problems for teachers and critics until they, first, begin to admit that language is in essence a social process (Vygotsky's influence) and, second, that, if language *is* a social process, then writing and reading must be seen dialogically, with one text containing many subtextual voices (21–40).

21. See Ira Shor's book on Freire in Works Cited for a collection of essays by committed teachers of reading and writing that moves in the professional directions that I have the space only to suggest in this essay. These essays speak in specific terms about reading-writing-speaking exercise sequences that will cause students to hear the many voices of the text they read, and to use those voices in combination with their own as they write.

Works Cited

Adams, J. Donald. *Copey of Harvard*. Boston: Houghton Mifflin, 1960.

Bakhtin, Mikhail. *The Dialogic Imagination*. Ed. Michael Holquist. Austin, U of Texas P, 1981.

Berlin, James. *Rhetoric and Reality: Writing Instruction in American Colleges, 1900–1985*. Carbondale: Southern Illinois UP, 1987.

———. "John Genung and Contemporary Composition Theory: The Triumph of the Eighteenth Century." *The Rhetoric Society Quarterly* 9 (Spring 1981): 74–84.

Bleich, David. "Cognitive Stereoscopy and the Study of Language and Literature." *Convergences: Transactions in Reading and Writing*. Ed. Bruce Peterson. Urbana, IL: National Council of Teachers of English, 1986. 99–114.

Booth, Wayne C. *The Rhetoric of Fiction*. 2nd ed. Chicago: U of Chicago P, 1983.

Brereton, John. "Sterling Andrus Leonard." *Traditions of Inquiry*. Ed. John Brereton. New York: Oxford UP, 1985. 81–104.

Bruffee, Kenneth. "Social Construction, Language, and the Authority of Knowledge: A Review Essay." *College English* 48 (1986): 773–790.

Connors, Robert. "The Rise and Fall of the Modes of Discourse." *College Composition and Communication* 32 (December 1981): 444–456.

Day, Robert. *How to Write and Publish a Scientific Paper*. 2nd ed. Philadelphia: ISI P, 1979, 1983.

Douglas, Wallace. "Rhetoric for the Meritocracy." *English in America*. By Richard Ohmann. New York: Oxford UP, 1976. 98–132.

———. "Barrett Wendell." *Traditions of Inquiry*. Ed. John Brereton. New York: Oxford UP, 1985. 3–25.

Freire, Paulo. *The Politics of Education*. Trans. Donald Macedo. South Hadley, MA: Bergin and Garvey Pubs., 1985.

————. *The Pedagogy of the Oppressed*. Trans. Myra Bergman Ramos. New York: Seabury, 1970.

————. *Education for Critical Consciousness*. Center for the Study of Development and Social Change. New York: Seabury, 1973.

Hirsch, E. D., Jr. *Cultural Literacy*. Boston: Houghton Mifflin, 1987.

————. *The Philosophy of Composition*. Chicago: U of Chicago P, 1977.

Lunsford, Andrea. "Essay-Writing and Teacher's Responses in Nineteenth-Century Scottish Universities." *College Composition and Communication* 32 (December 1981): 434–443.

Morson, Gary Saul, ed. *Bakhtin*. Chicago: U of Chicago P, 1981.

Mulderig, Gerald. "Gertrude Buck's Rhetorical Theory and Modern Composition Teaching." *Rhetoric Society Quarterly* 14 (Spring, Fall 1984): 95–104.

Ohmann, Richard. *English in America: A Radical View of the Profession*. New York: Oxford UP, 1976.

————. "Literacy, Technology, and Monopoly Capital." *College English* 47 (November 1985): 675–689.

Schuster, Charles I. "Mikhail Bakhtin as Rhetorical Theorist." *College English* 47 (October 1985): 594–607.

Shor, Ira, ed. *Freire for the Classroom*. Portsmouth, NH: Boynton/Cook, 1987.

Smith, Frank. *Understanding Reading*. New York: Holt, 1971.

Stewart, Donald. "Two Model Teachers and the Harvardization of English Departments." *The Rhetorical Tradition and Modern Writing*. Ed. James J. Murphy. New York: MLA, 1982. 118–129.

————. "Rediscovering Fred Newton Scott." *College English* 40 (January 1979): 539–547.

Thomas, Lewis. *Late Night Thoughts While Listening to Mahler's Ninth Symphony*. New York: Viking, 1983.

FIVE

Professional Writing Meets Rhetoric and Composition

JOHN BRERETON

There has always been a gap separating freshman composition from the advanced writing instruction—usually technical and business writing—that I shall call professional writing. The former is essentially a preparation for college, the latter a preparation for careers. That gap is widened by the desire to escape the low status imposed on the two fields within their academic setting, English departments. Furthermore, the two fields are old, complex, and not very well united; there are wide disparities within both camps, disagreements over priorities, methodologies, and allegiances. That said, I would like to examine one particular gap that separates composition from professional writing, the complaint that composition is a humanities subject and, thus, poor preparation for the kind of writing students will have to do on the job. I do so from a perspective that itself bridges gaps, since I direct technical and professional writing programs but have a background entirely in literature and rhetoric.

While some gaps may stem from a simple misunderstanding, in this case, close inspection reveals a wider gap than we imagined. What looks like a little coolness, or a modest academic wrangle, is I believe a reflection of some radically different assumptions underlying both fields. By examining what divides us, I hope we may arrive at a deeper sense of the complexities of writing research and instruction, and the beginnings of some ways to link two very disparate efforts.

At first, it seems easy to prove that no great chasms divide composition and professional writing. The latter is simply a subdivision of the former; composition/rhetoric is the field that analyzes and teaches nonfiction writing; professional writing (with its well-known divisions into business writing and technical writing) is one particular category of the larger field. But a significant portion of professional writing scholars regard themselves not as allies of composition scholars but as essentially different. To these professional writing specialists, composition has much more in common with creative writing and literature than it does with advanced pre-professional training. In their view, composition is far too humanistic and too academic. What they are claiming, though not in so many words, is that freshman composition is really literary. And rather than summarily dismissing such a claim, I want to examine it more closely, for I think there is a good bit of truth to it.

Critical comment on English department attitudes toward "applied" writing has been appearing in professional writing journals for at least the past two decades. For instance, Earl Britton's fighting title, "The Trouble with Technical Writing Is Freshman English" aptly describes his claim that composition, by emphasizing the wrong skills, provides poor preparation for advanced professional writing coursework and for the job market as well. Britton cites four main faults: (1) freshman composition stresses essays, which are seldom used in technical discourse; (2) freshman comp fails to confront the key technical writing situation: a knowledgeable writer addressing poorly informed readers; (3) composition teachers judge assignments on "quality of thought" rather than "communicative effectiveness"; and, (4) freshman composition stresses the inductive approach favored by literary essayists and ignores the deductive approach (main point first, backup later) common to professional writing.

In a similar vein, J. C. Mathes, Dwight Stevenson, and Peter Klaver note that English departments are not the best places to teach professional writing. They warn that when engineering programs send "students to English departments to learn technical communication, they risk having their students taught principles that are in conflict with engineering principles" (332).

Thomas A. Lang, in the December 1987 issue of the *American Medical Writers Association Journal*, claims that the current generation of technical writers are "such bad communicators because they were taught writing in the tradition of the humanities, and they have applied this orientation to technical writing, which requires a fundamentally different orientation" (3). And Lang states that "... most innovations driving technical writing today come from other disciplines, such as psycholinguistics, cognitive psychology, instructional technology, human factors engineering, typography, and organizational communication. Technical writing is not one of the humanities because its new research base is from the cognitive and perceptual sciences, not from the humanities" (4–5).

Finally, in the January 1988 *Journal of Technical Writing and Communication*, Arabella Lyon asserts that the humanities and technical writing have drifted far apart. While once, in the Renaissance, the term "humanities" was elastic enough to encompass the kind of specific, job-oriented writing today's professionals must do, the English department's version of the humanities has since degenerated into ivory tower studies in literature. Lyon contrasts this situation with the sciences and social sciences, which "interact with society and industry for funding and the application of their discoveries, [while] the humanities fail to interact with the world outside the tower" (55–56).

Though these writers by no means speak for all professional writing specialists, they demonstrate pretty clearly that a gap exists. And while there are serious problems with each of these authors' assertions, I would like to suspend judgment for a while in order to explore the notion they all share: that technical writing is not a humanities subject, while regular composition is.

Lurking behind this claim, I believe, is the old distinction between education and training, the former a broad, liberating introduction to culture, the latter a narrow, highly specific concentration on technique. Liberal arts people have always viewed education as positive, training as negative, while many businesspeople have done the opposite. I see a similar difference in attitude underlying the criticism of composition; those most concerned with immediate payoffs—the professional writers—tend to undervalue the education side, while composition specialists, even if they are not aware of it, tend to emphasize long-range educational ends. Nowadays, of course, we associate the humanities with a particular kind of education, the liberal arts, in which the link between careers and academic preparation has been broken. To be sure, this is something of a myth, a modern invention; a good case can be made that the traditional, pre-nineteenth-century humanities curriculum was a very narrow, highly focused training. Despite some exceptions and despite many lofty statements about the role of liberal learning, a humanities education was for centuries extremely concentrated—on construing classical texts in their original languages, on mastering dialectic, on proper elocution, on mathematics, on memorization. It was also highly career oriented: one prime reason for rhetoric's importance was that those in college—future profes-

sors, lawyers, legislators, and clergymen—needed training for public speaking. In other words, Lyon has a good case when she claims
that the humanities, having drifted away from their origins, have
lost their connection to the job demands of the modern world.

And though at first it seems odd, it is not hard to see why the
freshman composition curriculum looks literary to many professional writing specialists. Freshman composition at its best is much
closer to traditional humanities courses than to what professionals like to term "hard-hitting," "useful," "down to earth," "real
world" writing instruction. Professional writing people correctly see
that traditional composition is primarily an introduction to the art
of thinking on paper, a course that breaks down stereotyped, stock
notions in order to allow for richer personal expression. The most
prominent type of modern course, that embodying a process approach, seems particularly aimed at the kind of inward speculation
and weighing of potentialities that makes for a creative, fulfilled
person. It's no accident that composition theorists like Moffett,
Elbow, and Emig value the slow, creative writing approach and
stress introspection, multiple drafts, and discovery techniques. Or
that Berthoff stresses the active role of the imagination in the
making of meaning. Or that some of the best modern rhetorics and
readers (e.g., Bartholomae and Petrosky's *Ways of Reading*) emphasize a critical attitude toward writers and the contexts of
communication.

Professional writing specialists understand such approaches,
but often regard them as suitable only for the early stages of writing
instruction, far removed from advanced preparation. And that
seems to be a key to the big gap between the fields, the claim that
since the thinking and writing required in freshman composition
are simply different from the thinking and writing required in highly
focused professional writing courses, they are two distinct kinds of
writing.[1] To a professional, writing instruction that stresses the
search for a subject through freewriting, revising to determine the
"center of gravity" (Elbow's term), Peirce's triadicity, or a concern
with voice and style is humanistic, literary education, rather than
down-to-earth professional training. And though professionals con-
cede that such approaches help younger students in beginning
composition courses, they are quick to distinguish between the
long, slow developmental process educators employ and the quick,
real world expertise their students need at the end of a business
or tech writing course.[2]

From the perspective of a professional writing faculty member, regular composition is only peripherally concerned with issues
of on-the-job writing: documentation; house styles; formats; graph-

ics; readers' needs. Professional writing specialists willingly describe themselves as concerned with a skill, a *tekne*, in this case a precise, clear-cut ability to communicate. They like to say they deal with "writing that works," or "practical rhetoric" (Lutz, Jarratt, Harkin, and Debs, 1987, 286).[3] On the other hand, composition is fundamentally humanistic, concerned with personal growth, values, and the development of intertwined abilities to read, write, and think critically. Put this way, the professionals are right. Most writing scholars would agree that composition, done well, is more like the other humanities courses—literature, philosophy, history—than like accounting, management, or engineering. And it is certainly not "real world," or practical, at least in the sense that professional writing claims to be.

For a similar perspective, think of how the standard composition course would appear to a business professional, a middle manager who must oversee twenty people as they handle English prose every day. Such a person would be on the firing line of the writing crisis, concerned intimately with everything from format to spelling to usage to punctuation to issues of audience and tone. To this middle manager responsible for turning out a certain amount of acceptable prose every day, the standard freshman English course seems pretty remote. The course seems first of all inextricably concerned with a student's college education; it exists primarily to prepare students for the work they will do in college. It is an introduction to the liberal arts, an in-depth discussion of one liberal art in particular, rhetoric. It is not in any sense "real world." It is useful, to be sure, just as many other college courses are useful. And its subject, writing, connects closely to a key job responsibility, which this executive calls "communications skills." Yet the executive needs people who know the house style and who can produce twenty to thirty pages of easy to edit prose per work week. To confuse the standard college composition course with the real world, job-oriented skill training needed to produce in this office is a ludicrous mistake.

Such a characterization of composition helps explain the constant potential for strong disagreements between these two fields. There is an intellectual chasm, a set of differing allegiances, one to an educational model fostered by centuries of humanistic education, the other encouraged by the day-to-day needs of a technologically organized society in which information processing carries a high premium. But besides this difference in allegiance lies a practical chasm as well, the difference in treatment within their academic setting, an English department. And, as inevitably happens with academics, intellectual distinctions imperceptibly merge with less exalted distinctions that have to do with the pecking order. At times it becomes difficult to separate the differences over content from the differences over status. We can approach the status issue by framing the distinction as a rough equation: as composition is to literature, so is professional writing to composition. That is, when one thinks of all the ways composition is regarded as a second-class citizen in its academic setting, something similar holds true for professional writing.

One measure of the validity of the proposition is how it holds up in light of the system of rewards that operate within English studies. At the centers of power in the discipline—in departments, colleges, publishing houses, professional journals, learned societies, and funding agencies—composition specialists are clearly well behind literary types, but professional writers are a good bit further behind. Their share of honors, grants, rewards, power, even of teaching schedules, depends entirely upon their personal abilities and not at all upon the natural claims of their subject matter. Now it may be argued that this is the situation of composition as well, but I submit that there are significant differences that enable composition people to build successful alliances with their colleagues in literature. As we explore the claim that composition courses are essentially literary, we cannot help noting the connections between composition and literature that also serve to separate the two from less "academic" pursuits:

1. *Ancient origin.* In the humanities, where age and tradition count, composition's history as an academic discipline is as distinguished as any, much more so than most. (In fact, literary criticism entered the college curriculum well after rhetoric had become established.)

2. *A canon of approved works, tested by time and known to all practitioners.* If literary critics and scholars can rely upon each others' common knowledge of major texts, so can composition scholars. One type of composition canon appears most prominently in textbook anthologies that play such an important role in teaching. Everyone recognizes the classic authors: Bacon, Swift, Hazlitt, Lamb, Emerson, Thoreau, Arnold, Huxley, William James, Virginia Woolf, Orwell, E. B. White, Thurber. Everyone also recognizes the "modern" classics: Steven Jay Gould, Lewis Thomas, Maya Angelou, Richard Rodriquez, John McPhee, Annie Dillard, and many others whose appearance can guarantee sales for a composition anthology. Need I point out that these are not "compo-

sition" authors but "literary" ones, and that a major reason for teaching their work stems from its literary excellence?

3. *A common vocabulary and a short list of "approved" approaches to the subject.* Composition Ph.D. programs embody such a vocabulary in their reading lists for the orals; all initiates must become familiar with concepts like Jakobson's communication triangle, "holistic testing," and Aristotle's different types of appeals. Over time, different approaches fall in and out of favor, but there is always a line between acceptable ways of conducting scholarly inquiry and those approaches that fall outside the pale.

4. *A tradition against which to position one's self.* If one may extend Harold Bloom's notion of the creative process—writers are always establishing themselves over and against their predecessors—something similar may be said about literary criticism, where new theories become established only at the expense of the old. Precisely the same may be said for composition studies, in which one approach must cede ground to another. It is not by chance, for instance, that Janet Emig's ground-breaking 1971 study, *The Composing Processes of Twelfth Graders,* begins with a whole section deploring the then-current attitude toward formal outlines. Composition studies may seem to outsiders to be broadly accumulative, piling up wisdom (it is hoped) by the work of many; close up, though, the scene resembles a battle, with critics establishing reputations by discrediting the older theories of others. And in the last two decades composition has had a field day, because so many of the old theories and approaches were ripe for attack.

5. *A common heritage.* Composition specialists were almost all trained in literature, and that training hasn't worn off. Even the new generation of composition scholars, those trained in rhetoric programs, has had an essentially literary background, especially since most rhetoric doctorates require at least half the coursework in literature. Besides the direct influence of courses, the common language of English departments is literary. (Of course, since many professional writing specialists have shared this common heritage, they too have been influenced from the literary side.)

6. *Shared critical texts.* From Aristotle to Bacon to Johnson to Coleridge to Bakhtin, critics of literature have been critics of writing as well; their work is important to both groups. So is work on the philosophy of language, narrativity, revision, canon formation, the reading public, sociolinguistics, reading theory, prose style, to name just a few areas of convergence. Well-trained composition scholars who know the major works on these subjects are not narrow

"educationalists" or social scientists; they are literary types who share the scholarly and teaching interests of their English department colleagues.

Given so many things in common, one has to ask why have we never really thought of composition as a form of literary instruction. The answer, I believe, lies in the way composition scholars have frequently approached their field—not as a liberal art unto itself but as a form of practice, a skill. For generations, composition specialists have been under the spell of the deal made late last century by English departments. Under pressure from increasing numbers of poorly prepared writers, colleges have employed a similar remedy: make all students take a composition course in order to improve their writing, and increase the size of the English faculty accordingly. Under the terms of this bargain, composition must improve student writing rapidly; one semester of college instruction must make up for years of poor preparation or neglect. Thus, composition staffs have for a century undertaken a constant search for results and have often been unable to see that their subject is, like literature, justified not by its immediate outcome but by the values it imparts, the traditions it embodies, and the thinking it inaugurates. That is, the composition course doesn't so much teach a narrow skill as initiate students into liberal learning. The quest for results has let composition staffs assume that their subject's justification lay in immediate impact; there has been a constant search for gimmicks, for quick fixes to lifelong problems. And the stress on practical outcomes was exacerbated by the fact that for generations composition was the course used to determine if students ought to stay in college or be flunked out. It is this depressing fact that lies behind a whole tradition of curriculum research, culminating in Shaughnessy's brilliant *Errors and Expectations;* Shaughnessy understood that the writing issues she addressed were developmental, concerned with liberal arts, not training, yet the political and educational context required immediate response. Until very recently, composition research, driven by the need for results, has been forced to look more to the curriculum, to teaching than to deeper study of rhetoric or communication processes.

In comparison, the context for research and instruction for most professional writing specialists is totally different. First of all, they are responsible not to their peers in the English department but to their colleagues in other disciplines; the successes and failures of their teaching and curriculum planning are seen not by those down the hall but by those safely tucked away in colleges of business or engineering. Furthermore, students who complete professional writing coursework are rarely judged by their communication skills. That is, professional writing courses might be as unsuccessful as freshman composition, but students don't flunk out of college because of low grades in technical or business writing. Most telling of all, the ultimate judges of a business or engineering program's success lie in the job market, where writing ability has little relation to initial placement. (It's often said that writing has nothing to do with landing a first job, but can be decisive in landing the second job.)

Ultimately, the natural allies of many professional writing scholars are not university colleagues at all, but professionals in the workplace. It is no accident that the most prominent organization of professional writers, the Society for Technical Communication (STC), is *not* academic; it is composed of and run by private consultants and professionals from government, business, and industry. It is also common for some of the best university-based professional writing scholars to do a large amount of outside consulting, where their expertise is often appreciated more than on their own campus. Unlike their counterparts in composition, many professional writing scholars find their true peers in the world of affairs, among people who are not educators.

Given how much that divides professional writing specialists from composition scholars, can anything be done to bridge the gap? Yes, there are many measures that may be taken.

1. *Composition and professional writing scholars can develop some common research agendas in order to understand the dynamics of prose in different settings.* In this area, professional writing is far ahead of composition research. Studies like Odell and Goswami's, Flower's, and Couture and Goldstein's begin from the premise of discourse embedded in a community, a concept only beginning to appear in composition research. And when composition researchers do acknowledge discourse as determined by communities, they look closely only at academic communities (e.g., students in school; see Perl and Wilson) or use as their data base the reports of ethnographic fieldwork (e.g., readings of Thomas Kuhn, Clifford Geertz, and Shirley Brice Heath) rather than original observation. Meanwhile, professional writing scholars are examining insurance companies, factories, and government offices. Everyone ought to recognize that professional writing research to date has been more successful in getting out in the field, and less bound by book learning.

2. *Professional writing specialists need to assume a critical stance toward their subject matter.* That means making their profession's discourse the subject of research, just as literary critics study criticism and the reading process as part of their scholarly work. It may be that professional writing people have made a Faustian bargain here; they will teach what has been determined by the engineers or the business faculty, but they will not criticize those faculties' limited conception of professional discourse. Professional writing specialists might be a little behind composition staffs, which are finally taking the lead in determining what should or should not be taught in their own courses. The key to academic independence is the right to shape one's courses according to the requirements of one's discipline, not according to some outside practitioner's notions. That is why writing teachers added to graduate faculties in law and business hardly ever emerge as genuine forces for change; they are kept too busy teaching within the law or business professors' narrow sets of requirements and are not expected to conduct serious research into their own discipline. At even the best law and business schools, writing is highly valued yet still regarded as a narrow skill, much as composition was until very recently.

3. *All English department scholars can increase their understanding of prose in action.* For example, most colleges have coursework introducing students into the main genres: fiction, drama, poetry. Why not nonfiction, which seems to be omitted, left floating out there unacknowledged? Professional writing and composition specialists could add such a course, recognizing its pertinence not just to their specialties but to the needs of their students and to the life of an English department. And professional writing and composition faculty could collaborate on defining such a course, writing its syllabus, and teaching it.

4. *Composition specialists need to resist their automatic tendency to treat prose aesthetically.* This is a natural outgrowth of the connections between composition and literature and may stem from the fact that most composition teachers were English majors. There is, of course, nothing wrong with looking first at prose's aesthetic qualities; there is, however, something odd about not knowing that one is doing so. Emphasizing the aesthetic side inevitably begs the question of effectiveness and limits the range of prose a writing course can examine. (Interestingly, many successful professional writers swear by masters of belletristic prose like E. B. White or Red Smith and regard Strunk and White as a sacred text. I would claim, with advertising

man David Ogilvy, that success in much professional writing comes *despite* fine writing, not because of it.)

5. *Course designers need to become more aware of their own bias toward the literary.* More and more colleges have adopted one of the current crop of belletristic readers (Hall and Emblen; *The Bedford Reader;* Atwan and Vesterman; all excellent collections embodying literary principles and nice examples of how composition is ultimately literary). The problem comes when such readers are viewed as the best way, or only way, of presenting the subject. When a highly belletristic reader becomes the single writing text for every freshman, it is a strong signal that literary qualities matter most in student writing. If course designers want this and are willing to defend it to their colleagues, fine. Too often, though, composition specialists adopt texts like these and still assume their course deals in skills and competencies alone, without any admixture of aesthetics and values. Ultimately, such designers don't realize how literary their courses actually are.

6. *Scholarly journals need to become more open to different points of view.* After years of discouragement, professional writers have felt so left out of the major scholarly journals that they have founded their own. And since academic specialization will increase if left unchecked, there is increasing danger that many of the best professional writing teachers will rarely appear in mainstream composition journals like *College English* or *College Composition and Communication*. It's even rarer to see professional writing articles in *Rhetoric Review* and *Pre/Text*. It seems incumbent on the editors of these journals to seek out articles from the best thinkers about professional writing, articles that can inform their audiences of the best writing being done in the field. And, to remind everyone of the equation "professional writing is to composition as composition is to literature," professional writing specialists are still required to cite literature from the larger "prior" field, composition, as well as to master the literature of their own, while it is not thought necessary for composition specialists to have mastered the literature of professional writing. It is time to require composition scholars to return the favor and learn what is happening on the other side of the divide. In fact, it may be that the quality of much new work in professional writing will force a good many composition scholars to sit up and take notice.

My modest suggestions for greater coordination grow from recent changes within the two fields. James Zappen's 1987 review of the literature on scientific writing demonstrates convincingly that articles from 1950 to the mid-1970s tended to stress the differences between classical rhetoric and scientific and technical writing. Since 1975, however, Zappen notes a marked shift; recent scholarly studies "emphasize the similarities" and also stress the connections between "the political/ethical and probabilistic character of contemporary science and technology and of the contemporary discipline of technical communication" (285). The thrust of this new scholarship is toward the humanistic side; it brings the resources of philosophy, history, rhetoric, and literary criticism to bear on issues of scientific and technical prose (business writing is not covered in Zappen's survey). In other words, despite the significant body of claims that professional writing is really sharply different from the humanities as currently envisioned, a careful survey of the literature on the subject reveals that modern scholarship is coming to see close connections between professional writing and rhetoric. Does this mean the critics are wrong about the divorce between professional writing and the humanities? Or does Zappen overemphasize the trend? Neither. There really is a tremendous unmet need for competent, well-prepared professional writers that the English departments' humanistically oriented programs cannot meet. On the other hand, the humanities themselves are in the process of transformation, becoming much more interested in broad questions of context and status. The traditional humanities have grown to include much more introspection, much more attention to the sources of their own knowledge. And one key to the knowledge of any field is its rhetoric.

Some of the most exciting thinking about prose is being done where the fields of professional writing and rhetoric intersect. The large scale analyses of cultural settings by Foucault, White, LaCapra, and many others provide one entry into the subject. Another, different perspective comes from scholars like Bazerman, Wells, Couture and Goldstein, Miller, Goswami, Odell, and a host of others who examine the context of professional writing. Another significant indication of this shift is Wisconsin's ongoing series in "Rhetoric of the Human Sciences," with works like McCloskey's *The Rhetoric of Economics*, James White's *Heracles' Bow: Essays on the Rhetoric and Poetics of the Law*, and Nelson's collection, *Rhetoric of the Human Sciences: Language and Argument in Scholarship and Public Affairs*. Such books, most of them not by composition or professional writing specialists, testify to the growing trend to examine issues of rhetoric, disciplinary boundaries, and professionalization.

The next step, I think, is to follow up this new interest in professional rhetoric by examining that least explored of areas, the writing done by professionals as professionals. To be sure, technical writing courses are premised on teaching certain well-known formats, since engineering students will write that way after graduation. And business writing courses have traditionally stressed the proposal letter and the memorandum of understanding, since business people are assumed to need such formats all the time. Until now, however, few professional writing specialists have examined these formats critically or subjected them to the kind of research that would yield results about the rhetoric of their professions. The opportunity for far-reaching, rigorous research is extraordinary. The question is, will English departments seize the chance and sponsor this research themselves, or will it fall to the lot of other, less textually oriented disciplines? Faculty in composition and professional writing have a strong common interest in fostering this kind of scholarship; if they see themselves for what they really are—experts in prose, in rhetoric, in discourse—they can begin to make their own subjects central to the discipline of English and to the ongoing research program of the university.

Composition and professional writing are indeed two distinct areas. The critics are right: composition is one of the humanities; it's literary, concerned with aesthetics, with values, with criticism. If current changes in research orientation continue, however, professional writing specialists may just find that they too can share many of these interests and qualities as well. Inevitably, professional writing will continue to look outward, toward careers and job-related abilities, but I think it's possible that it too may find a home in a new, broadened version of the humanities that is rich enough to encompass professional rhetoric as well.

Notes

1. Some would claim that this antagonism toward the process approach is about to change with the new generation of "process" oriented professional writing books. But the first of these, Paul Anderson's *Technical Writing: A Reader-Centered Approach* (San Diego: Harcourt Brace Jovanovich, 1987), is very far indeed from the slow, ruminative process espoused by Emig, Moffett, and Elbow, among others.

2. Ironically, many elements of the process approach—multiple drafts, peer editing, heuristics—are perfectly in keeping with demands of professional writing and indeed were in operation in professional settings long before they became popular in the college composition classroom.

3. Specialists from professional writing backgrounds use the loaded term "real world" rather freely, no doubt opposing it to terms like "ivory tower" that characterize overly academic pursuits. It is a sign of an

academic-practical gap, I suspect, that to many, "real world" seems self-evident, while to others it covers a multitude of assumptions.

Works Cited

Atwan, Robert, and William Vesterman. *One Hundred Major Modern Writers*. Indianapolis: Bobbs Merrill, 1984.

Bartholomae, David, and Anthony Petrosky. *Ways of Reading*. New York: St. Martin's, 1987.

Bazerman, Charles. "Scientific Writing as a Social Act: A Review of the Literature of the Sociology of Science." *New Essays in Technical and Scientific Communication*. Ed. Paul Anderson et al. Farmingdale, NY: Baywood Publishing, 1983.

———. *Shaping Written Knowledge: The Genre and Activity of the Article in Science*. Madison: Wisconsin UP, 1987.

Britton, Earl. "The Trouble with Technical Writing Is Freshman English." *Journal of Technical Writing and Communication* 4 (1974).

Couture, Barbara, and Jone Rymer Goldstein. *Cases for Technical and Professional Writing*. Boston: Little, Brown, 1984.

Emig, Janet. *The Composing Processes of Twelfth Graders*. Urbana, IL: National Council of Teachers of English, 1971.

Flower, Linda. *Problem Solving Strategies for Writers*. San Diego: Harcourt Brace Jovanovich, 1986.

Hall, Donald, and D. L. Emblen. *A Writer's Reader*. 5th ed. Glenview, IL: Scott, Foresman, 1988.

Kennedy, X. J., and Dorothy M. Kennedy. *The Bedford Reader*. 2nd ed. Boston: Bedford Books of St. Martin's Press, 1984.

Lang, Thomas A. "Technical Writing is Not One of the Humanities." *American Medical Writers Association Journal* 2 (December 1987): 3–8.

Lutz, Jean, Susan Jarratt, Patricia Harkin, and Mary Beth Debs. "Practical Rhetoric—The Art of Composing." *The Technical Writing Teacher* 14 (1987): 285–297.

Lyon, Arabella. "Paideia to Pedantry: The Dissolving Relationship of the Humanities and Society." *Journal of Technical Writing and Communication* 8 (January 1988): 55–62.

Mathes, J. C., Dwight Stevenson, and Peter Klaver. "Technical Communication: The Engineering Educator's Responsibility." *Engineering Education* 69 (1979): 332.

McCloskey, Donald N. *The Rhetoric of Economics*. Madison: Wisconsin UP, 1985.

Miller, Carolyn. "A Humanistic Rationale for Technical Writing." *College English* 40 (1979): 610–617.

Nelson, John, ed. *Rhetoric of the Human Sciences: Language and Argument in Scholarship and Public Affairs*. Madison: Wisconsin UP, 1987.

Odell, Lee, and Dixie Goswami, eds. *Writing in Nonacademic Settings*. New York: Guilford Press, 1985.

Perl, Sondra, and Nancy Wilson. *Through Teachers' Eyes*. Portsmouth, NH: Heinemann, 1986.

Shaughnessy, Mina P. *Errors and Expectations: A Guide of the Teacher of Basic Writing*. New York: Oxford UP, 1977.

Tebeaux, Elizabeth. "Redesigning Professional Writing Courses to Meet the Communication Needs of Writers in Business and Industry." *CCC* 36 (1985): 427–428.

Wells, Susan. "Auditing the Meaning of the MOVE Report" in Louise Z. Smith, ed., *Audits of Meaning: A Festschrift in Honor of Ann E. Berthoff*. Portsmouth, NH: Boynton/Cook, 1988. 151–160.

Zappen, James. "Historical Studies in the Rhetoric of Science and Technology." *The Technical Writing Teacher* 14 (1987): 285–297.

SIX

Concepts of Culture
Cultural Literacy/
Cultural Politics

KATHRYN T. FLANNERY

Culture is not only a way of seeing the world, but also
a way of making and changing it.

Arif Dirlik

Flux in mainstream culture is obvious to all. But stability,
not change, is the chief characteristic of cultural literacy.

E. D. Hirsch

All literacy is cultural, of course. Learning to write and read
is in part a process of socialization, which involves to some extent
the inculcation of the dominant ideology. But such learning is more
than that, more than the passive reception of societally approved
ways of behaving. Writing and reading are also the "product[s] of
collective human praxis" (Marcus 177) and are therefore dynamic
and changing and not fully under the control of any group or agency.
But if this is so, if all literacy is cultural, what then is the meaning
of the phrase "cultural literacy"? What sort of "culture" does such
apparent redundancy signal? Although in recent debate the rhetoric
supporting the concept "cultural literacy" borrows from the inclusive, anthropological or ethnographic sense of culture—culture,
that is, as a whole way of life produced by and producing all the

members of a given society—finally and tellingly it centers on culture understood as a select and stable portion from the complex and dynamic whole. The select portion may not be characterized in the rhetoric of nineteenth-century idealism as the "best that has been thought or written." But in calling for a "return" to an educational program that would better teach a "national" and "traditional" culture, and, in the process, purporting to merely describe a body of knowledge apart from class or systems of power, it is clear that advocates of cultural literacy reinscribe as politically neutral the culture and the literacy of the dominant.

The promises of such a "return" are great. E. D. Hirsch, for example, contends that "cultural literacy constitutes the only sure avenue of opportunity for disadvantaged children, the only reliable way of combating the social determinism that now condemns them to remain in the same social and educational condition as their parents" (xiii). Indeed, the promises of literacy campaigns have been great. Literacy has been touted as the paved road to greater wealth, a leg up the social ladder, the Way toward godliness and a better self. While literacy has been enabling for many people, in particular contexts and at particular moments in history, it is equally likely to have played a role in restraining, in domesticating, in disabling—again, in particular contexts and at particular moments of history (cf. Scribner 12). The grand claims made for literacy too often have proved empty (cf. Graff). Why is it then that such claims, such promises continue to get a hearing? Why, especially now when recent work in the field of literacy studies has begun to situate literacy in its social, economic, and political contexts, does an oddly decontextualized, depoliticized "cultural literacy" capture the public ear? One way to address these questions is to contrast the aims of "cultural literacy" with the aims of "cultural politics." Each hinges on very different notions or concepts of culture. In this essay I want to consider what effect such different concepts of culture might have on our understanding of literacy and our praxis as teachers of reading and writing.

Cultural politics entails a broad definition of culture, "understood as a whole 'way of life' or 'way of struggle,' " and a "consequent shift and expansion of the meaning of politics" (Batsleer 7). Everyday life and the concerns of ordinary people are thus recognized as fundamentally political, subject to critique and allowing of change. Cultural politics has as its concern what languages, what symbols are used to represent peoples' lives; how those languages and symbols work to contain or delimit; and what might be done to counter such delimiting and containing. Both the civil rights and the women's movements in this country serve as examples of cultural politics in their challenges to dominant ways of defining what is valuable in our culture—what is "smart," what is "beautiful," what is "art," what is "competence," indeed what is "literacy" and what is "culture." Such challenges are more than semantic exercises, if we understand the extent to which language operates to shape our understandings of the world and to shape our actions in the world. Such challenges are potentially more than a demand for a piece of the pie or a piece of the action; rather, in challenging fundamental ways of seeing the world, cultural politics attempts to reshape that world. The "pie" or the "action," in other words, ought not look the same or act the same or feel the same.

The challenge and program of change represented by cultural politics inevitably calls forth the answering reaction to protect and stabilize represented in cultural literacy. Cultural literacy, in other words, is in fundamental ways meaningful primarily in opposition to cultural politics. E. D. Hirsch is quite explicit in situating his project in just such terms. In discussing the compilation of the list of "what literate Americans know," he says that he and his colleagues

> tried to avoid any of the prescriptiveness that is inherent in cultural politics, the aims of which are fundamentally different from those of teaching literacy. A chief goal of cultural politics is to change the content and values of culture. But the principal aim of schooling is to promote literacy as an enabling competence (137).

While one might argue with Hirsch's notion that cultural politics (as opposed to cultural literacy) is prescriptive, for the moment it is enough to emphasize how, under the sign of empiricism-as-politically-neutral, Hirsch offers an innocent-seeming list, a simple "description" of what is out there as "background information" or "world knowledge" (2), presently only available to some, but to be made available to all. Although he has a clear aim to change educational policy, Hirsch presents his plan as if it were not aiming to change "culture." The apparent assertion that one can change educational policy (and consequently change educational practice) without changing "culture" seems contradictory. It would appear, in fact, that cultural literacy, which is intended to be apart from politics, is necessarily enmeshed in it from the start. The opposition Hirsch sets up between cultural literacy and cultural politics does not seem to hold.

Hirsch argues that "literate culture" transcends class, social group, and race. It does not, however, transcend national boundary.

"Literate culture is the most democratic culture in our land," Hirsch contends; "it cuts across generations and social groups and classes; it is not usually one's first culture, but it should be everyone's second, existing as it does beyond the narrow spheres of family, neighborhood, and region" (21). This "national culture . . . depends on a highly diverse vocabulary of communication rather than a coherent system of fundamental values and principles" (102). It is this national vocabulary that is teachable. "Value-neutral," this vocabulary—a word Hirsch uses interchangeably with "cultural literacy"—can support any political position, any religion, any ethical view. It is, Hirsch urges, "capacious and tolerant" (102–103).

Hirsch contrasts the national vocabulary (or cultural literacy) with "culture proper," which encompasses the "concrete politics, customs, technologies, and legends that define and determine our current attitudes and actions and our institutions." It is here, in "culture proper," that one finds "constant change, growth, conflict." Hirsch acknowledges that "cultural literacy" and "culture proper" interact, but treats "cultural literacy" as the stable essence or distillate of "culture proper" (103). The nature of the distilling process, however, is not made visible. Hirsch and his colleagues set out to "describe" current literate American culture, as if it were a coherent whole, as if it were an empirically available entity—a notion of culture, as we shall see, that is challenged by recent work in anthropology and literacy studies. "Description," Hirsch contends, "accords" with the principle of political neutrality. But Hirsch also recognizes that "even a descriptive list cannot be entirely neutral with respect to cultural politics." Such a list "must necessarily emphasize traditional materials, because widely shared information is not likely to be new." The act of interpretation— the act of necessarily interested reading and selection—while acknowledged here, is recharacterized as a natural effect of neutral description. Traditional materials, that is, are self-defining, and— importantly—inherently valuable: "The traditionalism inherent in our project may make the list seem to some an obstacle to desirable change. But wise change comes from competence, and that is what our list really addresses" (137). Interpretation, of course, takes place, but the political nature of that interpretation is effaced in the move to show the result of interpretation as the only possible "good" result.

Although Hirsch places cultural literacy in relation to culture proper—a gesture towards what he calls an "anthropological theory of education," and acknowledges the interpretative nature of describing a "national vocabulary," he nonetheless fails to recognize the full import of literacy as cultural. Hirsch may borrow language from sociology and anthropology and linguistics, but the concept of culture that dominates his discussion of cultural literacy is fundamentally a concept of culture as an empirically available "thing"—in this case, a list, a describable entity. And the crucial descriptor for this entity is "stability." "Culture proper" may be in constant flux, and "cultural literacy" may derive from "culture proper," but cultural literacy is itself characterized chiefly by "stability." In essence, Hirsch renders the relationship between "cultural literacy" and "culture proper" virtually meaningless.

But what difference might any of this make to teachers of writing and reading? What difference might a notion of culture make to our understanding of what we do in the classroom? Hirsch's liberal agenda—his desire to demystify literate culture and make literacy available more widely than it is at present—is no doubt appealing. His apparent call for a return to "content," with its affinity to recontextualizing reading and writing, might also sound a responsive chord. Indeed, Hirsch, among others, has brought into the public forum issues of import with which we as teachers need to engage. Unfortunately, the liberal agenda might well mislead us into thinking that what supporters of "cultural literacy" offer is a program for educational reform. That liberal agenda rests on a limited, if not reactionary, notion of culture, which leads not to demystification but to further mystification of literacy.

Hirsch's call for cultural literacy is one of a number of recent moves that Arif Dirlik characterizes as the "reaffirmation of the necessity of instilling in education a sense of the 'Western tradition' " (48). This reaffirmation is a response, as Dirlik sees it, to what might be called cultural decentering, the process by which diverse and competing groups in their multiplicity attempt to define "culture." "Culture" in this context would mean, as Dirlik suggests, "not a thing, but a relationship" (14). "Produced historically," James Clifford contends, culture is "contested, temporal and emergent" (18–19).

Decentering threatens traditional power relationships, threatens traditional forms of control. In a much publicized instance, Stanford University shifted the reading list of their Western culture course from traditional "great books" to what might be called a decentered list, one including women, minorities, and non-Western cultures. William Bennett, then Secretary of Education, condemned the change as capitulation to pressure from special interest groups. The specter of sixties-style "fragmentation" was raised to frighten educators (and parents) into resisting such a dilution of standards. The "English only" movement could be seen in similar terms: when schools acknowledge institutionally the diversity of their student population through multilingual programs, especially in communities where non-English speaking residents appear to outnumber English speaking, the fear arises that the English speaking center will not hold. In such arguments, "Western tradition" or "national vocabulary" or "cultural literacy" is offered up as a unifying principle, transcending (petty, political) differences that threaten our collective well-being.

What is confusing perhaps about such efforts to protect the center is that they are often couched in terms of opening up, making available, increasing access—on the surface, admirable goals. But if we look more closely, the rhetoric of inclusion is in fact part of an effort to protect the Club. It is, in other words, as if the way to preserve the Club were to admit a few Outsiders. If Outsiders could just learn to behave like Insiders—talk like them, know what they know, value what they value—there would be no trouble. Even if one were to accept this move to open the ranks to outsiders as sincere, and not merely a cynical effort to quiet dissent (as a move toward "co-optation", in sixties lingo), recent work in literacy studies suggests such efforts invariably fail. Simply put, educational policy that strives to admit Outsiders into the Club makes for bad pedagogy. In a very real sense the dichotomy Hirsch sets up between cultural literacy and cultural politics, between "developing an enabling competence" and "cultural change" is a false divide. Historical, ethnographic, and sociological studies in literacy suggest that you cannot have one without the other, you cannot develop (new) enabling competencies without cultural change. It is not just that the Club is inevitably changed, however subtly, by the very admission of Outsiders (which is true enough); it is that for literacy to happen, cultural changes must take place.

It might help at this point to concretize the discussion by turning to the work of two ethnographers of schooling, John Ogbu and Shirley Brice Heath. Together, they offer an effective critique of the concepts of culture and literacy embodied in the "cultural literacy" program, as well as an alternative practice available to teachers of writing and reading. In his study of the "cultural ecology" of "black school failure," Ogbu is concerned with "institutionalized and socially transmitted patterns of behavior interdependent with features of the [effective rather than physical] environment" (234). Just as Shirley Brice Heath's ethnographic study of literacy acquisition and use among working-class community members of "Roadville" and "Trackton" emphasizes the extent to which literacy acquisition occurs through the convergence of a number of cultural forces, so too does Ogbu treat literacy not as a privileged cultural force but as one force interacting with others.

Ogbu's study, like Heath's, serves as critique of the "literacy myth," that assumption that literacy leads causally and unilinearly to socioeconomic and political advancement.

Ogbu addresses the question of why a disproportionate number of black children fail in school. He is thus interested in part of the same population to which Hirsch's cultural literacy effort ostensibly is directed. But Ogbu understands literacy and culture in fundamentally different terms, which leads him to fundamentally different conclusions. Because he sees literacy as an integral part of culture—culture in its dynamic sense—the conclusions he draws from his study point to the need for changes not merely in the content of curriculum but in the way we perceive the relationship between schools and other social forces. Although Ogbu does not characterize his work as such, I would suggest that his study contributes to a "cultural politics," an effort to decenter definitions of literacy.

As part of a larger ethnography of urban and minority education, Ogbu reviews recent interpretations of black children's failure in school, from the deficit theory that holds black dialect to be inferior to standard English to more recent "mismatch theories" which see discontinuity between the communicative patterns of the school and those of the home. A recent version of the "mismatch theory" holds that the disproportionate school failure of blacks is attributable to dissonance between "their essentially oral culture and the literate culture of the white middle class represented by the public schools" (228–229). Ogbu finds such interpretations inadequate in part because they fail to distinguish adequately among minorities. They fail, in other words, to account for why black children more so than other minority children fail in school. In order to better understand such disproportionate failure—so that we can begin to consider changes in educational policy—Ogbu suggests we need to consider the "historical and macro-structural forces that shape classroom process under which children acquire literacy" (232).

Such a study would involve understanding the connections between school and societal forces (234). This "cultural ecology" would be concerned with the resources available to a given population, the ability to exploit those resources, and the level of technology ready to hand. A given environment requires "specific skills, knowledge, and other attributes" for adaptation and survival. Schools, along with childrearing practices, "are culturally organized to insure that children in a given population meet these criteria for adaptation" (235). In an industrial, bureaucratic economy such as ours, Ogbu explains, the schools teach children "the basic practical skills of reading, writing, and computation essential for almost every

subsistence activity in the economy;" they provide vocational training; model behaviors appropriate for participation in the work force;
and provide credentials for entry into the work force."

All of which seems straightforward enough, and apparently
compatible with Hirsch's conception of the role schools ought to
play. But Ogbu goes on to make clear that his research does not
suggest that the schools are merely *sources* or *repositories* to which
students go to learn if they have the opportunity, motivation, and
aptitude. Rather, he characterizes schools as culturally sanctioned
gatekeepers: "schooling is more or less a culturally institutionalized
device for allocating and rewarding individuals in a society's status
system, particularly in the economy" (235). In other words, the
schools—as culturally organized institutions—reproduce and reinforce the stratifications of the larger society. They provide access
to doors that are already beckoning, not to doors that are perma-
nently closed. Thus, Ogbu argues, the "normal" means for achiev-
ing upward mobility does not hold for blacks; blacks do not gain
access to jobs and housing simply by acquiring literacy ("cultural"
or otherwise). Literacy is not necessarily a ticket to anything.[1] This
is not to say that some students cannot "beat the system"—boot-
strap stories are a typical and defining part of American culture,
after all—but it is to say that educational institutions are organized
first and foremost not to train students to change the system but
rather to conform to it.

This is not a new idea, of course. But it is an idea that is easy
to ignore. If one begins by assuming that literacy is the road to
success, and that defining literacy is virtually an apolitical act, then
it is possible to propose solutions to educational problems that
ignore the socioeconomic and political forces that shape those problems. It is far tidier—conceptually at any rate—to ignore the complexities of schooling. But Ogbu's study emphasizes that if we are
really interested in reducing or eliminating disproportionate black
school failure (or, by extension, putting Outsiders more generally
in a position to acquire literacy), we cannot ignore the "cultural
ecology" of schooling. In other words, we cannot expect to change
much by simply reinforcing "traditional" curricular content.

Ogbu's study supports the notion that for literacy acquisition
to be successful there must be societal valuing of literacy as well
as actual and apparent uses to which literacy is put. Those uses do
not have to be job-related, as Scribner and Cole's study of the West
African Vai or Shirley Brice Heath's study of working-class Roadville and Trackton make clear. As long as there is some congruence
between the sort of literacy disseminated and the uses to which
literacy will be put in the community, most physiologically normal

individuals in a culture will acquire the appropriate literacy (Heath, "Functions" 22–23). But when there is dissonance between the literacy disseminated and the functions (or lack of functions) of literacy in a given community, community members may well see little reason to acquire the apparently nonfunctional skills. It is precisely this lack of congruence that Ogbu points out between the literacy taught in schools, which are governed by the dominant, white culture, and the occupational and social uses to which literacy is put in the black community.

Ogbu underscores the importance of some sort of congruence when he points out that black students have been encouraged to work harder in school when "civil rights [have] effectively expand[ed] black employment opportunities and other rewards for education, as they appeared to be doing in the 1960s." But, he adds, "a discouraging message is also communicated, namely, that without such a collective civil rights struggle, blacks automatically have fewer opportunities than whites to benefit from education" (239–240). Ogbu's study makes it clear that, at the least, blacks are not "disadvantaged" educationally because they have been deprived of access to some "national vocabulary."

Ogbu acknowledges that some efforts have been made to increase educational and economic opportunities for blacks. But such efforts "have not broken the job ceiling or significantly altered black expectations, especially among the lower segments of the black community" (242). Indeed, recent unemployment statistics under the Reagan administration, used to substantiate the claim that the U.S. economy is flourishing, continue to record the disproportionate number of black males who remain unemployed. Similarly, Ogbu charges that compensatory educational measures, while helping "many blacks to complete higher levels of schooling, to achieve greater functional literacy, and to improve their performance in classrooms and on standardized tests," remain "ineffective for or unavailable to the majority." They are, he contends, "essentially remedial and often based on misconceptions of the underlying causes of black school problems" (242).

It is not Ogbu's purpose in his essay to propose specific remedies for ineffective schooling, but he does offer some general guidelines for the direction school reform should take. These guidelines underscore the differences between an approach that sees literacy as fundamentally cultural, as interacting with, and in many ways dependent on, other cultural forces, and an approach that sees "cultural literacy" as a causal force that can somehow lead to "greater economic prosperity," "social justice" and "more effective democracy" (Hirsch 2). According to Ogbu, we need to develop ways to prevent learning problems, which will require

> a strategy that will simultaneously have to (a) consider the economic expectations of blacks as a cause rather than a consequence of the school failure and literacy problem; (b) eliminate the gross and subtle mechanisms which differentiate black schooling from white schooling; and (c) examine black perceptions and "adaptive" responses, including the problem of mistrust and conflict in black relations with the schools (242).

I suspect that as teachers, when we get this far, we might just prefer, momentarily, Hirsch's clarion call to economic prosperity, social justice, and more "effective" democracy to the much grittier task Ogbu sets before us, even if it means teaching the infamous list. But if we accept Ogbu's argument, or the argument of others in the literacy field, it is difficult to be dazzled by simple solutions that promise grand results. Instead, we need to confront what it might mean to develop the sort of strategy Ogbu proposes, not only with blacks but with all learners. It seems a herculean task to try to change social and economic conditions so that doors would be open and beckoning, so that multiple literacies would be valued in the workplace and available for the learning in schools. Perhaps a first step would be to recognize the complexity of literacy learning, to understand the extent to which literacy does not occur independent of a multiple of other cultural forces. Perhaps such recognition will prevent us from proposing simple solutions, however well meaning.

But recognition of complexity is not enough. Some change in practice is required. Shirley Brice Heath offers the teacher some assistance in reimagining classroom practice in light of an awareness of the complexity of literacy learning. She notes that it is "easy to claim that a radical restructuring of society or the system of education is needed" for "large scale and continuous" cultural changes to take place (*Ways* 369). But we cannot begin with the whole—indeed such efforts at "totalizing" solutions are themselves dangerous if we truly value difference and diversity. Heath suggests instead that we begin with what we can change, with what she calls the "information and bridging skills needed for teachers and students as individuals to make changes which [are] for them radical." We can then "point to the ways these cultural brokers between communities and classrooms can perhaps be the beginning of larger changes" (*Ways* 369).

Fundamental to Heath's approach is her understanding that the school is "not a neutral objective arena." Rather it is an "institution which has the goal of changing people's values, skills, and knowledge bases" (*Ways* 367). In her ethnographic study of two communities in the Piedmont Carolinas, Heath found that the schools traditionally had worked to change members of working-class and poor communities so that they would function in conformity to the values of "townspeople," middle-class white residents. Early on the millowners planned the schools "as places which preached the culture of the townspeople to make millworkers docile and receptive" (*Ways* 364). But members of the working class also saw the potential in schools to change their lives for the better, and indeed, even when schools were planned to "domesticate," they continued to embody the potential for something else, some manner of "empowerment."

Heath's experience working with the schools and community members serves as a striking example of how the potential for "empowerment" might be actualized, but also how fragile such efforts can be. This project was made possible first of all by the confluence of several factors (a confluence that emphasizes the "contextuality" of literacy learning), among them desegregation legislation that called for changes in educational policies and practices; the willingness on the part of school administrators to trust teachers to come up with creative solutions to problems of pedagogy brought out into the open by desegregation; and the availability of an outside catalyst in the person of Heath. The point to emphasize here is that Heath's project grew out of specific circumstances. And the ideas generated out of her project would necessarily have to be translated into other specific circumstances and revised according to those specific circumstances to be of use to other teachers. But that is part of the strength of her project, that it does not presume to offer a global solution, an easy fix for literacy disrepair. The very concrete specificity of her project is itself a reminder of the need to understand the local, complex circumstances in which learning takes place.

Perhaps the key concept in Heath's project is interaction—interaction between the language practices of schools and the language practices of communities, among various community members, between teacher and learners, among learners. "Unless the boundaries between classrooms and communities can be broken," Heath argues, "and the flow of cultural patterns between them encouraged, the schools will continue to legitimate and reproduce communities of townspeople who control and limit the potential progress of other communities and who themselves remain untouched by other values and ways of life" (*Ways* 369). While "towns-people" and "communities" are used in her text to signify specific groups, I think we can read the passage as referring more generally to the split between traditionally dominant groups in a culture and diverse Outsiders. For Ogbu it is the white middle class of Stockton, California, who often unconsciously work to exclude the black and poor members of the community from full participation in the school; or we might consider the university, which often resists being changed by women, blacks, and other ethnic and racial minorities.

Interaction, for Heath, involves, among other things, "embed[ding] class materials in the lives of the students" (*Ways* 355). In order for that to happen teachers must be able to learn *from* students. To get to the point where teachers can do so, however, Heath asks teachers to first become aware of their own "home" uses of language and how those uses or patterns enter into classroom practice. Having considered her own language behavior as *one* among many, the teacher then can help to put students in a position to become conscious of the functions of language in their own lives so that they can make those functions visible to the teacher and to each other. Students, Heath explains, are thus "engaged in a process of self-awareness by which they, in a sense, *re*constructed a social and cognitive system of meanings" (*Ways* 356). Students investigated their home environment, recorded conversation, and analyzed various documents from their environment in order to see and understand the "different ways of talking and knowing" possible; and they began to try out these different ways of talking and knowing in order to begin to explore the options available to them and the differences such options might make in their own lives (*Ways* 355).

What is particularly striking about Heath's approach is her concern that students begin to bridge the divide between home and school in this process of exploring various ways of talking and knowing. "A critical component in the process," Heath emphasizes, "was allowing children to articulate how what they knew related to what the school wanted them to know" (*Ways* 355). The outcome was not that students abandoned their home ways of using language in favor of school ways, but that students learned how to move among various ways of using language. If there was an alteration in use, it would appear the most significant alteration was in the school's opening itself up to the use of other forms of language, valuing those other forms, making them acceptable modes for learning.

In her study, Heath addresses elementary-level literacy learning. While some of the specifics of classroom teaching are applicable beyond the elementary level, college teachers of writing and reading need to recontextualize the ideas she offers, to translate them to the post-secondary context. It is not the purpose of this essay to offer detailed course plans, but it is possible to briefly suggest what an interactive approach might look like in an undergraduate reading and writing course. Such an approach accords well with collaborative learning models, with reader oriented theories, with non-canonical or anti-canonical choices of texts to be read, and with whole language approaches or meaning centered approaches to language learning (reading and writing to learn as the means to learn reading and writing) (cf. Harste et al.) "Embedding" learning in the lives of students seems to be part of a number of approaches to reading and writing, not only in "expressive writing" pedagogy but also in "academic writing" pedagogy, represented, for example, by the University of Pittsburgh's basic reading and writing course (cf. *Facts, Artifacts and Counterfacts*). Essentially, courses designed to break down the separation between "acceptable," traditional knowledge and lived knowledge, between the teacher as controller and chief judge of acceptable knowledge (as priest of the word) and the student as empty vessel (as novice), between creators of knowledge and receivers of knowledge are courses that create the possibility for change.

We can imagine many sorts of courses that could do such things and many sorts of contents that would lend themselves to courses for change in language learning. The hopeful aspect of Heath's study is that we as teachers are not powerless to alter practice. But what cannot be lost in a discussion of possibility is how hard it can be to work alone or work against institutional and political pressure. When Heath left Roadville and Trackton, the project fell apart. Teachers felt that the institution had moved to bureaucratize teaching in such a way as to make innovation difficult at best. Many left teaching altogether, disillusioned by the institution's rigidity. Others stayed on, attempting to retain some trace of the innovation and excitement that had been part of their experience in the study. Just as Ogbu's and Heath's studies emphasize, from the learners' perspective, how much literacy learning is a part of larger cultural forces, so too do they remind us of how our practice as teachers is shaped by political and socioeconomic currents over which we may feel we have no control.

While Heath points to the real possibility for change, she also reminds us that we cannot simply rely on the teacher's fall-back position of closing the classroom door. The issue then would seem to be how to reassert what Dirlik calls the "sense of culture as activity" (14). A recent Conference on College Composition and Communication call for papers suggested that as teachers of reading and writing we need to consider not only our practice in the class-room but also what impact we might have in public policy debates about education—in the English first movement, for example. Indeed, if we understand how fully "cultural" literacy is, we do need to concern ourselves with politics in and outside the classroom. We need to resist the seductiveness of a "cultural literacy" approach to teaching that separates "culture proper" from "cultural literacy," and in so doing attempts to cover over the "interestedness" of apparently apolitical, "neutral" lists of national knowledge. In declaring for a "national" list at all, advocates of "cultural literacy" act to quiet the multiple, divergent, decentered, local voices of learners *and* teachers. Literacy studies teach us that if we are engaged in literacy learning, we are necessarily engaged in cultural politics. The only question that remains is what cultural politics we serve.

Note

1. Ogbu is concerned with the specific conditions that contribute to what he calls disproportionate black school failure. But the general claim that literacy in and of itself does not necessarily lead to socioeconomic and political advancement has been made in a number of historical studies (cf. Graff, "Literacy, Jobs, and Industrialization"; Galtung; Davis) and in cultural studies (cf. Scribner and Cole). The assumption that literacy acquisition is an unalloyed blessing runs so deep in our culture, however, that challenges to it meet resistance from various camps.

Works Cited

Bartholomae, David, and Anthony Petrosky. *Facts, Artifacts and Counter-facts: Theory and Method for a Reading and Writing Course.* Portsmouth, NH: Boynton/Cook, 1986.

Batsleer, Janet, et al. *Rewriting English: Cultural Politics of Gender and Class.* New York: Methuen, 1985.

Clifford, James. Introduction. *Writing Culture: The Poetics and Politics of Ethnography.* Ed. James Clifford and George E. Marcus. Berkeley: U of California P, 1986. 1–26.

Davis, Natalie Zemon. "Printing and the People: Early Modern France." *Literacy and Social Development in the West: A Reader.* Ed. Harvey Graff. Cambridge: Cambridge UP, 1981. 69–95.

Dirlik, Arif. "Culturalism as Hegemonic Ideology and Liberating Practice." *Cultural Critique* 6 (Spring 1987): 13–50.

Galtung, Johan. "Literacy, Education and Schooling." *Literacy and Social*

Development in the West: A Reader. Ed. Harvey Graff. Cambridge: Cambridge UP, 1981. 271–285.

Graff, Harvey. Introduction. *Literacy and Social Development in the West: A Reader.* Cambridge: Cambridge UP, 1981. 1–13.

———. "Literacy, Jobs, and Industrialization: The Nineteenth Century." *Literacy and Social Development in the West: A Reader.* Cambridge: Cambridge UP, 1981. 232–260.

Heath, Shirley Brice. "The Functions and Uses of Literacy." *Literacy, Society, and Schooling: A Reader.* Ed. Suzanne De Castell, et al. New York: Cambridge UP, 1986. 15–26.

———. *Ways With Words: Language, Life, and Work in Communities and Classrooms.* New York: Cambridge UP, 1983.

Hirsch, E. D., Jr. *Cultural Literacy: What Every American Needs to Know.* Boston: Houghton Mifflin, 1987.

Marcus, George E. "Contemporary Problems of Ethnography in the Modern World System." *Writing Culture.* Ed. James Clifford and George E. Marcus. Berkeley: U of California P, 1986. 165–193.

Ogbu, John U. "Literacy and Schooling in Subordinate Cultures: The Case of Black Americans." *Perspectives on Literacy.* Ed. Eugene R. Kintgen, Barry Kroll, and Mike Rose. Carbondale: Southern Illinois UP, 1988. 227–242.

Scribner, Sylvia. "Literacy in Three Metaphors." *Literacy in American Schools: Learning to Read and Write.* Ed. Nancy Stein. Chicago: U of Chicago P, 1984.

———, and Michael Cole. *The Psychology of Literacy.* Cambridge: Harvard UP, 1981.

SEVEN

Between the Trenches and the Ivory Towers
Divisions Between University Professors and High School Teachers

JOY RITCHIE

As I write this article I'm aware that lurking here are words that call up and reinforce a constellation of divisions—professor/ teacher, male/female, privileged/inferior, relevance/irrelevance, scholarship/pedagogy, humanities/teachers college—that are all a part of the central division I'm attempting to address. The language I use, like the division I am examining, arises from the intellectual, social, and institutional values we are drenched in and from which we derive our very identities as teachers, professors, and persons. These values are so pervasive and illusive they prevent us from seeing around, over, and through them long enough to critique them. They cloud our vision, preventing us from seeing each other clearly, and from recognizing that those very social and institutional conditions that appear to divide us mask underlying similarities in our respective positions and common purposes in our professional lives. Until we begin to resist these values instead of resisting each other, the dichotomy will remain. Teachers and professors will continue the cycle of blaming and fictionalizing that characterizes the history of our professional interaction.

I want first to examine some of the manifestations of oppositions between school and university teachers and show how they are linked to the structure of our social institutions and the expectations those institutions hold for the function of education and the job of teachers and professors. I will also look at historical forces that have produced the institutions and epistemologies that frame teachers' and professors' lives and that ultimately dominate our view of reading and writing, of research, pedagogy, and of each other. Though our official roles in institutions may define us differently, we share purposes and problems that we must address together.

I believe both groups, university professors and public school teachers, buy into a dichotomous definition of our respective positions in education. We are all teachers of reading and writing, we tell ourselves. But despite our common membership in NCTE, our professional lives, structured by the institutions we work in, differ in important ways and set us in opposition to each other. Lucille Schultz and her colleagues in "Interaction among School and College Writing Teachers" document the history of open hostility and failure that has characterized most collaborative endeavors between professors and teachers. They attribute this failure to differing cultural conditions in our work—"time, material goods, rewards"—and to deeply held hierarchical beliefs about theory and practice. I certainly acknowledge that significant differences exist in the conditions under which we work, and I recognize, as do other writers in this book, the pervasiveness of the misperception that theory and practice are separable. However, I believe we must probe beyond that divisive way of looking at ourselves, which focuses on teaching load, the ages of students we teach, teachers' rigid, intense schedule and the relative flexibility of most professors' schedules, and the status we each hold in our communities. Those overt differences only mask more significant conditions that, if brought into view, may allow us to challenge those ways of thinking. Ultimately, the hierarchical structures we reside in deintellectualize and demean teaching at all levels and separate it from the production of knowledge. In institutions at all levels, teaching is often defined as "training"—the routinized transmission of information, a bureaucratic maintenance task—rather than a creative activity.

We define ourselves, teachers and professors, as different and separate, and we do so because we clearly recognize ourselves in the network of stratified relationships on which schools and universities, as social institutions, are constructed and from which the corresponding expectations for our behavior arise. Louis Althusser says we are "hailed by ideology," comparing our compliance with the roles institutions prescribe for us to our response when we're walking down a street and we hear a voice shouting, "Hey, you there!" We expect that the voice is meant for us (48). Simone de Beauvoir describes the way society's pervasive values ensure compliance among women and blacks to their "separate but equal" status. Artificial divisions are created and maintained by society, but they become fixed and uncritically affirmed as real, universal, preordained divisions. They can be resisted only at great cost, because renouncing that status means giving up the advantages and benefits of those roles, however limited and repressive they may be (xxvii). The system of beliefs and values that construct our lives keeps us from seeing our own complicity in maintaining the oppositions between us, and we perpetuate the cycle despite our best intentions.

Like high school teachers, I am a teacher of reading and writing, but the university expects me to be something more than that. The role of the university professor descends from a long tradition of the cleric, scholar, and free-thinker, and as a result, professors stand in a position of privilege that allows them to maintain a critical, speculative, metatheoretical and metapragmatic stance. Even though I complain about a busy schedule, I have time to do research and freedom to contemplate the implications of research for my teaching. My work is seldom routine, nor do I have to meet a set of strict guidelines in planning my courses or subject my students to standardized tests at the end of their study. No one has yet thought of a "national professor examination" to see that I am competent to teach the nation's young people. The university traditionally functions in our society as the institution that carries on the discovery, preservation, and interpretation of a body of specialized knowledge. Its secondary mission is to transmit that specialized learning to others and to teach others to carry on the tradition of research and scholarship. While many colleges and universities, like the one in which I teach, claim to value excellence in teaching, professional advancement is based on one's success as researcher and scholar, not on teaching.

Although at one time they too were called "professor," teachers in the schools have traditionally been treated quite differently, more like skilled or semi-skilled workers than professors. Their role is to transmit skills and information and maintain order rather than to act as contemplative scholars. Often teachers are not free to make decisions about instruction, and managerial restrictions force them to teach in ways that undermine their own knowledge and experience and run contrary to the way language learning occurs. But administrators, parents, even some teachers and students believe that schools can function better if instruction is systematized and packaged consistently and if teachers and students are held accountable through testing and the use of prepackaged instructional materials. In one large Nebraska school district, students are given standardized tests at the end of the school year, and both students' and teachers' performance is judged by the test results. Because society views schools in particular as places where young people are trained to function as workers and citizens, the teacher's duty is to see that students learn to behave in those roles, and some teachers model that same role for students to follow—fitting in, accommodating themselves as functionaries in the bureaucracy.

While in the university we maintain some degree of autonomy in scholarship and teaching, the scope of ideas within which secondary and elementary teachers work is increasingly restricted. As my colleagues and I contemplate Plato, Derrida, Langer, and Cixous in our colloquia, behaviorist conceptual and management schemes like Benjamin Bloom's taxonomy remain the organizing paradigm for the writing and literature curricula in the schools our children attend. Madeline Hunter's Instructional Design Model, which organizes instruction, students, and teachers into teach, test, reteach, retest cycles, and promises accountability for all, has become the standard management tool. This is not just a local problem. NCTE's "1988 Report on Trends and Issues" concludes that "testing is overwhelming the public school curriculum." Dixie Dellinger, in a recent talk at the annual National Writing Project Directors' Meeting, said the Performance Appraisal System and the Career Ladder Plan her state has adopted ensure that the state can determine whether she teaches how and what it prescribes. Despite all the contradictions teachers see in the behaviorist management structures governing their work, it is increasingly difficult for teachers to close their doors and engage in challenging exploration and inquiry alongside their students.

In both our worlds, the school and the university, we experience renewed pressure to divorce ourselves from pedagogy as a form of inquiry and, consequently, to accept definitions of our role as teachers that force a wider gulf between us. In the trenches, English teachers face more students, more demands to standardize their teaching, and more barriers to their function as intellectuals. But in the ivory tower we face similar, if sometimes more subtle, pressures to divert us from concerns with teaching, learning, and students. Professors in my department have been criticized for their overuse of informal journal writing in literature classes; other faculty members, who have devoted themselves to improving undergraduate education or to programs involving teachers and schools instead of to research, are not promoted. Like our colleagues in the schools, we are asked to make compromises in our teaching by increasing class enrollments in order to increase credit-hour production. Women in part-time, nontenure track positions are "entrusted" with a large percentage of the beginning composition courses taught in universities, an indication of the status of women and the status of teaching writing—about as close to the trenches as one can be without actually stepping out of the ivory tower. In the university, we, like secondary teachers, are "service" people who get students ready for the real work of literary scholarship. At the same time, the widespread acclaim given E. D. Hirsch's and Alan Bloom's books narrows institutional definitions of knowledge and scholarship and reinforces the academic status quo.

Thus we are divided, not because our mission is essentially different but because our institutions define teaching in reductive ways and diminish it as an intellectual activity. First, institutions value some forms of knowledge more than others. Stephen North argues in *The Making of Knowledge in Composition* that as teaching is routinized and standardized, an important source of our knowledge about teaching and learning—individual teacher practice and observation—has been stripped of value and credibility. Our "knowledge" in composition in the past twenty years has been acquired through teachers' attempts to solve problems as they work with students. Although our discipline has grounded its investigation in philosophy, psychology, and linguistics and has begun to reexamine historical antecedents for present practices, much of the knowledge base of composition rests on the work of those who, like Mina Shaughnessy, Ann Berthoff, Donald Murray, and Peter Elbow, join teaching to inquiry. But because it is not text based, this knowledge is accorded lower status in the university community. Teachers experience similar problems. They all know and can document in detail the powerful negative effects on their teaching and on students' learning when their classes are too large. Yet no one, not the school principal or the district curriculum coordinator or the Secretary of Education, gives credence to their "knowledge."

The hierarchical structures of educational institutions further accentuate the division between university and school teachers. As we accept the roles institutions prescribe for us, we accept the status those roles carry with them. In the educational pecking order, greater authority is bestowed on university professors, who are supposed to possess more knowledge than secondary teachers. Secondary teachers, in turn, have greater authority than elementary teachers. In addition, university professors believe the primary job of schools is to prepare students for the university; and when we think college students don't measure up, we blame their teachers. High school teachers blame junior high and elementary teachers for the failures of their students. Thus teachers constantly define their students' education and their own role in that education as preparation for the next higher level, for the reports students will write in eighth-grade English, for the admissions tests and the term papers required in college. Lines of communication between institutions are often so poor and practices become so entrenched that teachers are often teaching to a fiction of what they think the university or the high school or the junior high requires. The sacrosanct position held by the term paper in school writing instruction is an example. A high school teacher told me recently, "Half of the secondary teachers in this district don't realize they no longer need to teach students traditional footnote forms, that most academic writing uses much different forms of documentation, but they've always done it that way, and they still believe they would be doing their students a disservice if they didn't teach it."

The teacher/student relationship between university professors and school teachers further complicates communication. Professors in English and in education departments are the teachers of school teachers, setting up a vexed authority relationship that promotes an array of responses from teachers, ranging from reverence to resistance. In addition, the university, through in-services and projects like those Louise Schultz describes, has also been aligned with governmental and administrative attempts to reform schools and to change teachers' behavior, often in an effort to make schools serve the university rather than the larger community. Each of the series of educational crises we have seen in the past twenty or thirty years has left teachers with less autonomy. Although at times teachers acquiesce to the demands placed upon them by government, universities, and central administrations, many of them resist the attempts to influence and control their work. This resistance is nowhere more evident than in compulsory in-service and staff development programs, where cynical teachers barely manage to control their anger at the university people who come to lay one more new theory on them. No matter what the message of those in-services, teachers often view them as yet another attempt to take away their autonomy, to make demands on their time, or to devalue their knowledge.

Conflicting and stratified patterns of teacher education in this country further perpetuate divisions. Questions concerning who should teach teachers and what the nature of teacher education ought to be are a continuing source of conflict between university professors in teachers colleges and English departments, between universities and state departments of education, and between professors and teachers themselves. English professors, educated in traditional humanities departments, often graduate from Ph.D. programs in major research institutions as specialists in a particular period or genre. Teachers college professors more often move through a different career pattern, often working as teachers, then moving through graduate courses and eventually into doctoral programs in education. Within the university there is a clear hierarchy that says a degree in a specialized arts and sciences area is more scholarly and prestigious than that in the "professional" areas of business and education. Teachers colleges are regarded as "trade schools" or training schools emphasizing "how to" methods and lacking solid intellectual substance. The "teacher as functionary" rather than "teacher as intellectual" role is reinforced when teacher education courses emphasize the effective delivery of information and the use of evaluation and classroom management techniques that allow teachers to work efficiently within the institution and to remain in control of their classes. While English professors retain some prestige as scholars, their work, usually having to do with texts and manuscripts, is often considered "soft," irrelevant, and of little practical value to "real world" problems. Thus, many teacher educators feel that potential teachers do not receive adequate preparation for teaching by reading Chaucer and Shakespeare and listening to lectures on the history of the English novel.

Colleges of arts and sciences are ambivalent about, if not disinterested in, teacher education and only grudgingly provide subject area courses for potential teachers, because they believe the teachers' role is to prepare students for academic life and to carry on the intellectual tradition of the discipline. Although English departments dislike, and sometimes even ridicule, courses taught in English education, we fail to offer suitable alternatives. English departments often blame behavioristic teachers college faculties and school bureaucrats as the culprits who squeeze the humanities out of teaching. But when the subject of teacher education does come up in English departments, we say among ourselves, "If they had just done away with teachers colleges and let those students take all their courses in English departments, everything would be just fine." However, Richard Lanham reminds us that English departments that are ambitious to develop a reputation for rigor and scholarship always distance themselves as much as possible from teacher education (197).

As these hierarchies become the metaphors we live and

work by, the divisions they perpetuate lead to our mutual alienation. Ultimately, we devalue each other, and we speak in
mutually unintelligible languages. This is evident in the conferences we attend, the presentations we make, and in the journals we read and write for. I have given what I thought were
important and relevant essays from *College English* to teacher
colleagues. They read the articles and came back saying, "This
is useless, theoretical claptrap. How can I possibly use this in
my teaching?" Recently, a colleague received a scathing letter
from two high school English teachers concerning his article on
Lacan and composition in *College English*. They criticized him
because of the style in which he wrote, but they also charged
that essays like his reflect an increasingly elitist, esoteric image
of the journal itself. They concluded that his essay, and many
essays written by scholars attempting to get a promotion, are
calculated to reinforce the inferior status of teachers and to diminish the importance of their pragmatic concerns. On the
other hand, one of my colleagues recently expressed her reluc-
tance to store the department's copies of *English Journal* and
Language Arts in her office. She realized most of us would seldom read them because the articles do not speak to our situation and are considered "lightweight" or "atheoretical."
Teachers find our suggestions and our "theorizing" to be out of
touch, unworkable, irrelevant, or, at worst, exploitive. And university professors are often frustrated by the lack of interest and
patience teachers have for a careful examination of theory and
by their demand for quick "recipes" to take back to the classroom. An outsider attending our conferences and meetings and
reading our journals might indeed conclude that we are members of different cultural communities.

I believe we can only understand and resist definitions that
cast some of us as contemplative scholars indulging in mostly irrelevant theory and others of us as manager/trainers if we look at
the historical and political forces that shape and perpetuate that
dichotomy. While a number of writers, including Henry Giroux,
Stanley Aronowitz, Stephen North, and Frank Smith, have examined recent political forces that restrict and deintellectualize
teachers, some dangers arise from the way we read their arguments.
First, given our own immersion in dichotomous thinking, we risk
assigning teachers to an irreversible status as second-class people
who deserve the sympathetic and patronizing assistance of privileged university professors. One only needs to talk with teachers
and to visit some of their classes to know that this assumption is
inaccurate as well as counterproductive. Furthermore, while illu-

minating and accurate, the descriptions of the current problem as depicted by Giroux, Smith, and others give the reader some sense that these are only recent political developments.

Taking a longer look should give us enough of a sense of the past to allow us to talk about changing the current situation and to counter the deterministic, reductive view of teachers as pathetic workers and professors as unrestricted contemplatives. Paulo Freire argues that people must develop a critical consciousness about the historical, political, and social situation in which they exist if they are to be able to interrogate the oppressive social situation and work to liberate themselves from it. Like blacks, women, and minorities, teachers have been cut off from their history. Our view of American education usually comes from our own experience, from patriotic histories extolling the virtues of the institution, which nurtured a new enlightened democratic electorate and integrated masses of immigrants into American culture, and from nostalgia and myths perpetuated by the media and critics of education. Yet real historical, economic, and philosophical conditions shape our roles as teacher and professor.

I want to trace some of the conditions from which our institutional structures have evolved and which perpetuate the divisions we are bound by. Hierarchical authority structures and management mentality in schools are not new evils. We only need to remember Gradgrind in Dickens' *Hard Times* to see the precursors of our present situation. According to Paul Olson in "The Transformation to a Market Economy: The Role of Early Teacher and Compulsory Education," the origins of management systems and the view of "teacher as worker" can be traced to British and Scottish economic and social philosophies that were transferred to America in the early nineteenth century and continue to dominate our culture. Olson demonstrates that empiricist and capitalist economic philosophies, which arose from the Scottish Enlightenment and the English Utilitarian philosophers, provided the impulse for compulsory education and teacher training institutions. *A Nation at Risk* and other recent calls for educational reform are tied to the same values—progress, technology, and support for our nation's business and industry. Then, as now, our economic system required a domesticated workforce shaped through the proper educational methods. Schools today, with their emphasis on "time on task," programmed and mastery learning, bear a striking resemblance to late eighteenth-century British "monitorial" schools and teacher training academies, both formulated according to the notions of associationist psychology and *laissez-faire* economic theory. The new psychology said that by "habituation" people could be changed and their manner of thinking reshaped. Thus, Olson says, the preferred pedagogy for schools was highly authoritarian and competitive, with children grouped by ability, and instructed by intensive drill and recitation, all proper preparation for the workplace ("Transformation" 22–24).

An important point I find here is that the teacher was little more than an assemblyline worker who reproduced knowledge rather than creating it, who carried out a prescribed task, attempted to achieve specified quotas, and followed a consistent routine requiring little intellectual effort on her part. Nothing in the institutional definition of her role suggested that part of her job was to examine and critique the assumptions and philosophy of her job as teacher.

This system, like today's educational management systems, was supported by the same positivistic theory of learning that continues to dominate education at all levels. Literacy—the ability to read, write, and compute—was thought to consist of the accumulation, piece by piece, of a set of facts that one could reproduce and measure, just like the product of the assembly line. This model of education, with the teacher a skilled worker dispensing and assembling units of knowledge, suited well the purposes of increasing industrialization and the expansion of public education in the United States. Michael Katz's book *Reconstructing American Education* demonstrates that by the latter half of the nineteenth century the United States already had a well-developed formal, bureaucratic system of public education whose purpose was to socialize children, to maintain social order, and to train a skilled work force for a capitalist economic system. While elementary, and later secondary, schools were to produce a docile and unquestioning workforce, universities were primarily the training ground for the wealthy, the upwardly mobile, and the elite.

Hierarchical structures and positivistic philosophy dominated teacher education also. In "The Preparation of the Teacher: An Evaluation of the State of the Art," Paul Olson points out that "common school" or elementary teachers attended normal schools that, like the Scottish "training academies," taught teachers to drill students in basic literacy and computation skills. At the upper tier of the hierarchy was the secondary school, whose teachers were educated at the university in the traditional classical disciplines until late in the nineteenth century when newly formed education departments in land grant universities took over training of elementary and secondary teachers. Here we have the origins of the split between teachers colleges and humanities departments. Other factors contributed to the stratification of teachers educated in normal schools and those educated in universities. Olson says that normal school teachers were predominantly from lower-class and rural backgrounds; they were also female. By the middle of the nineteenth century, according to Michael Katz, male teachers could earn more in factories than in classrooms, and because of the increased demand for teachers and schools by the masses of immigrants, women provided a cheap supply of elementary teachers, and increasingly, of secondary teachers as well (12). Alison Prentice and others have described how "feminization" of secondary teaching has continued to keep the status, pay, and perceived authority of secondary teachers at a low level.

As teachers colleges developed within universities and state governmental agencies became increasingly powerful, they reinforced the hierarchical structure of education, the teacher-worker image, and the factory model of learning, and they further fueled a power struggle for control of teachers and schools that continues today. As faculty members of these new education departments sought to gain legitimacy and to accommodate themselves to the research and publication requirements of the university, educational psychology, influenced strongly in many institutions by behaviorist theory, gained preeminence (Olson, "Preparation" 19). One effect of this trend in my institution is the overwhelming numbers of faculty whose backgrounds are in educational psychology, compared to the two or three people who might call themselves historians or philosophers of education. English educators have found it difficult to survive in such an environment without making enormous compromises, and in some cases they have been replaced by generalists who are grounded in behavioristic psychology rather than traditional subject area knowledge, laying the groundwork for wider divisions between humanities and teachers college professors and students.

By the end of the nineteenth century, enormous pressure came from many quarters to change the direction of secondary schools from "fitting schools," preparing students for the university, to schools preparing students for life. In the first decades of the twentieth century, two particularly strong movements challenged the traditional view of education held by many liberal arts faculties. The first was the "progressive education" movement, which drew from several political, philosophical and psychological perspectives unified by John Dewey's work (Cremin). Dewey and his followers argued that schools should function more broadly, to prepare students to live and to function in a democratic society rather than to prepare them for entrance into the elite academies. Another movement, described by Raymond Callahan in *Education and the Cult of Efficiency*, grew out of the entrepreneurial spirit of the early twentieth century. From this movement arose a clamor of attacks by businessmen, including Andrew Carnegie, who called traditional high school education "mere scholastic education." They demanded that school be "a place to learn how to manufacture" (9) and that administrators and teachers become efficient managers rather than philosophers or scholars.

Along with teachers colleges and state agencies, English departments intermittently joined the on-going struggle to influence the nature of teacher education and to determine the content of secondary education. The emerging discipline of "English" became a natural battleground for the controversy. Arthur Applebee's history, *Tradition and Reform in the Teaching of English,* tells us that the struggle for control was well underway in the late nineteenth century as English moved to full disciplinary status. Beginning in the 1890s, numerous committees and review boards found that schools were not adequately preparing students for tasks required in college—the beginning of the cyclical crises in education more recently manifested in "Why Johnny Can't Read and Write," *A Nation at Risk, Cultural Literacy,* and *The Closing of the American Mind.* The demands in the late nineteenth century for better English teaching represented yet another university imposition on the schools, since the solution to the problem, as university English departments perceived it, was to use college entrance exams as a way of pressing change on schools. Through the Harvard Committee of Ten and the National Conference on Unification of Testing Requirements, university domination of the secondary English curriculum was at its strongest, leading to a long series of efforts to mandate standards for schools and culminating in the College Entrance Examination Board, established in 1900. Such testing became yet another way of solidifying managerial restrictions on teachers, positivistic learning theories, and the educational pecking order—only this time the impetus came from English professors, not from schools of education. The interest in scientific approaches to education along with emphasis on "practical" education—efficiency, standardized testing, and the factory/school model—perpetuated a Gradgrind conception of education that would continue to force learning into arbitrary segments, measure growth in terms of short-term quantifiable gains, and cut off teachers from the identities they might develop as serious readers, thinkers, and writers who exercise their abilities with autonomy.

We continue to be bound by these cultural and political forces. Their influences are manifest in English departments where a set of dichotomies—male/female, literature/composition, scholarship/

teaching—continue to be reinforced by underlying positivistic thinking and privileged versus inferior hierarchies. The problem lies deeper than the English department's lack of commitment to teacher education. The very structures of our discipline, the overt and hidden curricula of English departments, undermine the education of all English teachers, secondary or college.

English department faculties have been, and are presently, predominantly male, whereas the teacher force in secondary schools is largely female. Traditional instruction in English departments, like the departments in which many of us were educated, with erudite, revered male professors lecturing to docile students, fails to empower either female or male students. Even departments with feminists in the professoriate have provided little support for women or men in such traditional roles as teacher. Instead of serving as strong advocates for teachers and for the children they teach, feminist professors have often ignored or even denigrated them. And the stance they assume toward their own students has often been as bound by paternalism and tradition as that of their male colleagues. Too many have failed to heed the call of feminists like Adrienne Rich to ally themselves with those who have been silenced by political and social institutions.

Furthermore, the tradition of instruction in English studies corresponds more closely than we want to acknowledge with the tradition of eighteenth-century positivistic psychology and economic structures that have dominated American education. As English gained disciplinary status at the end of the nineteenth century, the strong positivistic strain led to two developments that have reinforced traditional lines of privilege and a conservative educational philosophy in English departments: (1) the emergence and sixty- or seventy-year entrenchment of what James Berlin has called "current traditional rhetoric" and (2) the privileging of literature and criticism and the corresponding denigration of writing and teaching.

In *Writing Instruction in Nineteenth-Century American Colleges*, Berlin shows the close parallels between the positivistic psychology and pedagogical strategies espoused by educational reformers in the nineteenth century and those still evident in schools and colleges today. Despite the developments in composition theory and research since 1960, positivistic ideas continue to dominate the view of language education held by many of my colleagues in secondary schools and in the university. The textbook selection committee of a nearby school district has just adopted a policy statement on language and writing that sounds like it was written according to the latest thinking among "new rhetoricians," but the textbooks they adopted, while giving over many pages to "the writing process," still contain large sections on traditional grammar. More alarming, the curriculum committee in my department recently spent several hours debating a proposal for a new "traditional" grammar course to be taught in the English department. It was defeated, but many of my colleagues who would not approve the teaching of traditional grammar continue to think of teaching composition as content-free skills, which the large group of mostly female, nontenure track, part-time composition teachers ought to be able to teach efficiently while the literature professors get on with their own more valuable scholarship.

Writing instruction in school and university is still considered less intellectually demanding and less valuable than literature study. Whatever the origins of this historical split between composition and literature—the loss of a "mutually shared epistemology" as James Berlin suggests ("Rhetoric and Poetics" 523), or a conception of literature as "a reality apart from ordinary reality," founded on a positivistic view of the world that conceives of some independent order of truth and reality (Lanham 21)—the result has been the privileging of literary texts. According to Raymond Williams, this sanctification has led to a denial of the very process out of which literature arises, that of actual composition, and to a further separation of reading and writing, not only from each other but from "the whole set of social practices and relationships which define writers and readers as active human beings . . ." (189).

Students, many of whom are potential school and university teachers, are educated within departments whose disciplinary structure is still the positivistic "field coverage" model that Gerald Graff describes in *Professing Literature*. Thus, the hidden curriculum of many English departments suggests to students that learning occurs as they are exposed to a series of parcels of canonical literature. This hidden curriculum also undermines much of what we know about human language development. It teaches students that only narrowly prescribed ways of reading, thinking, and writing are rewarded. Furthermore, in many literature classes little writing is required, and writing is often only valued as a product—to evaluate students' mastery of a certain body of "knowledge" and to see that they have assimilated, to some degree, the discourse of the discipline. English majors leave having experienced little that would prepare them to teach writing or to view writing and reading as interdependent.

For university professors, the privileging of literary texts leads to greater separation from teachers and, worse, to loss of a clear perspective on serious public issues concerning literacy in society today. Terry Eagleton argues in *Literary Theory* that the narrowing of literature studies has resulted in literature being separated from other cultural and social practices, making it an end in itself, isolated from the public realm. Research is most valued if it "makes a contribution to knowledge" about texts themselves, leading, as Richard Ohmann warns in *English in America*, to an ever accumulating, narrow, and specialized "knowledge" that does not lead back to the human experience beneath the texts (13–15). Only occasionally do literary scholars consider what happens to students or texts when we teach a given work. Only under pressure from feminists and minorities have they considered the political and social implications of the literature they ask students to study. Research that looks at people comes too close to the social sciences, and thus research in composition, which attempts to understand the human activity of writing, its history, and the political and social implications of teaching, is regarded as less legitimate, less "pure." Even among composition faculty we tend to stratify our research. Recently I was told, "Be as 'theoretical' as possible. Your writing will be more highly valued." Inquiry that focuses on pedagogy, even that which attempts to illuminate theory, is simply not considered to be as theoretical or as valuable.

Thus, the conception of teaching in university English departments reinforces the same positivistic management models that have long defined teaching in the schools: pedagogy is a simple matter of determining the best mode in which to deliver "knowledge" to students; it is separate from and far less important than the "content" we teach, and it demands little reflection and examination. In the schools, poor teaching is tolerated if classrooms are orderly and the objectives are covered. In the university, poor teaching is ignored if a faculty member produces plenty of "scholarship." The university dean who says, "Get your teaching in order, and get on with your research," once again reinforces the notion that teaching is something one can master by preparing lectures and assignments, and that it is mostly disconnected from inquiry, critical practice, and scholarship.

From this climate students graduate and become teachers in the schools, and in this environment future English professors are nurtured. Gerald Graff points to the virtue of the "coverage" model for English departments, with their multiple areas of autonomous scholarship: it has allowed departments to embrace a variety of subdisciplines and philosophical perspectives that might not ordinarily coexist. But he argues further that these groups often operate in virtual isolation, and departmental structures prevent dialogue and collaboration that might lead to discussion of underlying aims and methods among those varied groups. Thus, conflicting assumptions embedded in the discipline itself go unexamined, a critical view of education is obscured, and students and professors are "deprived of one of the central means of situating themselves in relation to the cultural issues of their time" (9). The traditional university English program, then, often fails to provide what students, prospective teachers, and professors most need—the opportunity to develop a sense of ourselves as "intellectuals," as people who can interrogate, challenge, and take control of the institutions within which we live and work.

Where does that leave us, English teachers in elementary and secondary schools, colleges, and universities? It leaves us embedded in a system of inequalities shored up by long-standing philosophical, economic, and epistemological structures. In schools and universities, we find ourselves seduced away from our students and from each other as we see our teaching devalued. And we find ourselves a part of an educational system and a society in which inequalities among people are widening rather than narrowing. These inequalities constitute the real educational and social crisis before us. The popular solution to these problems is a prescriptive dose of "the canon" for everyone, K–college, renewed standardization of the curriculum, and rigid evaluation. But this solution, arising from within hierarchical institutional structures themselves, promises only to strengthen and perpetuate inequalities among students, teachers, and communities.

We do have powerful alternative models for education that promise to enable rather than circumscribe, to dissolve distinctions rather than reinforce them. The National Writing Project, the "teacher-researcher" movement, and the "liberation" pedagogy of Paulo Freire turn hierarchical authority structures upside down and help professors, teachers, and students challenge them rather than become domesticated by them. These models allow students and teachers to build upon the knowledge and ability they possess and to engage in dialogue with each other in order to recognize multiple perspectives and to generate new ones. Students and teachers grow to recognize that they possess the knowledge necessary to question and resist existing structures and to transform their classrooms and their communities. Many people describe their experience in the National Writing Project in metaphors of rebirth, transformation, and salvation. Even in the most repressively "managed" school environments, I see teachers who find ways to resist regimentation and to adapt writing workshop strategies to their classrooms. As a result, teachers pass on to their students the same authority as writers and readers they experienced in the writing project. The teacher-researcher movement has a similar potential to reduce teacher cynicism about research and to transform teachers' image of themselves from reproducers of information to innovative investigators.

These programs are not successful because they bring teachers to the university and allow them to dabble again in the activities of the scholar, although that can also be important for some teachers. Instead, they are successful because they transform dichotomies and break down inequalities by allowing school and university teachers to work together with equal authority as writers and thinkers. They affirm teachers' knowledge as practitioners instead of trying to change them into "scholars" of a different sort. The Writing Project and the teacher-researcher movement argue that participants have authority because they have developed among them a valuable body of knowledge working with students. Sharing and examining that knowledge revitalizes all of us as teachers. Professors and teachers also are empowered because they have grasped and formulated for themselves the "theory" behind their teaching and are no longer dependent on what Ann Berthoff calls "recipe swapping." Those teachers, in turn, teach in ways that encourage their students to become inquirers in the classroom rather than functionaries who passively reproduce a standardized body of knowledge. In such classes the hierarchical relationship between teachers and students is diminished and distinctions among students based on privilege are reduced.

Efforts like these make me somewhat optimistic, but not entirely. Miles Myers' article "Institutionalizing Inquiry" notes that educational reformers do not even mention teacher research in their plans for change, and only a handful of school districts in the entire country have made it a part of their educational agenda. I also have some serious reservations about our motivations when we bring teachers to universities to make them researchers. Do we want to make teachers into researchers to allow them to accept our way of thinking? With Ann Berthoff ("The Teacher as REsearcher"), I want to know whose questions they are pursuing. Whose theory controls the assumptions underlying that research, and who is formulating the research methodology? This movement will be as bankrupt as traditional educational research if it becomes just another way to gain new funding for the work of a few professional researchers, like the Center for the Study of Writing at Berkeley seems to have become. New orthodoxies take their place quickly in the power structure. If in writing workshops and classroom research endeavors, both in the university and in our K–12 classes, we do not allow teachers and students to understand, critique, and operate within and against the environments in which they learn and teach, including ours, we serve them no better than traditional educational programs of the past.

History demonstrates too clearly that changes in education occur slowly and capriciously. Theories of social and linguistic change show us that conflict always exists between the normative forces of what Bakhtin calls "authoritative" discourse and forces of generative, innovative, "individually persuasive discourse." Teachers at all levels must decide whether to participate in producing the tension, resistance, and opposition from which change can occur. Although we live and function within institutional and societal frameworks that define us as skilled worker or as transmitter of knowledge, we also have the potential to resist, challenge, and reshape those definitions. That resistance and restructuring must occur in the politics of classrooms, departments, colleges, schools, and districts. We frequently delude ourselves into thinking that teaching and scholarship are above politics. Politics is "out there," beyond the walls of the school or university. We want to believe that teaching is simply a matter of deciding which textbook we use or whether we teach Shakespeare in tenth grade or how to structure our next graduate seminar. But the way we organize our graduate seminar or our eighth-grade class inevitably has social and political implications for our students' lives. In our classes, students are "hailed by ideologies" from which they find it difficult to escape.

Whether we are fifth-grade language arts teachers, eleventh-grade English teachers, specialists in eighteenth-century literature or in the history of rhetoric, we must continually reexamine the assumptions underlying our teaching and research if we hope to create change. We must pose and answer such questions as: What are the political, ideological, and pedagogical implications of my research and scholarship? Does what I do in the classroom reinforce inequalities? Does it empower all students by allowing them to articulate various perspectives and to question, examine, and challenge their own *and* my perspective? Or does it actively silence them or merely numb them into passive submission? We must question the definitions of literacy that structure and inform our teaching—literacy that is univocal, monological, defined as a narrow list of artifacts to be constantly preserved, or multi-dimensional, evolving, and including the expressions of people in our communities. If it is the latter, then we must work to restructure educational environments to nurture diversity and complexity rather than merely reproducing a static literacy of the powerful and privileged.

Asking and posing answers to questions such as these is a political, often subversive, activity that can lead to new structures in schools and universities and to revitalized roles for us and our students. But we cannot take on this activity without examining carefully our own present marginal positions and recognizing that to take on new roles, we must shed others. I think particularly about those of us who are working to secure tenure and promotion in English departments and to legitimate rhetoric and composition studies. After twenty years of establishing at least a rudimentary core of theory and practice, many university composition teachers are moving off into more heady realms, examining our roots in the history of rhetoric, looking to feminist, poststructuralist, Marxist, and social psychological theory to help us understand the historical and philosophical base for our pedagogy. As we move in these directions we move toward more ambiguity, more of the speculative "pure play" Richard Lanham describes (27). This is a healthy development, but it can also be dangerous. Scholarship and research that make us more acceptable to our colleagues in literature may also distance us from teachers and from crucial issues in education.

As a university composition professor I can say that the institutional pull away from marginal status toward legitimacy and acceptance is very strong. It is very easy to be seduced into thinking that I can be more effective if I work within a trickle-down philosophy of language education—teach my students, do my research, and hope that the effects of my work will eventually make their way down to students and teachers in the schools. Elementary and secondary teachers face similar choices. Some teachers feel they cannot afford to resist the possibilities for advancement offered if they become teacher/leaders, instructing their colleagues in new mastery learning programs, or if they take courses in educational administration rather than writing workshops. Our position reminds me of Virginia Woolf, locked out of the university library, the bastion of traditional forms of knowledge. She recognized that perhaps it was better to be locked out rather than take on forms of thinking that were not her own and that discounted her own experience (*A Room of One's Own*). Better to live outside the power structure than to live with the divided consciousness of those who seem to reside within but who are constantly jolted by the reality of their exclusion from it. Like second-generation immigrants, we face the problem of assimilating into the mainstream culture of our discipline at the price of divesting ourselves of our cultural heritage. And even when we do that, we may achieve no real power, but only the "separate but equal" power that institutions define for us.

We have one further choice. Elementary and secondary teachers, untenured professors, writing teachers, women—a union of

those of us who already have limited power within institutions—
can consciously stake out a place on the margins of the trenches
and the Ivory towers. This is a stance we see other disenfranchised
people taking—lesbians, gays, native Americans, blacks—holding
something of themselves apart, preserving their heritage, their
identity. I am not proposing a new separatism, a new opposition.
I am suggesting that we place ourselves in a different relationship
to power and legitimacy in the institutions we continue to work in.
Standing on the margins, we remove ourselves from a position of
ambiguity, of continual striving to be what we cannot be and instead
join with people who also stand outside the power structure and
who, for that reason, can question established assumptions, envi-
sion alternative structures, and work to create new forms of be-
longing and becoming. It is not a comfortable position. Because it
doesn't promise the same benefits and potential legitimacy, few of
us may choose to remain in such a position. But the margins of
power provide a vantage point from which we can see ourselves
and our institutions more clearly, a place from which to begin a
dialogue with each other and to transform the structures that perpetuate divisions and inequalities among us and our students.

Works Cited

Althusser, Louis. *Essays on Ideology*. Thetford, Norfolk: Thetford-Verso,
    1984.
Apple, Michael, ed. *Cultural and Economic Reproduction in Education*. Lon-
    don: Routledge, 1982.
———. *Ideology and Curriculum*. London: Routledge, 1979.
Applebee, Arthur. *Tradition and Reform in the Teaching of English*. Urbana,
    IL: National Council of Teachers of English, 1974.
Aronowitz, Stanley, and Henry Giroux. *Education under Siege*. South Had-
    ley, MA: Bergin and Garvey, 1985.
Bahktin, Mikhail. "Discourse in the Novel." *The Dialogic Imagination*. Ed.
    M. Holquist and C. Emerson. Austin: U Texas P, 1981.
de Beauvoir, Simone. *The Second Sex*. New York: Random House, 1952.
Berlin, James. "Rhetoric and Poetics in the English Department: Our
    Nineteenth-Century Inheritance." *College English* 47 (1985): 521–
    533.
———. *Writing Instruction in Nineteenth-Century American Colleges*. Carbon-
    dale: Southern Illinois UP, 1984.
Berthoff, Ann E. "The Teacher as REsearcher." *The Making of Meaning:
    Metaphors, Models, and Maxims for Writing Teachers*. Portsmouth, NH:
    Boynton/Cook, 1981.
Callahan, Raymond. *Education and the Cult of Efficiency*. Chicago: U of
    Chicago P, 1962.

Cremin, Lawrence. *The Transformation of the School.* New York: Random House, 1961.

Dellinger, Dixie. "Where Does the NWP End and the Real World Begin?" *The Quarterly* 10 (1988): 1–3.

Eagleton, Terry. *Literary Theory: An Introduction.* Minneapolis: U of Minnesota P, 1983.

Freire, Paulo. "Letter to North American Teachers." *Freire for the Classroom.* Ed. Ira Shor. Portsmouth, NH: Boynton/Cook, 1987.

Graff, Gerald. *Professing Literature.* Chicago: U of Chicago P, 1987.

Lanham, Richard. "One, Two, Three." *Composition and Literature: Bridging the Gap.* Ed. Winifred Horner. Chicago: U of Chicago P, 1983.

Katz, Michael. *Reconstructing American Education.* Cambridge: Harvard UP, 1987.

Myers, Miles. "Institutionalizing Inquiry." *The Quarterly* 9 (1987): 1–4.

North, Stephen. *The Making of Knowledge in Composition.* Portsmouth, NH: Boynton/Cook, 1987.

Ohmann, Richard. *English in America.* New York: Oxford UP, 1976.

Olson, Paul. "The Preparation of the Teacher: An Evaluation of the State of the Art." *Education for 1984 and After.* Ed. Paul Olson, L. Freeman, J. Bowman. Lincoln, NE: The Nebraska Curriculum Development Center, 1972.

———. "The Transformation to a Market Economy: The Role of Early Teacher and Compulsory Education in the English-Speaking World." (forthcoming).

Prentice, Alison. "The Feminization of Teaching in British North America and Canada, 1854–1875." *Histoire Sociale-Social History* 8 (1975): 5–20.

Schultz, Lucille, et al. Interaction among School and College Writing Teachers: Toward Recognizing and Remaking Old Patterns." *College Composition and Communication* 39 (May 1988): 139–153.

Smith, Frank. *Insult to Intelligence.* Portsmouth, NH: Heinemann, 1988.

Suhor, Charles. "The 1988 Report on Trends and Issues–NCTE Commissions." Urbana, IL: National Council of Teachers of English. 1988.

Williams, Raymond. "Cambridge English Past and Present." *Writing in Society.* Thetford, Norfolk: Thetford-Verso, 1983.

Woolf, Virginia. *A Room of One's Own.* New York: Harcourt Brace, 1928.

EIGHT

Tenure, Status, and the Teaching of Writing

WANDA MARTIN

In our line of work, there are two possibilities. You can be a member of the regular, tenure-track faculty, with voting status in the department, a teaching load that takes into account your other obligations, and your name on the department directory. Or you can be a part-timer, with no vote, a teaching load limited only by the number of papers you can possibly read in a weekend, and your name on an index card taped to the door of the office you share with one or more others of the same status. That is to say, there is the possibility of being Somebody, or of being Nobody.

Most English departments look like pyramids, with the most senior faculty—those holding and protected by tenure—teaching the most advanced, most specialized courses, which are usually also those with the smallest numbers of students. Typical class maxima for graduate and upper-division undergraduate courses are fifteen to twenty-five, but many courses, especially in smaller programs, do well to draw the five or six needed to avert cancellation. Every semester, some of these classes fail to garner the needed enrollment, and the faculty member is bumped down, down, down, into God forbid, Freshman English. Generally, professors in such situations are gracious; they put the best possible face on it and may even claim to hold no particular preference for teaching Seventeenth-Century Poetry over teaching composition. But given any choice at all, they will always seek an advanced composition course over one for freshmen, and a second semester freshman course over a first. English 101 is Hell.

At the bases of such pyramids, we find vast numbers of students in beginning courses, virtually all of them focused on instruction in writing rather than on the study of literature. These are taught almost exclusively by junior faculty on the tenure track, graduate students serving apprenticeships in the hope of getting on that track someday, and full- or part-time lecturers who can never hope for the protection of tenure. Many members of this latter class possess professional credentials equal to those of the tenured and tenure-track faculty but are constrained by a variety of circumstances from obtaining tenurable positions. In my own department, at least ten of the thirty lecturers hold the Ph.D., half a dozen more are A.B.D, and all have M.A.s, most with additional hours. The part-time faculty is not a holding tank for those not yet ready for the job market, nor a refuge for the incompetent. By and large, these people are professional teachers of writing, writers and scholars themselves, often qualified to teach a far larger range of courses than is available to them. But they are in general disregarded by their "regular faculty" colleagues, who as a group are unaware of their numbers, their credentials, and their contributions.

The conditions under which part-time teachers work are difficult, whether the individual hopes eventually to find a full-time position or intends to work part time indefinitely. Lack of access to necessary office supplies and secretarial help, limited availability of typewriters and strictly limited access to copying, inadequate or nonexistent office space, dilatory scheduling practices, sudden changes of appointments, departmental communications that unconsciously exclude—simply forget—part-time people, are common aggravations, but they are only signs of the larger and more troublesome reality: these people are not conceived as department members but as menials, employees like the janitors, whose work is simple, requiring no particular preparation and no important expertise.

The hiring practices that result in such departmental structures are generally justified by commonsense appeals to economy and administrative flexibility. It is pointed out that tenured and tenurable faculty members carry responsibilities other than teaching, which justify their relatively higher salaries per course taught. Such people form the backbone of essential programs for majors and graduate students and must be available to meet those needs. Since professors are expensive and most departments are short-handed, while part-timers are both cheap and plentiful, it makes economic sense to staff the numerous sections of elementary-level courses with the latter. No use paying for a Cadillac where a Volkswagen will do. Furthermore, enrollments for such courses are difficult to project accurately, so staffing with part-time people, who are guaranteed nothing, provides necessary flexibility to cut or expand offerings as enrollments and administrative pressures dictate.

While perhaps rational from a narrowly administrative point of view, such arrangements create far more problems than they solve if the department's goals include not only covering all the necessary classrooms but also providing a coherent curriculum in writing, taught by people who regard themselves as members of a humane community. While the annoyances and indignities suffered by part-time teachers are the most visible of these problems, professorial faculty lose credibility with deans, administrators, and taxpayers when it is clear that the bulk of the teaching is being done by apprentices and temporaries. Students complain that curricula taught partly by closely supervised "staff" and partly by faculty members who are free to shape their courses lack coherence. In programs controlled by standard syllabi and exit exams, students find just cause for complaint when Professor So-and-So, teaching by her own lights, fails to prepare them for the final. Most important, the gap in status between those who teach writing and those who study and teach about literature makes it nearly impossible for departments to engage in the rethinking and redefinition that would carry them into the future intact.

The issue of membership is central: the structure I have been describing systematically excludes from full membership more than half of the people teaching, and they are the ones who account for well over half of the student contact hours. Even if paper clips were freely available, even if everyone had a typewriter that worked, the distinction between the tenurable and the nontenurable would still, and in a much more important way, guarantee exclusion from membership for this substantial fraction of the faculty. People who are not "regular faculty" are not eligible to serve on committees that set policy for the department, do not attend department meetings, have no votes. Some departments grant token, representative membership on selected committees. In my experience, only the committee that governs the Freshman English program is substantially affected by the influence of part-time teachers. The interests and concerns of part-time teachers are nowhere represented in the deliberations of the departments, save when their state of exploitation is being ritually decried during the annual frenzy of budget reduction. This is the politics of the English department: the few govern while the many serve. If, as we claim when we say we are committed to the humanities, our mission is to initiate students to the body of knowledge, methods of inquiry, and ways of evaluating experience that constitute Western culture, we must examine whether we send those students contradictory messages in our lectures and in our practice.

If learning to write compositions is so vital an educational experience that every college in the university requires it, why do professors find the teaching of it beneath their dignity, unworthy of their scholarship? Why is a writing course for twenty-five freshmen worth only one-third or one-half as much money as a course in Milton for six graduate students, or a course in poetry writing for twenty advanced undergraduates? Why do professors, most of us literature specialists, hold all the power while others, paid piecemeal, hired semester to semester, carry most of the responsibility? The institution that thinks it can teach in opposition to its own politics is deluding itself.

We may profitably begin looking for answers to these questions in the history of American higher education, a history that Walter P. Metzger traces back to the universities of the Middle Ages. Originally, he points out, the masters were essentially independent scholars, and universities had the character of guilds. Then, scholarly tenure equaled privilege—exemption, security, protection— for a class defining itself as separate from the larger population by virtue of its learning, and demanding

> through the device of incorporation (variously termed *communitas, collegium, societas, consortium*) the right to elect their own officers and representatives, to sue and be sued as a single juristic person, and—above all—to enact the rules and regulations to which they and those who dealt with them had to conform (96).

Over time, states, churches, universities, and scholars have changed, and their relations have changed along with them. In this country, the earliest universities began almost as seminaries, dedicated to passing on to an elite class of students the received body of knowledge that would make them cultivated men, properly prepared to enter business or the professions. Access to higher education was strictly limited, as was society's view of its purpose.

As Myron Tuman documents in *A Preface to Literacy*, by the time of the Civil War, even elementary education was far from universal:

New England recruits in the Northern army averaged only 5.2 years of schooling by midcentury, and the figures were considerably lower in other regions. Nearly twenty percent of the recruits from Kentucky, Tennessee, the coastal slave states, and Canada had never attended school, while nearly half had done so for only three years (45).

The transition from a frontier and agrarian society with a small class of educated people into an industrial culture that attempts to educate all its members has kept us divided and confused, older concepts of mission and faculty roles colliding head-on with new demands. The developments of the nineteenth century—widespread industrialization, the need for a more skilled and intellectually flexible workforce, the need to systematize new knowledge to foster the further development of industrial technology—led to a broadened view of higher education. While studying and transmitting the knowledge of the past remained important, newer institutions, particularly those started under the land grant laws, demanded that scholars conduct research to create new knowledge as well. Further, these agriculturally oriented schools tended to privilege the positivistic views and methods of nineteenth-century science. The notion of the cloistered retreat where people of intellect and discrimination could share their concerns was overwhelmed by the view of the university as engine of progress and social change.

Metzger characterizes the modern American tenure system, which he dates to the 1913 founding of the American Association of University Professors, as judicial, intended primarily to protect academics against unjust dismissal. He sees the impetus for this new model in social forces at work around the turn of the century that

> ushered in the age of the professional: the appearance of the political activist on the faculty; the growth of ideological conflict between academic social scientists and trustees of wealth; the emergence of an "academic freedom public" with high sensitivity to complaint; the inclusion of this public into administrators' significant world (138).

The dismissal of economist Edward A. Ross from Stanford University at the behest of sole trustee Jane Lathrop Stanford because his economic ideas and his efforts to influence public policy offended her private values seems to have been a significant precursor to organization of the AAUP; and it provoked the profession at large to demand, not always with success, faculty involvement in dismissal decisions. This is a far cry from the atmosphere of the simulated family that Metzger tells us characterized relations at Harvard in its earliest years.

In the last 120 years, this country has changed from one in which few people possessed the ability to read and write into one in which virtually every citizen expects to be able to earn a college degree if she or he so desires. But we do not all agree what such a degree is or should mean. The continuing critique of students' skills upon entering college, documented by Mike Rose in "The Language of Exclusion"; the cyclic rise, fall, and rise of remedial education; the periodic calls for a return to standards of excellence, all reflect our efforts to reconcile fundamental ambivalences about the nature and purpose of higher education. And the gulf between tenured and nontenurable faculty members is only another symptom of our uncertainty.

Certainly in our contractual arrangements with the institutions that employ us we differ vastly from the magisterial guilds of medieval Europe, not least in that to admit a woman to such membership would have been unthinkable. But the medieval heritage persists. Academic status is not fundamentally a matter of contractual protection but of self-conception. The metaphors tell all—the "ivory tower" in which we reside, the "real world" out there, for which we try to prepare our students though we would not want to live there ourselves. Academics still see themselves as outsiders, noncommercial creators and disseminators of knowledge, still hearkening to the religious origins of the university.

The professoriat tends to think of itself as a kind of priesthood, to which only the elect are admitted, which will study only the elect texts, which must set its own standards and make its own rules, by which both the membership and those who deal with it ought to be governed. The elect are mostly male, even now—the struggle for equal employment of female academics continues despite laws prohibiting gender discrimination and lawsuits documenting and penalizing it. A 1977 article by sociologist Hugh Gardner asserted that "[t]here are actually a smaller proportion of women on tenured college faculties today than there were in 1931" (52). That such a struggle is necessary underlines the existence of the professorial self-concept I have described. That it has been started reflects the changes underway in higher education.

The developments of the last three decades have created rough going for the priestly self-concept, especially among English professors. As Metzger and other researchers (Leslie, Kellams, and Gunne; Chait and Ford; Abel) document, the 1950s and early 1960s

were a time of breathtaking expansion for higher education in the
United States. With that expansion came increased pressure to
come down from the ivory tower and provide the kinds of education
that the real world required if this country was to remain the world's
leading industrial democracy.

When the generation that fought World War II came home,
it possessed the GI Bill, some years of hard experience, and the
ambition to go to college and make something of itself. The subsequent boom years; the rush to improve education, especially in
science, which followed the Soviet satellite launch of 1957; the
expansion of opportunities and expectations for minorities resulting
from the civil rights campaigns of the early sixties; and those veterans' Baby Boom children reaching college age in the mid-sixties
expanded the number of potential college students, fueling a great
increase in the resources committed to higher education and in the
number of professors employed. According to Metzger, the professoriat numbered about 70,000 in 1930, nearly half a million in
1973. Drawing from several sources, Emily Abel reports that
"[b]etween 1960 and 1970, the number of faculty in four-year
institutions expanded 138 percent" (3). Summertime, and the tenure was easy. More than one professor hired and tenured during
that period has commented to the effect that "about all you had
to do was keep breathing."

During that same period, "the number of college students
jumped from 3.8 million to 9.2 million" (Abel 2). And the increase
was not just in numbers but in kinds of students to be served. If
the World War II veterans came to college in large numbers, hungry
to earn degrees and find themselves a place in the America of the
Dream, they also came mostly white, overwhelmingly male, and
experienced in doing the difficult and the unpalatable. Not all
possessed the skills they needed for college, and many institutions
resurrected mothballed remedial programs to meet their needs
(Lunsford 8). But these students shared the values of the academic
establishment. They came to learn what college had to offer.

Their offspring grew up expecting to attend college, under a
barrage of information depicting the college graduate as inevitably
much more affluent and enjoying a much more satisfying life than
his diploma-holding neighbor. Somewhere along the line, college
had stopped being a finishing school for young men on their way
into the professions and had become the place to get the necessary
credentials for A Successful Life. These students were still mostly
white, mostly middle class. Although they sometimes raised troubling questions in challenging ways, they shared the values of their
masters to a large degree, and they had the skills.

The students brought to college by the success of the civil rights movement, many of whom entered under the open admissions plans that proliferated in the late sixties and early seventies, were another matter altogether. The changing structure of the job market was not lost on minority leaders, who made universal access to higher education a chief demand. As Abel points out, "It was also the demand to which state officials may have preferred to respond, for they could create the illusion of upward mobility through education far more readily than they could effect fundamental social and economic changes" (3).

These new students tended to be black, Hispanic, native American, or Asian. Many were poor, and most had been schooled in neighborhoods where the PTA didn't hold bake sales to raise money for language labs. They came from a different part of the country than college students had generally come from before, and they were, if not proud, at least a little defensive of their values and backgrounds. In the Introduction to *Errors and Expectations*, Mina Shaughnessy catches the mood of the faculty who faced these students.

> Not surprisingly, the essays these students wrote during their first weeks of class stunned the teachers who read them. Nothing, it seemed, short of a miracle was going to turn such students into writers. Not uncommonly, teachers announced to their supervisors (or even their students) after only a week of class that everyone was probably going to fail. These were students, they insisted, whose problems at this stage were irremediable. To make matters worse, there were no studies or guides, nor even suitable textbooks to turn to. Here were teachers trained to analyze the belletristic achievements of the centuries marooned in basic writing classrooms with adult student writers who appeared by college standards to be illiterate. Seldom had an educational venture begun so inauspiciously, the teachers unready in mind and heart to face their students, the students weighted by the disadvantages of poor training yet expected to "catch up" with the frontrunners in a semester or two of low-intensity instruction (3).

This also was a boom time for graduate education. The expansion in undergraduate populations meant both increased numbers of students qualified for graduate school and increased demand for holders of advanced degrees to teach all the undergraduates. Abel reports that the graduate student body more than tripled between 1960 and 1975, growing from 314,000 to 1,054,000. In 1970 alone, almost 30,000 Ph.D.s were awarded and, by 1976, annual production had risen to 34,000. . . . Over 25 percent of all humanities doctorates ever awarded in the United States were conferred during the 1960s and over 44 percent during the following decade" (2).

Gardner, writing in 1977, points out that this growth reflects not just a touching faith in the benefits of higher education but a scandalous failure of universities to plan rationally.

For almost a decade now, American higher education has been turning out new college teachers about twice as fast as new jobs have opened up for them. In the last five years alone, according to Labor Department estimates, more than 125,000 new Ph.D.s have graduated for whom no jobs exist. By 1985 that number is expected to reach nearly 400,000. In fields like English, languages, philosophy, and history, where 90 percent of the jobs are in teaching, only 20 percent of the Ph.D. graduates are hired each year (49).

These excess college teachers were, as Gardner wrote, finding positions in the academic equivalent of migrant farm labor. The economic troubles beginning in about 1966, largely attributable to government efforts to finance the war in Vietnam without anyone having to pay for it, visited the colleges and universities as well as the factories and department stores. An era of retrenchment followed the frantic expansion of the preceding decade and a half, an era that saw reductions in force, layoffs of tenured professors, lawsuits over these dismissals, and a general resurgence of administrative control over staffing decisions.

In its 1972 report, *The More Effective Use of Resources: An Imperative for Higher Education*, the Carnegie Commission on Higher Education "recommended that colleges and universities employ increasing proportions of nontenure-track faculty to retain 'flexibility' during a period of declining or shifting enrollment" (Abel 69). And that they have done. Between 1972 and 1978, while full-time faculty was growing by 18 percent—from 380,000 to 448,000—the number of part-timers increased 73 percent—from 120,000 to 208,000. In a more recent study, based on data gathered by the National Center for Education Statistics, Judith M. Gappa estimates that in 1977, 34 percent of faculty members were classified as part-time. According to EEOC reports, 7 percent of those were tenured or eligible for tenure (10).

Not very many tenured faculty members remain marooned in classrooms with basic writers, or even with freshmen entering the regular composition sequence. Through the combined effects of all the forces discussed above, freshman writing courses are now overwhelmingly taught by graduate students and part-time lecturers. Many of these still fit Shaughnessy's description—"trained to analyze the belletristic achievements of the centuries"—but only some of the graduate students among them still expect eventually to be delivered. The majority know they are composition teachers, regard the teaching of writing as suitable employment for the professionals they know themselves to be, and are puzzled by the unwillingness or inability of their departments to accord them status commensurate with the service they render.

The departments' dilemma is partly administrative: all faculty have to be protected by tenure, but each department has only so many lines, so it must use part-timers to accomplish all the teaching it is obligated to do. Although the people hired on part-time appointments are willing and able to do this work that others find distasteful or difficult, departments cannot tolerate their working anything like full time, lest they claim *de facto* tenure. Although many, perhaps most, of them know enough about the tenure system to find *it* distasteful and would be delighted to have opportunities to compete for simple full-time teaching positions with no more guarantees than a yearly contract and benefits comparable to those accorded to clerical staff, institutions generally cannot find a place in their organizational charts for such positions. Faculty must be protected by tenure; people who teach in tenure-granting institutions must be faculty; and so it goes. The only way to get the teaching done without running afoul of the system is to create positions that don't really exist, employees who don't really work for us. At this point, the problem ceases to be administrative and becomes clearly political. Political in the sense that it becomes necessary to examine whose interests are being served, and at whose expense.

The tenure system as we know it in this country arose as protection for the freedom of speech of an elite class of intellectuals in a society and at a time when such protection was essential. And no one, surely, would argue that academic freedom is in less need of protection now than it was in 1913. But in addition to protecting academics' freedom to explore new ideas, tenure in its present form often protects very small teaching loads, unfettered choice of what courses to offer without much regard for efficient use of resources, and comparatively wide leeway, in the form of course releases, for a variety of nonteaching activities—research, travel, and journal editing, to name a few. Tenured academics control their time and choose their activities to an extent virtually unknown among other classes of salaried workers. One of the activities tenured people least often choose is teaching writing courses.

Most of the basic teaching that supports that class now is done by a class of laborers on an industrial model. I say this because most of the English departments with which I am familiar depend heavily on the student credit hours generated by enrollments in freshman-level "service" courses to justify their size and their budgets. Thus, they invest part of the resources gained in part-time instruction and take profit in the form of small classes and leisurely teaching lives.

Meanwhile, lecturers carry loads of from three to seven (depending on how many jobs they have) classes per semester, usually with about twenty-five students in each. They earn roughly $1200 to $2000 per class, with little or no access to employee benefits. A lecturer of my acquaintance earned $21,000 before taxes in 1987 by the simple expedient of teaching fifteen sections of English 101 and 102 at three campuses. Leaving the building on Friday afternoon, he was often heard to say he was "off the clock," not acknowledging for the moment the stack of student essays he invariably carried with him.

And like other industrial workers, these teachers legitimately worry about what labor relations experts call "deskilling." No department I know of would think of instituting a common syllabus and uniform final examination for all the sections of Shakespeare, The Comedies. Yet such arrangements are routine in freshman writing programs, and they are commonly explained as quality control measures. This is not to argue against the program coherence and reliability of outcomes that may also result. It is simply to point out that freshman writing is in general viewed by departments as a fundamentally different enterprise from the rest of the department's work: an assembly-line endeavor, essentially remedial, not especially demanding on the intellect, taught by interchangeable workers, managed by composition specialists, the segment of the regular faculty whose status is most dubious.

The very existence of such specialists, and of graduate programs to educate them, coincides with the influx of nontraditional students to the colleges and universities. The upper classes, nostalgic for the days of belles lettres and the elite academy (which, ironically, most of them never really knew), resent and resist the changes in the mission and the student body of higher education.

The growing managerial class—composition specialists, program administrators—do their best to offer coherent programs despite unstable budgets and a constantly changing and demoralized teaching force. Composition teachers meet their classes, duplicate handouts at their own expense, and wonder what new assault on their professionalism each new administrator, each new semester, will bring.

Since the problem is only partly administrative, administrative action can provide only partial solutions. Certainly it would help if ways could be found to provide secure and dignified employment for those on whom we rely to teach our beginning students. Some institutions have made a start in that direction, offering full- or part-time instructorships with set terms, arranging for lecturers to have some access to benefits, and including part-timers in collective bargaining units. These institutions are to be praised for their efforts, and every department that employs part-time faculty members should launch similar initiatives.

The larger problem, however, will not be solved by treating the coolies better, and it would be a mistake to bend all our efforts toward what are finally only stopgap measures. Our society's long-simmering confusion and debate over the purposes of higher education has come to a boil in the modern English department. If such departments are to proceed into the future intact, rather than fragmenting into programs on Literature, Communication, Rhetoric, and Writing Across the Curriculum, they must address the confusion directly and find ways to synthesize the antagonistic parts of their missions.

In *Textual Power: Literary Theory and the Teaching of English*, Robert Scholes offers a structuralist analysis of what he calls the "English apparatus." He begins by defining the problem in terms of two oppositions:

> First, we divide the field into two categories: literature and non-literature. This is, of course, an invidious distinction, for we mark those texts labeled literature as good or important and dismiss those non-literary texts as beneath our notice. This distinction is traversed and supported by another, which is just as important, though somewhat less visible. We distinguish between the production and the consumption of texts, and, as might be expected in a society like ours, we privilege consumption over production (5).

Is it this privilege—the prestige accorded to the consumption and explication of the sacred literary texts—that underlies the status system I have been examining and that must be challenged if writing and its teachers are to become integrated with the rest of the department? Scholes argues that both distinctions can readily be seen as superficial and inept, and that at least part of the resolution lies in learning, and teaching our students, that the heart of the matter is not to worship some texts and scorn others but to question texts of all kinds in order to make them meaningful in their various contexts.

This kind of change will be difficult if literary scholars persist in what Maxine Hairston recently called their mandarin attitude. The literature/non-literature distinction, Hairston argues, arose in the effort to establish respectability in the university and protect literary research from competition with the sciences. If, by definition, respectable texts must be detached from the world and its purposes, she goes on,

> I do not see how expository writing programs can long exist in a healthy condition within a department whose power structure holds this value. The very essence of rhetoric and composition is that it is worldly, pragmatic, contingent, and dynamic. . . . It does something, and writing teachers are engaged in the practical, everyday work of teaching large numbers of people a craft they think is going to be useful to them.

In that article, Hairston puts her finger on an issue that is central in this matter but too complex to explore fully here—the role of research and its relation to teaching. In the nineteenth century, when the university as we know it was emerging, one of its chief purposes was to educate the workforce, but another was to systematize knowledge, to conduct organized inquiry whose outcomes would contribute to the advancement of industrial culture. The pursuit and publication of research in all fields—one of the major endeavors of faculty members and perhaps the most important criterion on which most of them are judged for tenure—has become one of the main distinctions between universities and other kinds of institutions offering higher education.

Because English departments have for so long been departments for the examination of sacred literary texts, the standards for and respectability of literary research are well established. Because the teaching of the craft of writing has been largely relegated to underlings—graduate students of literature and part-time teachers—research into how writing is accomplished and how it can be taught is suspect. Only a few composition specialists make it into the tenure-track ranks where resources are available for research. The crowning irony is that part-timers—whose labor pays for so much of the research that is done—are excluded from doing any, whatever their interest might be, and are then penalized by the system for this very lack of intellectual proprietorship. We appreciate you, says the faculty, for keeping the freshmen at bay. But you can't expect equal status; after all, you're only teachers, not scholars.

That attitude fails to recognize an important fact of modern life in the academy: society's expectations of us are changing. If higher education was first to provide cultivated men for the professions, and then to educate the workforce for the Industrial Age, one of its central functions in the late twentieth century is surely to broaden access to opportunity by providing education to an increasing segment of the population. Although some of the open access programs of the 1970s have shriveled under the rhetoric of "excellence" in the 1980s, the growth of evening and weekend programs and the continuing influx of adult and other nontraditional college students bespeaks a broad public perception that the way to improve one's life is through higher education. A man laid off by a large corporation yesterday was quoted in this morning's newspaper to the effect that it isn't really so bad because now he can finish his college degree.

The tight budgets that most people and virtually all government agencies (I include public universities in that class) have suffered in the 1980s have also put the public in the mood to question what it gets for its money. Recent calls for the abolition or modification of tenure are symptomatic: the public is coming to believe itself ill-served by its system of higher education. People living and working in the world know they and their children need to know how to read and write—consume intelligently and produce efficiently—the kinds of texts they encounter in that world. They are impatient with what they often see as an "egghead" academy where their hard-earned money is spent by esoteric people on esoteric pursuits.

I would be the last to argue that literary study is not valuable, or for a reversal of the present hierarchy, with composition privileged over literature. But it is certainly time for English departments to come to grips with present reality, to try to reconcile the roles of research and teaching, reading and writing, creation and interpretation. As we attempt such reconciliations, we will find ourselves, I think, with a much broader sense of the department's mission, as a center for the study of texts and their creation. Such a definition of mission will recognize that the society that supports us expects us to educate all its children, not just those who share our fondest interests.

Then writing program administrators will not need to look for homes outside the department, but can work within to bring all the resources of literary study to bear on the teaching of writing. Then literary scholars will recognize that when students learn to read carefully and write intelligibly in Freshman Composition, they are not being programmed with skills they should have acquired earlier but are in fact taking the first steps toward the critical acuity we hope they will show later, whether they study Shakespeare, political science, or mechanism engineering. And then it will be fruitful to talk again about the status of part-time faculty.

Works Cited

Abel, Emily. *Terminal Degrees: The Job Crisis in Higher Education*. New York: Praeger, 1984.

Chait, Richard P., and Andrew T. Ford. *Beyond Traditional Tenure*. San Francisco; Jossey-Bass, 1982.

Gappa, Judith M. *Part-Time Faculty: Higher Education at a Crossroads*. Washington, DC: ERIC Clearinghouse on Higher Education, 1984.

Gardner, Hugh. "Ph.D.s: Migrant Workers of the Academy." *Mother Jones* (May 1977): 49–52.

Hairston, Maxine. "Some Speculations about the Future of Writing Programs." *Writing Program Administration* 11 (1988): 9–16.

Leslie, David W., Samuel E. Kellams, and G. Manny Gunne. *Part-Time Faculty in American Higher Education*. New York: Praeger, 1982.

Lunsford, Andrea A. "Politics and Practice in Basic Writing." Unpublished manuscript, 1985.

Metzger, Walter P. "Academic Tenure in America: A Historical Essay." *Faculty Tenure: A Report and Recommendations by the Commission on Academic Tenure in Higher Education*. San Francisco: Jossey-Bass, 1973.

Rose, Mike. "The Language of Exclusion." *College English* 47 (1985): 347–359.

Scholes, Robert. *Textual Power: Literary Theory and the Teaching of English*. New Haven: Yale UP, 1985.

Shaughnessy, Mina P. *Errors and Expectations*. New York: Oxford UP, 1977.

Tuman, Myron. *A Preface to Literacy: An Inquiry into Pedagogy, Practice, and Progress*. Tuscaloosa: U of Alabama P, 1987.

NINE

A Marriage of Convenience
Reading and Writing in School

HEPHZIBAH ROSKELLY

I'm watching my two-year-old nephew watch "Sesame Street." Today is brought to us by the letter "K." Oliver walks to the television to point and say the letter aloud to me. Then suddenly, he turns and runs out of the room, returning a minute later with a coloring book of the twenty-six letters. He turns the pages until he finds the one Grover has just explained to Big Bird. He has laboriously colored the letter—written it—in a bright purple. "K," he says again, with a satisfied smile. And he should be satisfied. He has read and written, simultaneously almost, and with a clear prescient sense of connection that seems to need no explanation. Reading shapes his writing just as writing directs his reading, and in this way Oliver interprets his expanding world.

With some important exceptions among special populations, by the time students reach college, they have written and read a lot. They've mastered the skills of literate communication in their primary and secondary education and will proceed to refine them in college. They will read more and with more efficiency; they will write more and with more sophistication. But some of their teachers, and later, their employers, will be concerned by the passive way they read and write, by their seeming willingness to regard their reading and writing as completely separate from their real lives. These students will have difficulty in making important con-

137

nections that show them to be active thinkers—connections between their reading and writing in various contexts, between the
process they use to read and the one they use to write, and most
of all between their experiences outside and inside the classroom.
Somewhere between "Sesame Street" and Freshman Composition
children lose that sure sense of organic integration that makes reading and writing part of the larger activity of living. Oliver knows
something that the college student has forgotten.

In *The Fate of Reading* Geoffrey Hartman remarks on the growing separation between the acts of reading and writing as part of a
larger discussion of the role of interpretation and criticism in an
increasingly fragmented culture. Hartman fears the loss of the
"dream of communication" shared by readers and writers in the
past. As perspectives on interpretation multiply, Hartman argues,
reading is becoming more and more narrowly conceived and writing
consequently more service oriented, directed toward explaining
ways of reading. In this new *mal du siecle,* the two activities drift
apart:

> It is now not possible to read some kinds of writing—concrete
> poetry or extreme experimental prose, for example—though
> it is quite possible to analyze them and construct by that means
> something readable: a metanarrative. One can foresee, how-
> ever, an era where writing will be as semi-automatic as reading
> is now. Writing and reading would be competitive rather than
> mutually reinforcing activities (272).

Clearly, Hartman is disturbed by his vision of a future where writing
interferes with reading as an interpretive mode, where interpreters
read only to find topics for their own discourse. He locates this
future just on the horizon: "Those who read merely to find a starter
for their own performance are already close to that productive
state," he warns (272). The new world will be a bedlam for humanists, if a paradise for technocrats, with resource people and
retrieval systems a substitute for audience and memory. Dominated
by mechanisms they don't control or understand, interpreters will
write and read in the constricted ways that have come to pass for
literacy.

To Hartman, the separation between the two activities of
literacy is killing reading: "Writing appears as productive, activist,
material; reading as passive, accumulative, retrograde—the most
recalcitrant of bourgeois idealisms!" (272). I think Hartman is right
to be anxious, though his worry about the death of "retrograde"

reading at the hands of "productive" writing is not only precipitous but paranoid. Writing is not prospering at the expense of reading; both seem to me to be at risk and not because, as Hartman implies, print and culture have exploded so violently that they have little chance to work together. Pedagogy is at the heart of the reading and writing problem, though Hartman would like to diminish its role in the problem or in the solution: "As if a pedagogy accommodated to the pressures of a particular community were the best we could hope for" (viii). Reading and writing, the most traditional "subjects" paired in school, in fact have made a bad match. Wrenched apart by skills teaching and patched together in curriculum plans and textbooks, reading and writing are not so much learned together as taught together. They are combined unequally, by tradition or surface similarity and not by what they together contribute to a learner's interpretation. The cause, and the result, is an underlying separation between the two that infects the way students think of reading and writing in school. The dichotomy arises, ironically, from the pairing itself—where an unequal partnership obscures the fact that both processes are directed and produced by the force of the imagination.

The earliest experiences of schoolchildren match reading and writing poorly. Most primary school teachers are trained in reading, but few have specialized, similar training in writing. It's hardly surprising that teachers make connections between the two acts by inserting writing into their reading instruction. "Read this tall tale," teachers say. "Now write one of your own." Or "Read to the bottom of the page. Close your book. Now write what you think will happen to the donkey." Occasionally, older students are asked to "explain what you feel" about a text or to "pretend" to be the author or the story's protagonist in an imitation exercise. Contrary to Hartman's expectations, writing doesn't kill reading, overtake or replace it. Writing time is simply time subtracted from reading time. Nevertheless, this reading/writing time is based on a principle, though a faulty one, of connection between the two acts. The teacher assumes a similarity between the processes by placing writing after reading; students are expected to use one set of skills to produce another set. Unfortunately, research shows that this expectation is frequently unmet in the classroom, for children often end up disliking, and failing to perform, the interrupted reading task as much as the interruptive writing.[1]

In high school and college classrooms, assignments in reading and writing follow much the same pattern. Mirroring Hartman's definition of reading in the technological age, students read to reconstruct or decode an unfamiliar language, and they write to demonstrate their mastery over that strange language. In this environment, reading is diminished, but appears prior and primary, inasmuch as it directs the writing that will follow it; writing appears consequent and adjunct, as it follows in substance the reading which occasioned it. The college reader or literary anthology in the writing class is typical of this kind of pairing: the reading in those texts is fuel for students' composing processes as they read, decide, and record their decisions in an academic essay. Students explore the content of their reading in discussions of character, theme, plot, conflict—the most common kind of assignment—or they imitate the forms they read, either by mimicking surface features or rhetorical ones. These assignments assume that if a student *really* reads, she'll be able to *really* write because she'll have something to write about. These kinds of writing-from-reading tasks constitute the bulk of assignments students get in high school and college English classes, and the message they send is that reading controls writing. If writing gets more attention in classrooms, it's because it's visible, the tangible sign of reading having taken place. The student has read to locate a performance in writing, just as Hartman fears, but the writing is no more active and productive than the reading which preceded it.

This unequal, often uneasy partnership between the acts of reading and writing illuminates an underlying dichotomy in teaching literacy. I discovered how pervasive this dichotomy was while teaching a course for English majors preparing to teach in high school. My students had been studying theories of reading and of the writing process, and, to clarify their own reading of these theories, they listed on the board the characteristics that separated reading from writing, aiming to take issue with the divisions. "Reading is easy/writing is hard" headed the list, followed by a group of words that all expressed a similar notion about reading and writing, pairs like "receive/give," "mental/physical," "passive/active." The group quickly disposed of the "easy/hard" split and disputed the other distinctions as well. But the students remained uncomfortable with their own arguments; they kept talking about a difference that theories of composing didn't explain, a difference closely related to their own experiences in becoming literate. What the discussion came down to was at once simple and difficult to resolve. Reading and writing are divided by the most obvious of factors: one is internal and the other external.

It seems to me that the way reading is taught in schools, paradoxically as "prior" and as "passive," is the result of a continuing belief in the venerable but still very spry Cartesian division between mind and body. Reading is necessarily of the mind because it requires no physical, observable markers to accompany it. Writing is just as necessarily of the body because it is defined entirely by the observable physical effort that produces it.[2] Hartman acknowledges the destructiveness of the dichotomy with his anxious complaints about the death of "passive" reading at the hands of "active" writing. Richard Rorty goes much further than Hartman in attempting to dissolve the dichotomy, and so his arguments have some relevance to the reading/writing split found in much of the literacy instruction in schools. In *Philosophy and the Mirror of Nature*, Rorty looks at the work of three anti-Cartesian philosophers—Wittgenstein, Heidegger, and Dewey—in order to call into question the hypothesis that the mind reflects reality and that mental and physical activity are therefore opposed states. "I would hope to have incited the suspicion," he remarks, "that our so-called intuition about what is mental may be merely our readiness to fall in with a specifically philosophical language game" (22). He heightens that suspicion by going on to list features philosophers have taken as indicators of the mental rather than physical and systematically deconstructs the list by showing how beliefs about language ability as "mental," for example, are matters of conscious decision rather than some *a priori* truth.

What Rorty is after, and this is the reason he chooses the particular trio he does to help him make his case, is a philosophical recognition of knowledge as relative, speculative, and historically determined, rather than a system that defines the most objective reflection of reality as knowledge. I don't want to follow the line of Rorty's argument against Cartesian dualism much further, except to say that his lengthy attack establishes the continuing influence of his argument in philosophy and inevitably pedagogy. John Dewey, perhaps Rorty's strongest witness in his attempt to break down Cartesian distinctions, shows how the metaphor of mind as the eye of nature results in a mind and body separation and in a received notion of knowledge as immutable. Dewey's statement illustrates how the Cartesian dichotomy works against an integrated conception of teaching reading and writing.

> The theory of knowing is modeled after what was supposed to take place in the act of vision. The object refracts light and is seen; it makes a difference to the eye and to the person having an optical apparatus, but none to the thing seen. The real object is the object so fixed in its regal aloofness that it is a king to any beholding mind that may gaze upon it. A spectator theory of knowledge is the inevitable outcome (39).

"Spectator knowledge" is just the kind of knowledge that dominates practices in both the teaching and learning of reading and writing. Students read to learn about the "real object," to see it as clearly as they can, and they write to prove to teachers just how clear their mental mirrors have been while they were reading. Teachers use the "real object" as their standard for evaluating their students' writing, and their reading. Those students who are the best spectators of the objects they see, and of their teachers' mirrors, are almost always successful. Their adept passivity, which manifests itself in a subversion of their own interpretive power in favor of teachers' and texts' "real objects," is rewarded. As an educational theorist, Dewey argued that the spectator knowledge is destructive to learning, and later work in composition and reading has validated his claims that students need to be participants in their own learning. The notion of reading as passive has been fervently opposed by reading specialists like Frank Smith and literary theorists like Louise Rosenblatt; and composition specialists from Janet Emig to Peter Elbow have pointed out the myth of writing as necessarily active.

Mark Twain made the same point long before any of these critics were writing about the insufficiency of traditional ways of regarding the acts of reading and writing. In *The Adventures of Tom Sawyer*, Tom's classmates cap their school year with a demonstration of their writing and reading expertise in commencement addresses. The young ladies who compete produce original compositions with titles like "Friendship," "Forms of Political Government Compared and Contrasted," "Heart Longings," "The Advantages of Culture." These compositions, of course, are based on only the vaguest of ideas about the topic and only the most rigid ideas about the forms the topics should accommodate themselves to. "No matter what the subject might be, a brain-racking effort was made to squirm it into some aspect or other that the moral and religious mind could contemplate with edification... [with] a gush of the language and lugging in by the ears particularly prized words and phrases" (191–192). Twain knew there was a problem with the way Tom's teacher, Mr. Dobbins, taught reading and writing to his students. The "glaring insincerity" of these productions wasn't sufficient to fault them, "and never will be sufficient while the world stands, perhaps," Twain comments. In fact, insincerity seemed to be a virtue, for the most pious composition was inevitably delivered by the "most frivolous and least religious" girl in the school.

Tom Sawyer's classmates could be seen as sad examples of what happens when reading and writing are separated in function in the way Hartman fears. In fact, Percy Boynton's textbook *Principles of Composition*, a college handbook first published in 1916, uses the Tom Sawyer passage as an illustration of what happens when students fail to limit topics and read about them. "What Tom's friends fumbled with on that historic occasion is the kind of subject that will always be attempted as long as youthful students consult nothing but their own inexperience" (11). Boynton admits that "it is right that the student who deserves the name should want to puzzle out on paper his relation to himself, to the culture for which he has come to college, to the society of which he is a member." But that desire should only be gratified if "the written product is based on definite reading and is definitely limited in scope" (16). Boynton's words are echoed often in composition textbooks today, for he is promoting the same one-way relationship between reading and writing that teachers accept still: more reading makes for better writing.

On the surface, modern students seem pretty much like Tom Sawyer's friends. They read without recognizing context at all, or with recognition of nothing but, and they seldom consider their own place in the transaction. They use a highlighter pen to mark the progress of their interpreting—as they look for form, for thesis sentences, for major points and less major details so that they can reproduce what they've decoded. This process defines school reading for most students, and the yellow marker that flies across the page is usually a profoundly passive activity, which will be passively reconstructed in a written text.

But there is a difference. Hannibal's students shape reading and writing together despite their teachers. Forced to perform, they take note of the essential act of mind that directed their compositions' production and delivery. They know that to write is to read, and that to do both is to imagine purpose. Because they have constructed compositions based on the way they imagined their purposes—constructed as they construed, as Ann Berthoff says—the compositions succeed. Admiring friends, proud parents, ministers, and judges sit in the hall murmuring, "How sweet," "So true," and the prize is awarded to a composition so eloquent that "a Webster himself might well be proud of it." The writer has done her job—written her essay with one eye trained out and ahead to the performance she will deliver for that audience and one eye trained inward and back to the myriad examples of commencement addresses she has heard, read, and been instructed to imitate. This sort of cross-eyed vision might not have helped her see better, but she links reading and writing together with purpose and coherence as a way to help her interpret. I suspect that if she *had* read deeply about "life" or "earthly pleasures" or even "forms of govenment," as Boynton and no doubt contemporary composition instructors would advise, her composition would have been no less general or banal. She would have read about her topic in precisely the same way she wrote about it, with a rigid but finally effective notion of how her reading would fit her purpose.

Reading can't guarantee writing or give it a rationale. To teach reading and writing together requires a movement away from establishing which element of literate behavior is prior and which subsequent. It requires a reemphasis or a reclaiming of the imagination as the forming activity that shapes both reading and writing. Boynton acknowledges—maybe a little grudgingly—the role of the imagination in interpretation: "There is no more virtue in dumbly rereading what one already knows than there is in daydreaming, book in hand, and attempting to absorb information by contact. Indeed, as between ways of wasting time, it is rather more profitable to look out the window, where something may happen to wake one up, than to gaze at a page which does not contain anything new" (16). Boynton may not have perceived that passive reading might be the result of something more than repetition, but he did see that looking away, even daydreaming, might awaken a student to the possibilities of a text.

Seeing the imagination as a mediating principle between the interpretive acts of reading and writing breaks down the mind/body dichotomy that limits the teaching of literacy by treating writing as the physical outcome of the mental reading process. It's puzzling to me that in his attack on Cartesian dualism Rorty all but ignored the philosopher who could have provided the most support for his case against such distinctions.[3] C. S. Peirce exposed and rethought either/or distinctions in many areas of thought, including science, linguistics, and mathematics, as he called on philosophy to look beyond ideas and reactions to them and toward the principles that put concepts into relationship. These principles Peirce called "thirdness." Two juxtaposed items—thought and language, sign and signifier, science and humanities—are bound by some principle that draws them together, and the only complete philosophy, the only one that carries the possibility for truth, is one that explores the mediating factors, the "thirds," that relate ideas. "To say something is similar," Peirce explains, "means that some occult power from the depths of the soul forces us to connect them in our thoughts after they both are no more" (385). For Peirce, that means that surface differences or similarities or an emphasis on skills or characteristics is an inadequate philosophical perspective. The power of thirdness is that it uncovers concepts that allow thinkers to break down the dichotomies that signal limited ways of knowing. Peirce found that the perception of triadicity allowed connections to be made between science and art, evolution and psychology, object and symbol. The spark that illuminates ideas provides new ways of thinking about them. The "occult power" Peirce describes becomes a new construction not a simple amalgam, a new concept arising after the initial pairing is no more.

For teachers interested in "reconciling" reading and writing, Peirce is profoundly useful. One of his explanatory analogies suggests how. Comparing the three aspects of ideas (firstness, secondness, thirdness) to a gunpowder explosion, Peirce writes, "Nature herself often supplies the intention of a rational agent in making Thirdness genuine and not merely accidental; as when a spark as third falling into a barrel of gunpowder as first, causes an explosion, as second" (366). I see the explosion; I know gunpowder was placed in the gun. But I *assume* the spark that makes the relationship; I don't even think of it. Reading and writing are seen too often in a similar cause-effect combination, with reading as the gunpowder and writing the explosion. As a teacher of reading and writing, I know like Peirce's observer that there's a connection between the two, but the explosion I read—students' compositions—or the kind of gunpowder I've handed out—assigned readings—keeps me from noticing the spark. Peirce's triadic concept of ideas allows me to imagine the spark and discover more profound relationships than cause and effect or traditional similarity, which have combined reading and writing in my classroom. Attention to the similarity between them, or teaching them as cause-effect as though they progressed in an evolutionary continuum from reading to writing, are both inadequate methods to develop an integrated theory of interpretation that places equal emphasis on reading and writing. Those links exhibit what Peirce calls "thinking in seconds," and they only perpetuate a dichotomy that makes writing the outcome of reading, both passively encoded and reproduced by learners.

This is what Oliver knows that his teachers will miss, and that he later, sadly, will forget. Reading and writing are connected by the imaginative act that produces them. The scholars in Hannibal let writing direct reading as they fit purpose to form. Oliver let reading become the end result of his writing as he located purpose in performance. But neither Oliver nor Tom Sawyer's friends simply perform; they transform what they do by combining it with what they need. Reading and writing, as isolated products, are not the goals; the goal is to know—and then to have that knowing recognized. Perhaps one of the easiest classroom strategies to locate the imagination as the "third" R in literacy is to nurture oral speech in reading and writing.

To escape the yoke of similarity that binds reading and writing in school, teachers need to explore Peirce's "third" by using strategies that illuminate reading and writing as mediating, symbolic acts, both representing and explaining the interpretive process. This act of symbolic construction is imaginative, the living force of the active mind at work. And it is purposive, determined by intention or desire. Kenneth Burke, one of the philosophers Hartman looks to for solutions to the problems of a quasi-literate world, insists that the principle of symbolic action governs human behavior. "We all symbolize," Burke maintains, and that truth suggests how reading and writing must be connected with the imagination in schools as the symbolic action governing the processes of reading and writing. "Terministic screens," one of Burke's metaphors for the interpretive process, explains this symbolic activity more precisely. Terministic screens are the angles an interpreter takes on experience, angles whose degree is determined by the language of the particular screen. The screen directs interpretive energy into one channel or another, allowing the interpreter to symbolize and resymbolize experience in a number of different ways. If imagination directs the acts of reading and writing, reading and writing might be seen as terministic screens themselves, "languages" chosen as methods for coming to knowledge.

The movement between reading and writing, with imagination as the third or mediating point, dissolves the mind/body, passive/active dichotomy that makes reading and writing only a marriage of convenience in teaching. As Burke's work suggests, the imagination is an act, not just a state of being, a force that initiates, juxtaposes, brings together processes. As far back as Plato, the imagination is shown to work in this mediating way between ideas. In the *Phaedrus*, it is Will—or the imagination—that reconciles opposing forces within the soul.[4] Socrates describes the soul as a triad, with the will standing between reason and appetite, and uses the metaphor of a charioteer trying to control two horses. "With us men it [the soul] is a pair of steeds that the charioteer controls; moreover one of them is noble and good, and of good stock, while the other has the opposite character, and his stock is opposite. Hence the task of our charioteer is difficult and troublesome" (246B). Though one horse is good and the other bad, and the work is hard, the soul learns lessons of love through the struggle. The charioteer drives his team most effectively by learning when and how to draw the reins on the dark horse. "And so it happens time and again, until the evil steed casts off his wantonness; humbled in the end, he obeys the counsel of his driver. . . . Wherefore at long last the soul of the lover follows after the beloved with reverence and awe" (254E). The combination of reason and desire in the soul allows the will to find its power.

Teachers make the imagination the goal in reading and writing when they allow writing to precede reading, or assign journals as products as well as processes, or encourage marginal comments and dialectical notebooks, or form small groups to read aloud and write together. The imagination as mediating principle lets pedagogy put mind and body, reason and sense to work together, lets teachers make of reading and writing a true union rather than a lifeless marriage. In the *Phaedrus,* the soul sprouted wings when it contemplated the beloved, communicated and consummated that love by exercising the will, its imaginative power. Reading and writing don't have to be conveniently paired by custom in schools. Students can learn to exercise their imaginations, and even childhood wisdom, as they read and write in an individual and communal search for truth, which is at the heart of the composing act.

Notes

1. For a good discussion of the teaching of literacy in the elementary school, see Lucy Calkins, *The Art of Teaching Writing* (Portsmouth, NH: Heinemann, 1987). Her work in classrooms shows how reading and writing are equally compromised by teachers' insistence on making writing secondary and interruptive.

2. Of course, the mental/physical dichotomy has been partially dissolved by both reading and writing theorists. Studies of the reading process in works like Eleanor Gibson and Harry Levin, *The Psychology of Reading* (Cambridge: MIT P, 1975) and Frank Smith, *Understanding Reading* (New York: Holt, Rinehart, 1978) take note of the physical manifestations of the reading process, including eye and brain movements. There have been innumerable studies of the writing process that explore the "mental" aspects of the physical production of texts. Two of the most important are Donald Murray, "Internal Revision: A Process of Discovery," *Research on Composing,* ed. Charles Cooper and Lee Odell (Urbana, IL: National Council of Teachers of English, 1978) and Ann E. Berthoff, *The Making of Meaning* (Portsmouth, NH: Boynton/Cook, 1982).

[3]Rorty makes only a few glancing references to Peirce, one in a footnote that misreads Peirce's allusion to "man's glassy essence," a figure Peirce used to confirm (not deny) the interdependence of mind and matter. See *Philosophy and the Mirror of Nature* (Princeton: Princeton UP, 1979), 42, and Peirce's "Man's Glassy Essence," *Chance, Love and Logic* ed. Morris Cohen (New York: Barnes and Noble, 1923). His omission of Peirce is all the more puzzling since the selections of Dewey's work that Rorty chooses clearly show Dewey's debt to his mentor, Peirce.

4. As it changes the reason and appetites, the will as a force is linked to the imagination through its transformative power. Hartman uses the terms more or less interchangeably. "The will remains, whether we call it honorifically, the imagination, or deplore it as 'the self whose worm dieth not, and whose fire is not quenched.' " See *The Fate of Reading* (Chicago: U of Chicago P, 1975), 260–264 for Hartman's discussion of the role of imagination in criticism.

Works Cited

Boynton, Percy. *Principles of Composition*. Boston: Ginn, 1975.

Burke, Kenneth. *Counter-Statement*. Berkeley: U of California P, 1968.

Dewey, John. *The Quest for Certainty*. New York: Harper & Row, 1960.

Hartman, Geoffrey H. *The Fate of Reading and Other Essays*. Chicago: U of Chicago P, 1975.

Peirce, C. S. *Selected Writings*. Ed. Philip P. Wiener. New York: Dover, 1979.

Plato. *Phaedrus*. Ed. Edith Hamilton and Huntington Cairns. Princeton: Princeton UP, 1961.

Rorty, Richard. *Philosophy and the Mirror of Nature*. Princeton: Princeton UP, 1979.

Twain, Mark. *The Adventures of Tom Sawyer*. Kingsport, TN: Grosset and Dunlap, 1946.

TEN

Content(ious) Forms
Trope and the Study of Composition

PHILLIP K. ARRINGTON

. . . the theory
Of Poetry is the theory of life,

As it is, in the intricate evasions of as . . .
—Wallace Stevens
"An Ordinary Evening in New Haven"

"Trope" isn't the first word on the lips of many teachers of composition these days. We usually think tropes are mere "figures of speech," a sometimes dangerous, and frequently abused, stylistic tic. Perhaps this is because, in reimagining writing as process, we have been unable to transcend our own "negative rhetoric" about style (Rankin 12). So it remains a low-level concern, absorbed into the clean-up maneuvers of editing and proofreading. Our textbooks, if they mention figures of speech at all, simply repeat this conventional wisdom. With some notable exceptions, of course: Ann Berthoff warns her students not to use "a metaphor unless you can use it to think with; don't use it as icing" (*Forming* 194). Sound counsel, except that metaphoric "icing" does tell us something about the writer's thinking, the vague mixing of desire, evidence, and belief. Some, like myself, would go farther and claim that this icing may be *all* we have "to think with."

Granted, the more conventional meaning of trope has a long and venerable tradition, as old, or older, than Plato or Aristotle. The meaning and the tradition meet and reinforce the classical division of the rhetorical process into two basic steps: finding something to say (the invention of content, in this case, arguments) and saying it (the forming and stylizing of content). Tropes, obviously, were of relative importance in the second step, but quite consistently excluded in the first. This division, of course, presupposes the even more familiar separations of content from form, idea from image, and literal from figurative meaning. And it's precisely these separations that many critics and scholars today question, if not attack.[1] Out of this dialogue emerges a meaning of trope that has yet to make much impact on the study of composition, even though many of our most widely respected theorists vigorously urge us to embrace the complex interplay of thought and language, form and content. And out of it emerges a chance not only to "bring style back into style" within composition circles (Rankin 12), but also to help us understand that how we, and our students, talk and write about our "content" shapes how we know it. And this in turn may help us to recover the "theory of poetry" as a "theory of language," if not "life," which is to say the imaginative grounds of thinking, writing, and meaning itself.

Some Twists on the Well-Dressed Thought

We've heralded and debated the "paradigm shift" presumed to have taken place in composition. We've rediscovered invention in the ruins of ancient rhetoric, and we've adopted ever more radical, phenomenological assumptions about thought and language than our classical predecessors (Knoblauch). Yet the split between form and content survives. It underlies and supports what Robert Zoellner calls the "think-write" model of composition. We discuss and even evaluate our students' writing as if it were a verbal centaur, half "form," half "idea." And we teach invention, prewriting heuristics, or outlining as those discrete stages where we "think" before we "write."

So we easily separate thought from language and literal language from its tropes. Yet, in 1930, I. A. Richards argued that " '[t]hinking' is radically metaphoric. Linkage by analogy is its constituent law or principle, its causal nexus" (*Interpretation* 48). Later, Richards will proclaim that "the study of metaphor, through

metaphor, should become...a central and governing part of
the study of language," noting that metaphors come into our language as soon as human beings "pursue their further-than-
referential aims" (*Speculative* 41). Which, if we're candid, is more
often than not.

Richards rightly calls our attention to the inventive power of
metaphor. But metaphor is but one embodiment of the tropic principle. Even so, as Karl Wallace notes, in our efforts to revise the
topoi of classical rhetoric, metaphor and the other tropes were cur-
iously omitted. Why, Wallace asks, privilege the classical *topoi*, or
our modern, "cognitive" translations of them, as generators of content and not metaphor, or imagery? Indeed, as many modern rhetoricians are now asking, why not privilege all the tropes? The same
spirit that leads Richard Coe to ask "who took the form out of the
process?" leads me to ask, "who took style out of invention, form
out of content?"

One may answer that we've inherited these age-old dichotomies from those classical rhetoricians who needed to "rationalize"
rhetoric so it could remain respectable and useful for philosophy.
Although classical rhetoricians did not neglect "form" in their understanding of "process," they did restrict tropes to *elocutio* or
"style," where they were not always distinguishable from figures
of speech or thought. As a stylistic category, tropes included many
lexical and phrasal indirections. Some—metaphor, irony, and per-
sonification—are familiar. Others—metonymy, synecdoche, hyperbole, metalepsis—are more exotic and frequently confused.
Over the centuries, the exact number of these forms has varied.
Quintilian describes a dozen; Bede, forty-one. Much later, Peter
Ramus and Giambattista Vico keep the number at four—metonymy, irony, metaphor, and synecdoche (Howell 116, 168). And
we're still arguing over how many tropes there are (though the set
of four has gained many followers) or which ones are most important, most valued (usually, metaphor wins this contest).

But these arguments distract us from a more important modern
twist: a small, seemingly superficial, part of rhetoric now appears
in various disciplines as our name for the "deepest" of our "deep
structures." According to Hans Kellner, tropes "...have become
a kind of *lingua franca*, bridging linguistics, rhetoric, poetics, philosophy, criticism, and intellectual history" (15). Many other fields
could be added to his list: sociology, anthropology, history, music,
psychology, and, only recently, in Frank D'Angelo's work, composition. In any case, Kellner's hyperbole seems partly justified.
Trope has become our "philosopher's stone," our long sought "key
to the mystery of texts" (Kellner 14).

Why the lowly trope? Kellner feels that critics have "inflated" trope's importance to keep step with "the broadly structuralist mood of the times" and to respond to the "pressure" critics feel "to discover a 'missing link' " between tedious analyses of small chunks of discourse and the broader, macroscopic analyses of texts as fables of a time, place, and culture (14). But the search for this missing link has led to our recognizing the complex poetry of *all* language, the imaginative ground of *all* meaning. Tropes seem to be a useful way for us to describe "the dance of discourse" (Phelps), the way meaning plays out its work and works out of its play.

Harold Bloom reminds us that "every critic necessarily tropes the concept of trope, for *there are no tropes,* but only concepts of tropes or figures of figures" (Stevens 393). Bloom characteristically overstates his point. But he makes us aware that our preference for the sartorial concept of trope—as stylistic "dress"—seems the necessary outcome of certain epistemological assumptions which philosophers since Plato have insisted rhetoric make. Our most persistent critical troping of trope in Western rhetoric is of a piece with the trivialization of style.

This persistence, as it turns out, obscures a more subtle pattern in trope's meaning. At that precise moment when rhetoric (or its now emerging double, composition) seems to become *nothing but style, nothing but the tropes and figures that, during the Renaissance, consumed it, the ground is cleared for trope to reappear as central to thinking and meaning.* This pattern coincides with the apparent epistemological break modern rhetoric makes with its classical precursors over the separation of form from content. Fundamental to the "rational metaphysics," which "teach[es] that man becomes all things by understanding them (*homo intelligendo fit omnia*)" (Vico 88), this dichotomy now supports a "rational paradigm" of discourse in which language serves reason, logic (Fisher). So, it becomes possible to imagine that the invention of content precedes and subsumes how content is expressed, style. Thinking comes *before* speaking and acting, just as Mind comes *before* Body and is above Body, as if *logos* were the parent and master of language rather than simply one its many rebellious children (Derrida). With the body outside of and subsequent to the mind, language can be situated outside of thought, as can rhetoric, style, and trope. From such logocentric assumptions springs rhetoric's own grammar of the composing process: invention, arrangement, style, memory, and delivery, and the more recent and frequently criticized linear model of composing some of us teach: prewriting, writing, and revising.

However, a quite different and more expansive meaning of trope emerges from what Giambattista Vico calls the "imaginative metaphysics," out of which the rational metaphysics comes and to which it often returns. This metaphysics "shows that man becomes all things by *not* understanding them (*homo non intelligendo fit omnia*)" (Vico 88). As such, tropes become language's primary enactment of our "not understanding," our highly meaningful evasions.

Our earliest senses of what a trope is anticipate Vico's. Unlike *topos* or *figura*, trope is a word naming either a "motion" or an "action," not a "thing": the "natural" motions of the sun at winter and summer solstice and the human (hence, cultural) action of the farmer as he turns his plow at the end of a furrow. Out of the first sense come the tropisms of science—en*tropy*, photo*tropism*—and the "heliotrope," as Jacques Derrida calls it, of Western philosophy—our imperfectly perfect metaphor for describing how the "light/sun" of knowledge and truth appears and disappears in the tropic "darkness" of language. Out of the second come *boustrophedon* and *strophes*. The turn of the plow reappears in the ancient Greek practice of turning a line of written script from left to right and right to left on alternating lines of a page and in the choric practice of turning from one side of the orchestra to the other.

Once classical rhetoricians borrow the term to describe verbal action, trope will name "places" where meaning turns. Yet, as if foreshadowing contemporary critics, they imply that such turnings are from place to place. Modern theorists have exploited this implication to trace the running to and fro of discourse, the weaving and interweaving of texts, the ongoing and unwinding series of "turns" in "plots" we invent to structure and interpret experience. These plots, Walter Fisher suspects, are as essential to, though less obvious in, arguments, theories, and scientific treatises, as they are to poems, novels, and plays. All have "stories" to tell because stories, replete with "turning points," are fundamental to the human experience of time. So Fisher proposes a "narrative" model of discourse which, he argues, subsumes the "rational" one because *logos*, as Hayden White argues, is "merely a formalization of tropical strategies" in stories and myths that continues to "prefigure" how both philosophers and scientists make discursive sense of the objects they want to describe and explain (17).

Once these turns are formalized as enthymemes and syllogisms, tropes themselves become ornaments of style, adornments that rhetors use to "dress" up content because the ability to speak and write in this "uncommon" manner displayed their social status, culture, and education. But there was also the embarrassingly obvious appearance of tropes among poets, the poor, the uneducated, necessary for expressing emotion, for naming what had no name (Howell 117).

This troubling fact partly explains classical rhetoric's ambivalence toward tropes and style, from the moment philosophy masters it and so represses rhetoric's poetic origins. Even after this happens, rhetoric was not entirely loyal to the philosophical assumptions it had to serve. It couldn't surrender the very tropes of style without which the "truthful" content lacked body. Without them, it couldn't present itself effectively, as Aristotle knew, to the "eye" and "ear" of the audience. As such, the *energia*, "lifelikeness," "movement," and *enargia*, "vivid, colors" of verbal performance, like the *evidentia* so important to Erasmian "copia," relied on the stylistic effects tropes could create. They could *show* what *logos* could only tell. And so they remained for many classical rhetoricians: ambiguously suspended between the rhetor's will to embellish and show off his social status, his cultural refinement, and the "natural" necessities of naming the unnameable which the *poiesis* of language allowed.

Quintilian's clumsy attempt to save tropes from being reduced to mere wordplay is a key instance of this ambiguity. When he must distinguish trope from figure, he surrenders to the prevailing assumptions of his predecessors. But before that, Quintilian, who deeply influenced Erasmus, admits that tropes altered meaning, not just words. Nor were they restricted to words or phrases. They could, as linguists and modern literary critics have now shown, stretch throughout an entire speech or text. So out of Quintilian's rescue attempt come two definitions of trope, not one. The first, and more revisionary of these, Quintilian sacrifices on the altar of a philosophical rhetoric. The other, of course, continued to dominate much of what followed.

Quintilian's ambivalence about tropes, like his ambivalence about style for the sake of style, is, writ small, rhetoric's own. Rhetoric's "paradigm shifts" over the centuries, despite our disavowals, prefigure composition's vacillations between our emphasis on product (form, style, grammar) and process (thinking, forming, revising). Jonathan Culler, for instance, imagines these shifts as the "paradox" implicit in "the nature of the situation rhetoric [and, now, composition] is trying to describe" ("On Tropes" 607–608). If effective language is "artistic," rhetoric idealizes tropes, style, the "literary" side of itself, and so spills into "poetics." Yet true art must not "show." It must remain subservient to the content it expresses, the effect it tries to create. So rhetoric idealizes invention, the "clear" language of "truth," without trope or deviation, and so spills into logic, philosophy, and science. For Culler, the "relationship between structure [tropes and conventions] and event [persuasion] is incalculable." This is rhetoric's fate: forever to al-

ternate in defining its "substance," from language (style, tropes)
to the persuasive "event" language is supposed to create (invention, *topoi*).

Culler, of course, fails to account for trope's other traditions
in ancient Greek scepticism or medieval hermeneutics. Aenesidemus called the sceptic's elaborate arsenal of heuristic strategies
tropoi. Their function: to open up and overturn any philosopher's
claim to "absolute" knowledge, thereby preserving the freedom to
think "otherwise." Tropes, as St. Augustine presents them, were
the triggers for and the justification of exegetical glosses, explica-
tions, and commentaries on Scripture. Reading texts tropologically
was the indispensable first step in escaping the carnality of literal
interpretation—so much so that it constituted, in Augustine's Christian rhetoric, an entire program of education and the single most
important "invention" strategy for the exegete. Later, like their
exegetical counterparts, medieval composers troped the accepted
musical and lyrical formulas of liturgies, thereby making a trope
the primary means of creative expression in medieval music (Van
Deusen).

In these other traditions, trope means something more than
simply dressing up a thought. Aenesidemus and Augustine, not
Aristotle or Quintilian, may be the more influential—and unacknowledged—precursors shaping trope's expanded meaning today.
But neither quite anticipates Vico's widely acknowledged influence.
Vico "reads" in the tropic strategies of language the cyclical patterns
of human consciousness and cultures. "All the first tropes [meta-
phor, metonymy, synecdoche, and irony] are corollaries of [a] poetic
logic." These, Vico explains, are "imaginative class concepts," the
basis of human thinking (128–131). Even the later development of
"rational" consciousness, in Vico's scheme, presupposes the master
trope of irony to distinguish the "as if" of tropes from the "is" of
literal meaning.

Admittedly ambiguous and arbitrary,[2] Vico's fourfold, recursive scheme, to many critics, corresponds to many explanations of
"how" we know: Aristotle's principles of memory and eighteenth
century revisions of these principles into "laws of mental association" (resemblance, contrast, contiguity, and abstraction); Kant's
categories of thought; Marx's theory of ideological development;
Freud's "dreamwork" strategies (condensation, displacement, representation, and secondary revision); and Piaget's stages of cognitive development—to name but a few. For Kenneth Burke or
his disciples, Hayden White and Harold Bloom, Vico's scheme of
tropes has an "inherent narrativity" (Kellner 27). Each trope implies and contains the next, and the order of turns can variously

repeat itself at different moments in a culture's or a writer's development. This "narrativity" complements, and could quite possibly complete, Fisher's ambitious effort to synthesize "two traditional strands in the history of rhetoric: the argumentative, persuasive theme and the literary, aesthetic theme" within an encompassing narrative paradigm of discourse (2). These strands, we know, have not only divided rhetoric against itself but also divided English departments from speech departments, and, within English departments, the teaching of composition from the teaching of literature. Even though modern theorists differ on the exact order of these turns, or on whether these turns are individually willed, the imagination's "defense mechanisms" (as Bloom would have it) or systemic to language's deconstructive impulses (as Derrida or de Man would argue), they agree on one point: a trope simultaneously unites "how" we know and "what" we know because what we know always implies a way of knowing it. For Burke and White, naming and describing the world presupposes verbal translation, a series of tropic perspectives, within a given text or series of texts. Whatever strange object or event we know and write about can be metaphorically seen in more familiar terms. If that object is abstract, like the mind, we can metonymically reduce it to physical attributes or dimensions, to causes and effects, or correlations of these. Or we may see it synecdochically, as a representative part (microcosm) of a whole (the macrocosm of history, culture, and so on). Or we may play these perspectives off against each other, seeing ironically what one misses in what the other includes, and vice versa.

For Bloom, it's someone else's prior interpretation of that world, and not the world per se, the writer must turn to her own uses. Compared to his scheme of tropes, Burke's and White's looks Edenic, their troper an Adam come new and innocent to experience. Bloom's troper seems more like Caliban. The world is already someone else's tropes of it, which partly explains why Bloom grounds his tropic scheme in Freud's psychology of defenses. For Bloom, knowing begins in irony, not metaphor. Writers subvert the priority of whatever meaning precedes their own by imagining it isn't there so theirs can be. Or they defend themselves by reducing and limiting its meaning (metonymy), by substituting a partial meaning for the whole (synecdoche), or inflating or deflating their own work by inflating/deflating their predecessors' (hyperbole, litotes). As ultimate defenses, they can reverse relationships of inside and outside (metaphor) or turn the tables on the previous meaning so that it seems they, not their precursors, invented it (metalepsis).

These two schemes, while offering different stories of how

the human imagination turns whatever is "out there" into a "version" of itself, both subvert the sartorial trope of trope, emphasizing the inventive dimensions of style and stylizations of invention. The hard-won wisdom is to recover, however tentatively, the *poiesis* of meaning from the fateful split philosophy and science has tried to make between form and content, invention and style. This *poiesis*, need I stress, is quite visible in our own efforts to define what a trope "really" is, for we both enact and embody this internal principle of change every time we describe, analyze, or otherwise perform a dance of discourse. "Language," notes anthropologist Roy Wagner, "allows meaning to be projected and resonated outside of the mental microcosm [of thought, mind, self] via sensuous means" [sounds, images, letters] and thus "establishes... a single referential standard for projected and internally performed perceptions" (136–37).

The key phrase I would stress is "performed perceptions." As an act, trope mediates the conventional and the invented dimensions of what we perceive. Without the first, we could not recognize a trope, even though the convention itself may also be a "dead" or forgotten trope. Without the second, we couldn't make sense of new experiences. To trope, then, is neither totally a process of subjective expression (as Bloom seems to argue), nor totally an impersonal play of signs, cut off from human intention, history, and cultural context (as many deconstructionists are fond of claiming). It requires both an individual imagination and the more public conventions of discourse. So defined, trope has no precise "structure, system, or mechanism" because, as Roy Wagner argues, it "embodies" structures, systems, and mechanisms, performing meaning and commenting on the performance (126). It's thus impossible to "construct a position outside tropology from which to view it" or to avoid tropes as we analyze them (Culler; "Turns" 209). Both efforts are certain to fail because, as Wagner reminds us,

> the trope of meaning encompasses the meaning of trope: neither nature and culture, nor God and man, nor any of hundreds of other symbols constitutes the core of a human culture. Rather, its contained and containing form does; the core of every culture is the single idea, or epoch, of humanity. (141)

Trope and the Teaching of Composition: Questions and Possibilities

Fine, the unrelenting pragmatist may say, but what does all this have to do with the complexly "human" (or "inhuman," as the case may be) culture of classrooms we inhabit, or with our students' struggles to write, or our struggles to teach them? What good is it?

Difficult as it is to answer these questions, given the highly theoretical nature of much that's been written about tropes, I would reply that the greatest value of trope for the composition teacher is the degree to which it forces us to confront the irreducibly rhetorical and literary dimensions of our language, whatever we're writing about. Which is to say only that the study of tropes helps us become more self-conscious about how writers "see" and "re-see" the meanings they try to create.

To see trope as an act, a performance whereby meaning emerges through the mediation of language, reaffirms, in one sense, Ann Berthoff's central pedagogical principle: "we teach students *how* to form by teaching them *that* they form" (*Forming* 2). This is no small thing. When Berthoff speaks of the "atonceness" of composing, she is trying, in that Joycean trope, to recover the fusion of the "what" and the "how," the mediation of form and content ("Recognition" 28–29). Trope also seems related to James Britton's telling phrase, "shaping at the point of utterance," except that this "shaping" may already mediated by a prior shaping. From the tropic perspective, writers don't think of ideas and then dress them in a language of tropes. The ideas or content may already be tropes from the start. In this way, tropes may correspond to the recursive nature of "cognitive moves." But they may also correspond to far less "conscious" patterns in thinking, to symbols and plots internalized in living in a specific culture at a specific time.

It may also be that the "recursive" moves of writers—their turning back and forth, from making to revising meaning (Perl)—embodies at the purely physical level the "discursiveness" of meaning in texts, their capacity to "wander," move, and transform themselves in Protean fashion. This may be why, when we try to describe composing, we have so much trouble separating the telling from the tale, writer from text, processes from products. Even more importantly, it may be why our talk about a text's "flow," "movement," and "direction" makes sense: because it implies that there's a "process" embodied within the textual artifact, which readers can map.

What does this mean for the classroom? For one, it suggests we need to stop thinking of style as "icing," separate from invention, and pay more attention to the tropes our students perform and what these tell us about how they know what they're writing about. A brief but suggestive example must suffice. In an early working draft reviewing two articles on journalistic ethics, one of my students happened to use twice the well-worn metaphor of the "cookie jar" to describe the effect of journalists being caught using the techniques of creative writers in their "factual" reports. I could've red-inked this phrase as a trite cliché or ignored it as mere "expressive" icing. But I didn't. Instead, I suggested that she might try to use this phrase as an organizing motif throughout her review. In her second draft, she took my suggestion to heart, extending the "cookie jar" metaphor throughout her review, giving it a new twist each time it appeared, until finally it became laden with bemused irony at the fact that the journalists in question seem almost to enjoy being caught and punished for raiding the fiction writer's techniques. In short, the final draft of the review became her own allegorical revision of the cookie jar trope as a way of making sense of the ethical questions, fraught with irony, she explored.

My point is that the tropes that appear in students' writing are not simply to be treated as low-level concerns, as stylistic "icing," but as an opportunity to help students become conscious of and exploit them to discover what they can help them discover. They can be used "as a technique of reflection and operation of research" (Richards, *Speculative* 41), not just stylistic embellishment.

In fact, tropes seem to enact, in small, the directions of thought implicit in the much criticized and often misunderstood "methods of development" in expository writing courses—comparison, cause and effect, division and classification, exemplification, and so on. These "methods" re-emerge in the heuristic called "cubing," yet both suggest that every heuristic, whatever faddish name we give it, encourages the same multiple styles of thought embodied in tropes. Hence we may not be simply teaching invention, but styles of invention—some that suit students' personalities and learning "styles" and some that don't.

The possibilities of transforming meaning is, in short, what I am suggesting teachers find in trope's modern definition. These possibilities are best studied and taught by helping students find the turning points in their own texts and in their own processes: those moments when they're struggling to find out, not what, but how they mean what they've written. The intrinsic mutability of how we make meaning suggests that students could read and rewrite a story as an argument, or an argument as a story, a theory as a poem, or a poem as a theory. These transformations would reinforce different ways of knowing and writing about the same subject, exploring it, turning it around, upside down, inside out, outside in, and so, as we discover ways to "figure" and "re-figure" them.

Such turnings may operate even in those typically "academic" acts of discourse: paraphrasing, summarizing, synthesizing, analyzing, and evaluating. As verbal acts, each assumes one or several styles of thinking. Paraphrasing, often dismissed as a mechanical procedure and restricted to research papers, remains an important act of translating another writer's act of discourse into our own, often requiring numerous tropings of the original to do this (Arrington, "Dramatistic"). Summarizing, on the other hand, to some extent dependent on the tropics of paraphrase, seems to privilege metonymic reduction of a text to its essential features. Synthesizing, on the other hand, appears to privilege metaphor (finding similarities in differences) and synecdoche (parts for wholes, wholes for parts). Analysis, meanwhile, seems to depend on metonymic and synecdochic turns and evaluation on hyperbole, litotes, and metalepsis.

Tentative as these speculations are—and they are only that, speculations—they remind me of how often I find myself now, in working with students in either their planning stages, or after they've written a draft, talking of the "turns" they did or didn't make or could make. In short, I'm recognizing and at last using a language that acknowledges that the "creative" side of all writing "grow[s] out of combinatorial activity—a placing of things in new perspectives" (Bruner 210).

This realization has made me increasingly conscious of the tropic activity in the "professional" discourse published about composition. Consider the dichotomy of theory/research vs. practice. Practice is what we "do" and theory and research is what we "think" and "know" about what we do. The dichotomy, it turns out, repeats the metonymic separation of form from content, the literal from the figurative. Theorists and researchers become "heads," and teachers, "hands," "bodies," in composition studies. Theorists and researchers generate "content," "ideas," while teachers express this content. Hence, we speak of "styles" of teaching but seldom, or not enough, of the "styles" of "theory" and "research." And in so speaking, we repeat the old lie: literal content here, forms and figures there.

Carry the trope further, and we "thicken" our reading, as Clifford Geertz would say, of how we "translate" (a Latin synonym for trope) theory into practice and practice making theories. We find ourselves relearning the hard lessons: we don't teach writing or reading without at least a tacit "theory" of language and discourse, however conscious, however limited. Our doing, as teachers, often generates the conflicts and problems we think about and try to understand as theorists and researchers. Fewer of us, perhaps, learn the other lesson—that "theory" is a practice—because many composition teachers, like literature teachers, feel a strong "resistance to theory" (de Man 3). Yet, theory is an act of "seeing," too, derived from an overwhelmingly powerful metaphor in Western culture—the *theatrum mundi*. The "governing gazes," to use Janet Emig's phrase (160), allow composition theorists to look upon writing, its teaching, as gods look upon the cosmos, as theatre-goers look upon the stage—from a distance, yes, but a distance necessary for the play to unfold, be "seen."

There are in this trope many social and political implications that I leave for another time. Yet, as I've argued elsewhere, many arguments among theorists and teachers about the composing process "reduce," if they reduce at all, to how we imagine this process, our different "versions," or tropes, of what we see. The arguments are, in short, different ways to "read" the phenomenon we study and teach, each as limited as the next. Troped this way, theories become our field's "visionary" poems in whose rhetoric trace the "stealing back and forth" of our cultural "symbols of authority" (Burke, *Attitudes* 328–38). And to understand theory making fully, we would not, unlike Stephen C. Pepper, speak only of the "root-metaphors" of composition theory but the "dance" of tropes within those theories.

This recognition, I believe, "thickens" Lester Faigley's otherwise admirable effort to classify, analyze, and evaluate three theories of composing—"expressive," "cognitive," and "social"—that now "compete" for our attention, our allegiance, and that shape much of today's teaching, research, and scholarship. Like the critical theories M. H. Abrams examines, each of Faigley's theories of composing is a "prodigous synecdoche" (31). Each imagines the whole complex "process" in terms of one of its parts—expressivists, the Self; cognitivists, Mind; and social theorists, Community. These "god-terms" do indeed imply different "versions" of composition pedagogy (Berlin 766). But, by definition, any "version" of these processes necessarily involves "turning" away from one theory and toward another and so permits a "re-turn" of the theory we oppose in the one we make.

If Faigley's explanation seems too thin, it's because he hasn't paid enough attention to "how" the language of composition theories performs and invents the stories of the "processes" they describe. Nor has anyone tried to describe fully the intricate evasions of one theorist's revisions of another. Theoretical "competition" can also be troped as theoretical "cooperation." No theory of composing, and no implicit pedagogy, like no one word in a sentence, like no trope, has meaning apart from its relationship to others. And those relationships can be analyzed as tropes because tropes are acts of inventing and reinventing relationships among and within the terms theorists use.

Consider, for example, composition's ironic swerve away from its precursor, rhetoric, its reductive characterization our parent discipline (Hairston; Knoblauch and Brannon). It is not simply that composition wishes to assert or validate itself within the social and political brokering of the academy. Rather, it may be the way a "belated" field opens an imaginative space for itself, denying that part of its past it most compellingly affirms.

Consider, too, the twists and turns that "make knowledge" in the "society" of Composition. Each of Stephen M. North's communities—Practitioners, Historians, Philosophers, Critics, Experimentalists, Formalists, Clinicians, and Ethnographers—relies upon "modes of inquiry" its members typically accept as valid. This can only make us wonder about the modes of troping embodied in the discourse each community privileges. My point simply is this: the published texts of teachers, scholars, and researchers are as much, if not more, about "making meaning" than "making knowledge." To understand the second we can't ignore the first. The knowledge of "researchers"—Experimentalists, Clinicians, Formalists, and Ethnographers—depends heavily on sensory data and "clear-cut inferential and implicative structures" (Fisher 4). But their discourse assumes a way of making meaning, a way of telling their "stories," in the data they so elaborately collect, represent, and, most importantly, "read."

Three brief but suggestive examples must suffice. If "Formalist" researchers such as Linda Flower compare actual composing behaviors to an abstract model, does their discourse privilege tropes of resemblance—metaphor, simile, and allegory? Do Experimentalists, seeking causal or correlative patterns in their data, prefigure this data through to metonymy? And do Philosophers, Historians, and Critics, relying on texts and the dialectic of argument and interpretation, prefigure their knowledge through irony—dialectic's "master trope"? Does this help us understand why it so often seems that scholarly inquiry, unlike, say, researcher inquiry, seldom "progresses" in the strict, nineteenth-century sense of scientific progression?

Such would be my tropings of some all-too-familiar tropes, placing them in new perspectives. But obviously tropes raise questions for which we don't yet have answers. How, for example, might we "test" each theoretical scheme of tropes? And how long would it take? What about writers' handling of textual sources? At his most lucid, Bloom defines trope as "a stance or ratio of revision" to "defend against other tropes," adopted for "path-breaking into

[our] own inventiveness" (Stevens 395, 11). Which leads me to ask, how does a writer invent a "stance" vis-a-vis another's text? Does Bloom's model of tropic "misprision" explain or predict how students "misread" texts, their own, others', or our assignments— also "texts"—to create those stances? Would his scheme help us to differentiate "strong" from "weak" misreadings students perform? Would it explain "the degree to which a writer appeared to make the teacher-set task his or her own," even if the task is one of revising their own texts on freely chosen subjects (Britton; "Composing" 14)? Would it yield different profiles of how writers revise texts than Nancy Sommers or Mimi Schwartz provide or, more significantly, from Bloom's perspective, how they write from textual sources (Kennedy)?

And what of trope's uses as a stylistic taxonomy? Do some writers rely on specific styles of thinking, or do they "develop" as Vico describes? If so, how easy is it for writers abandon these styles and learn new ones? Or, again, do they adopt different styles at different times, and how? Could tropes be at all useful in describing students' different learning styles or the teaching styles of their instructors? And must students have teachers and textbooks who mirror their own styles of learning to benefit from their instruction?

No one, to my knowledge, has yet fully explored these questions in composition. Others will surely arise. I've done little more here than explore them. Whether any of them proves "useful" must come in time, and with much difficulty. The *poiesis* of meaning is what we're trying, however tentatively, to discover in the verbal tricks we play, upon ourselves and others. For Wallace Stevens, "[t]his trivial trope reveals a way of truth" (16). That "way of truth" may lead us to understand and be aware of the all-too-human "evasions of as."

Notes

1. Just to get a sense of the cross-disciplinary interest in trope in the social sciences, see the collection of studies by cognitive psychologists on figurative language, edited by Honeck and Hoffman; the social and anthropological essays on metaphor and other tropes, collected and edited by Sapir and Crocker; and the extended anthropological studies by Turner, Fernandez, and Herzfeld.

An exhaustive list of all the scholars and critics of specific tropes, tropology, and specific tropologists that have influenced my own essay is virtually impossible to include. However, readers may sample the diversity of the recent literature by consulting the work of Bryan (on Vico), Culler (on metaphor, trope, and persuasion), de Man (on tropological readings), Grossman (on Hayden White's tropology), Harlos (on Gerard Genette's concept of a figurative rhetoric), Holdcraft (on irony), Hollander and Perri (on the figure of metalepsis or allusive "echo"), Logan (on tropological readings), Miller (on Piaget's tropes), Nadel (on biography's tropic scheme), Paul (on figures), Quinn (on the four master tropes), Rice and Schofer (on tropes and figures), Ricoeur (on metaphor), Saunders (on de Man's tropes), and Van Deusen (on the musical trope of medieval liturgy).

2. See my "Traditions of the Writing Process" and "Tropes of the Composing Process."

Works Cited

Abrams, M. H. *The Mirror and the Lamp: Romantic Theory and the Critical Tradition.* 1953. New York: Oxford UP, 1974.

Aristotle. *De Memoria.* Trans. J. I. Beare. *The Works of Aristotle.* 12 vols. Ed. W. D. Ross. Oxford: Clarendon, 1908–1952.

———. *The Rhetoric of Aristotle.* Trans. Lane Cooper. Englewood Cliffs, NJ: Prentice, 1960.

Arrington, Phillip K. "A Dramatistic Approach to Understanding and Teaching the Paraphrase." *College Composition and Communication* 39 (1988): 185–197.

———. "The Traditions of the Writing Process." *Freshman English News* 14 (1986): 2–4, 9–10.

———. "Tropes of the Composing Process." *College English* 48 (1986): 325–338.

Augustine. *On Christian Doctrine.* Trans. D. W. Robertson. New York: Library, 1958.

Berlin, James A. "Contemporary Composition: The Major Pedagogical Theories." *College English* 44 (1982): 765–777.

Berthoff, Ann E. *Forming/Thinking/Writing: The Composing Imagination.* Portsmouth, NH: Boynton/Cook, 1982.

———. "Recognition, Representation, and Revision." *Rhetoric and Composition: A Sourcebook for Teachers and Writers.* Ed. Richard L. Graves. Portsmouth, NH: Boynton/Cook, 1984. 27–37.

Bloom, Harold. *Agon: Towards a Theory of Revisionism.* New York: Oxford UP, 1981.

———. *A Map of Misreading:* New York: Oxford UP, 1975.

———. *Wallace Stevens: The Poems of Our Climate.* Ithaca: Cornell UP, 1976.

Britton, James. "The Composing Process and the Functions of Writing." *Research on Composing: Points of Departure.* Ed. Charles R. Cooper and Lee Odell. Urbana, IL; National Council of Teachers of English, 1978. 13–28.

————. "Shaping at the Point of Utterance." *Reinventing the Rhetorical Tradition*. Ed. Aviva Freedman and Ian Pringle. Urbana, IL: National Council of Teachers of English, 1980. 60–65.

Bruner, Jerome S. *Beyond the Information Given: Studies in the Psychology of Knowing*. Ed. Jeremy M. Anglin. New York: Norton, 1973.

Bryan, Ferald J. "Vico on Metaphor: Implications for Rhetorical Criticism." *Philosophy and Rhetoric* 19 (1986): 255–265.

Burke, Kenneth. *Attitudes Toward History*. 3rd ed. 1937. Berkeley: U of California P, 1984.

————. *A Grammar of Motives*. 1945. Berkeley: U of California P, 1969.

Culler, Jonathan. "The Turns of Metaphor." *The Pursuit of Signs: Semiotics, Literature, Deconstruction*. Ithaca: Cornell UP, 1981. 188–209.

————. "On Trope and Persuasion." *New Literary History* 9 (1978): 609–618.

D'Angelo, Frank. "Prolegomena to a Rhetoric of Tropes." *Rhetoric Review* 6 (1987): 32–40.

————. "Rhetoric and Cognition: Toward a Metatheory of Discourse." *Pre/Text* 3 (1982): 105–119.

de Man, Paul. "The Resistance to Theory." *The Resistance to Theory*. Minneapolis: U of Minnesota P, 1986. 3–20.

Derrida, Jacques. "White Mythology: Metaphor in the Text of Philosophy." Trans. F. C. T. Moore. *New Literary History* 6 (1974): 5–74.

Emig, Janet. "Inquiry Paradigms and Writing." *The Web of Meaning: Essays on Writing, Teaching, Learning, and Thinking*. Ed. Dixie Goswami and Maureen Butler. Portsmouth, NH: Boynton/Cook, 1983. 159–170.

Empiricus, Sextus. *Outlines of Pyrrhonism. Scepticism, Man, and God*. Trans. Sanford G. Etheridge. Middletown, CT: Wesleyan UP, 1964. 31–128.

Erasmus, Desiderius. *On Copia of Words and Things*. Trans. Donald B. King, et al. Milwaukee, WI: Marquette UP, 1963.

Faigley, Lester. "Competing Theories of Process: A Critique and a Proposal." *College English* 48 (1986): 527–542.

Fernandez, James W. *Persuasions and Performance: The Play of Tropes in Culture*. Bloomington: Indiana UP, 1986.

Fisher, Walter R. "Narration as a Human Communication Paradigm: The Case of Public Moral Argument." *Communication Monographs* 51 (1984): 1–22.

Geertz, Clifford. *The Interpretation of Cultures*. New York: Basic Books, 1973.

Grossman, Marshall. "Hayden White and Literary Criticism: The Tropology of Discourse." *Papers on Language and Literature* 17 (1981): 424–445.

Hairston, Maxine. "The Winds of Change: Thomas Kuhn and the Revolution in the Teaching of Writing." *Rhetoric and Composition: A Sourcebook for Teachers and Writers*. Ed. Richard L. Graves. 14–26.

Harlos, Christopher. "Rhetoric, Structuralism, and Figurative Discourse: Gerard Genette's Concept of Rhetoric." *Philosophy and Rhetoric* 19 (1986): 209–223.

Herzfeld, Michael. "Closure as Cure: Tropes in the Exploration of Bodily and Social Disorder." *Current Anthropology* 27 (1986): 107–120.

Holdcraft, David. "Irony as Trope, and Irony as Discourse." *Poetics Today* 4 (1983): 493–511.

Hollander, John. *The Figure of Echo: A Mode of Allusion in Milton and After.* 1981. Berkeley: U of California P, 1984.

Honeck, Richard P., and Robert R. Hoffman, eds. *Cognition and Figurative Language.* Hillsdale, NJ: Erlbaum, 1980.

Howell, Wilbur Samuel. *Logic and Rhetoric in England, 1500–1700.* Princeton: Princeton UP, 1956.

Kellner, Hans. "The Inflatable Trope as Narrative Theory: Structure or Allegory?" *Diacritics* II (1981): 14–28.

Kennedy, Mary Lynch. "The Composing Process of College Students Writing from Sources." *Written Communication* 2 (1985): 434–456.

Knoblauch, C. H. "Modern Rhetorical Theory and Its Future Directions." *Perspectives on Research and Scholarship in Composition.* Ben W. McClelland and Timothy R. Donovan. New York: MLA, 1984. 26–44.

Knoblauch, C. H., and Lil Brannon. *Rhetorical Traditions and the Teaching of Writing.* Portsmouth, NH: Boynton/Cook, 1984.

Logan, Marie-Rose. "Rhetorical Analysis: Towards a Tropology of Reading." *New Literary History* 9 (1978): 619–625.

Martin, Wallace. "Floating an Issue of Tropes." *Diacritics* 12 (1982): 75–83.

Miller, Keith. "The Tropes of Jean Piaget." *Freshman English News* 16 (1987): 9–11.

Nadel, Ira Bruce. "Biography and Four Master Tropes." *Biography* 6 (1983): 307–315.

North, Stephen M. *The Making of Knowledge in Composition: Portrait of an Emerging Field.* Portsmouth, NH: Boynton/Cook, 1987.

Paul, Anthony. "Figurative Language." *Philosophy and Rhetoric* 3 (1970): 225–248.

Pepper, Stephen C. *World Hypotheses: A Study in Evidence.* Berkeley: U of California P, 1942.

Perl, Sondra. "Understanding Composing." *College Composition and Communication* 31 (1980): 363–369.

Perri, Carmela. "Knowing and Playing: The Literary Text and the Trope Allusion." *American Imago* 41 (1984): 117–128.

Phelps, Louise Wetherbee. "The Dance of Discourse: A Dynamic, Relativistic View of Structure." *Pre/Text* 3 (1982): 51–83.

Plato. *The Collected Dialogues of Plato Including the Letters.* Ed. Edith Hamilton and Huntington Cairns. Princeton: Princeton UP, 1961.

Quinn, David. "The Four Master Tropes as Informing Principles." *Hispania* 66 (1983): 242–252.

Quintilian. *Institutio Oratoria.* Trans. H. E. Butler. 4 vols. Cambridge: Harvard UP, 1922.

Rankin, Elizabeth D. "Revitalizing Style: Toward a New Theory and Pedagogy." *Freshman English News* (1985): 8–12.

Rice, Donald, and Peter Schofer. "Tropes and Figures: Symbolization and Figuration." *Semiotica* 35 (1981): 93–124.

Richards, I. A. *Interpretation in Teaching.* 2nd ed. 1930. New York: Humanities, 1973.

———. *Speculative Instruments.* Chicago: U of Chicago P, 1955.

Ricoeur, Paul. "The Metaphorical Process as Cognition, Imagination, and Feeling." *Critical Inquiry* 5 (1978): 143–159.

———. *The Rule of Metaphor: Multi-disciplinary Studies of the Creation of Meaning.* Trans. Robert Czerny. Toronto: U of Toronto P, 1977.

Sapir, J. David, and Christopher Crocker, eds. *The Social Use of Metaphor: Essays on the Anthropology of Rhetoric.* Princeton: Princeton UP, 1977.

Saunders, Ian. "Criticism and the Object of Explanation: Paul de Man's Trope of Interruption." *Southern Review* 18 (1985): 49–64.

Schwartz, Mimi. "Revision Profiles: Patterns and Implications." *College English* 45 (1983): 549–558.

Sommers, Nancy. "Revision Strategies of Student Writers and Experienced Adult Writers." *College Composition and Communication* 31 (1980): 378–388.

Stevens, Wallace. *The Collected Poems of Wallace Stevens.* New York: Knopf, 1974.

Turner, Bryan S. *The Body and Society: Explorations in Social Theory.* New York: Basil Blackwell, 1984.

Van Deusen, Nancy. "Origins of a Significant Medieval Genre: The Musical 'Trope' up to the Twelfth Century." *Rhetorica* 3 (1985): 245–267.

Vico, Giambattista. *The New Science.* 3rd ed. Trans. Thomas Goddard Bergin and Max Harold Fisch. 1948. Ithaca: Cornell UP, 1970.

Wagner, Roy. *Symbols That Stand for Themselves.* Chicago: U of Chicago P, 1986.

Wallace, Karl R. "Topoi and the Problem of Invention." *Contemporary Rhetoric: A Conceptual Background with Readings.* Ed. W. Ross Winterowd. New York: Harcourt Brace, 1975. 112–123.

White, Hayden. *Tropics of Discourse: Essays in Cultural Criticism.* Baltimore: Johns Hopkins UP, 1978.

ELEVEN

Rewriting Composition as a Postmodern Discipline
Transforming the Research/Teaching Dichotomy

JAMES THOMAS ZEBROSKI

Perhaps there is no stranger dichotomy for the untenured faculty person (aside from the dichotomy of "tenured versus untenured" faculty) than the common distinction constantly made in the modern university between "research" and "teaching." Whether at a big school or a smaller university, the dichotomy is pervasive in spite of all protestations to the contrary. At the big "research institution," there is much official concern for upgrading undergraduate instruction, but the fact is that getting tenure is largely a matter of "research"; that is, the number of publications— the more the better. All else is secondary, including written and oral testaments by students to the quality of their classroom experiences and scads of high-numbered, pencil-blackened dots on machine-scored "evaluation" forms, blithely, anonymously, and too often mindlessly, cast upon the waters at term's end.

At the smaller school, where the faculty is constantly being told "we are a teaching institution," the dichotomy between research and teaching is no less real. Rather, it is the second term of the dichotomy that is embraced. And again, the administration often asserts that it wants high-quality faculty who are current in their fields and are active professionals. But if one tries to find time in the schedules of teaching and committee work typical at such schools to read even the Sunday *New York Times*, let alone a book from one's field of specialization, or to get recognition, let alone financial support, for presenting at national conferences, one quickly discovers that the "research versus teaching" dichotomy is alive and well at smaller universities and colleges too.

Embedded deeply in our collective mind is that despicable bit of proverbial dogma that passes for wisdom in twentieth-century, technocratic U.S. society—"Those who can, do; those who can't, teach." In the modern university, "doing" has to do with "research," the creation of scholarship, the adding of knowledge to the field, *not* "teaching," which is seen as a transmissive, essentially secondary activity.

Stephen North, in his recent book *The Making of Knowledge in Composition*, has recognized the epistemological and political consequences of the research/teaching dichotomy. In a laudable attempt to make sense of the diversity of the discipline of composition and, in fact, to transcend the dichotomies, North argues that one reason for the increasing split between research and teaching in composition is that intensifying and exaggerating the dichotomy has been useful to certain people. Dichotomies, then, are social constructs. They fulfill ideological functions; they don't exist "in nature." Rather they come into being—they are institutionally constructed—and continue to exist because they are helpful in the exercise of power; that is, they are of great use to people who have power and want to retain it, or to those who do not have power but want to fight for it.

North goes on to recite the narrative that researchers and scholars in composition have frequently told the public over the last twenty to thirty years. By telling a story that places the failures of mass literacy in the United States on the backwardness of practitioners, researchers have distanced themselves from the problem and have been able to persuade the federal government, foundations, and corporations of their own worthiness. Funds, positions, and not a few careers have come out of this "story" of crisis in literacy and by the dichotomizing of research from teaching, by the distancing of researchers from teachers.

It seems that some of the recent commentaries on North's book have bypassed this poststructuralist, Foucault-like dimension of North's argument and his acceptance of "narrative" as an evocation and enactment of power relations, institutionally situated.

Narrative, the stories we tell our professional selves—often put forward as accounts of empirical reality, as factual history—can have very important rhetorical and political effects. North astutely notes, ". . . crises are invoked for political ends, and they are invoked in the form most convenient, and according to the criteria most useful, for the invoker" (324). So university "researchers" have too often assailed "practitioners" for the primitiveness of their practice. In the process, many university "researchers" have benefited from the resulting grants, projects, institutes, academic positions, and improved status.

North himself tries to surmount the research/teaching dichotomy by elevating practitioners to equal partnership in the making of knowledge, arguing that the practitioner, no less than the researcher or scholar, is constantly involved in the making of knowledge, that practice is in fact a mode of inquiry.[1] North specifies how practitioners create, assimilate, evaluate, preserve, and share knowledge through "lore." So North tells his own story of the fall and redemption of the practitioner, which reverses the one told over the last two decades by composition researcher/scholars.

This is a radical notion, and North has already met a fair amount of resistance. The power of North's narrative can be gauged by how fashionable and intense North-bashing is becoming in some quarters of the "society of Composition." While I would tell the story somewhat differently, for the purposes of this essay I want to accept North's general storyline.

In the next section of this essay I want to add a story to the one North tells, a related story but a broader one, a story that "contains" North's narrative of the rise of Composition as a subplot. I am suggesting that not only do dichotomies like "research versus teaching" serve ideological functions in a specific institution, but that dichotomizing itself, as we experience it, is a historically specific activity—an activity part of the much broader stream in Western twentieth-century intellectual history named "modernism."

After very briefly recounting some of the "story" of modernism and its continued effects on our thinking, I want to propose that Composition, because it is a postmodern discipline (perhaps the first?), is necessarily going to find the reigning dichotomies, and even the very act of dichotomizing, wanting. In the final section of this essay I will illustrate how I try to use these understandings to transform the research/teaching dichotomy in my own composition classroom.

In 1916 a network of trenches cut Western Europe in two.

In 1916 a network of discourses cut five hundred years of Western intellectual history in two.

From the Swiss Alps to the North Sea it ran. The trenches divided Europe and the world.

On 21 February the Germans attacked the French at the eastern edge of the trench line near the town of Verdun. More than 600,000 soldiers died during the battle of Verdun, in which the only military objective was to bleed the other side white. Numbers, cold numbers, old numbers. But these were people, the best and the brightest of the younger generation, slaughtered in new and horrifying ways. More French and German soldiers were killed in 1916 in the single battle for Verdun than the total number of American soldiers killed in World War II.

The battle—itself a misnomer in this war of attrition—never really ended but was simply displaced around 24 June when the battle of the Somme began at the Western end of the trench line. There the British attacked dug-in German defenders, who had been issued that perfect weapon of modern mass-produced war, the machine gun. In the first *hour* of the battle of the Somme, 30,000 British men were slaughtered; by day's end 60,000 had been cut down. The battle of the Somme bled on until November.

And the result of this "carnival of death," as Malcolm Cowley calls it, of this "death on the production line" (Cowley 4)? After four years of trench warfare, until the final year of the war, advances by either side amounted to no more than eleven miles.

Paul Fussell, in his superb discussion of the legacy of the Great War to modern life and thought, describes the Somme battlefield sixty years after these events.

> Today the Somme is a peaceful but sullen place, unforgetting and unforgiving. To wander now over the fields destined to extrude their rusty metal fragments for centuries is to appreciate in the most intimate way the permanent reverberations of July 1916 (Fussell 69).

In 1916 the Paris edition of Ferdinand de Saussure's *Course in General Linguistics* was published. During 1916, Roman Jakobson, founder and president of the Moscow Linguistic Circle, was in his second year of studies at Moscow University. Through 1916, Viktor Shklovsky and his colleagues were thinking through the fundamentals of a literary theory that would subsequently be named Russian formalism.[2]

Modernism was certainly in the air well before the turn of the century, though there is little agreement among the various accounts locating modernism's origins. There is even intense debate about whether there is such a thing as modernism or whether it is simply an umbrella, or bucket, term.[3] No matter.

If the break in Western life and thought can be represented by Picasso's 1907 creation of "Demoiselles d'Avignon," which ended over five hundred years of representationalism and "realism" in painting and initiated the project of Picasso and Braque to capture the modern in the bits and pieces and fragments of collage, then the modern mind became fully embodied in the slaughter of 1916, with the binary opposition of French to German, of Us to Them, with signifiers detaching from signifieds, with a very literal dissociation of sensibility.

Breakup and reconstruction.[4]

Using "transparent form to explore basic inner structures" (Kuh 38).

Simplifying, breaking up, reducing.

Searching for, capturing the essence.

Piercing outer coverings; penetrating to inner form.

"To examine more fully, to penetrate more deeply, to analyze more thoroughly, to enlarge, isolate . . . not merely to reflect our world, but in fact to interpret it" (Kuh 15).

High modernist art (and thought) is "characterized by shattered surfaces, broken color, segmented compositions, dissolving forms and shredded images" (Kuh 11).

The modernist mind is at work in the elusive quest for the smallest, most elemental subatomic particle, the basic building block of the entire universe. The modernist mind is at work in the attempt to remake philosophy into the structured investigation of the syntax of individual propositions, in the belief that a philosophy that is not superstitious metaphysics is only about the use of concepts, of words, since "use" equals "meaning." The modernist mind is at work in T. S. Eliot's "objective correlative," which tries to "build" feeling/perception by building basic verbal things; in Eisenstein's films, which explode image into image, creating the new "unit" of montage; in theories of language that search for phonemes, "kernal" sentences, "structures"; in literary practices that attend to only the purity of the "work itself."

High modernism after 1916 is a drive to get back to the basics. It is, as Hal Foster calls it, a will-to-purify (190). Among other things, it is a move to purify the language of the tribe. It is a strategy to deal with the chaos created by slaughter and political and technological revolution, by attending only to what is essential and unchanging—form, and the form of forms: structures. Modernism is a sort of intellectual fundamentalism that is one response to the events of the day. Out of a dichotomized world came the dichotomizing mind. Peculiar to this century is the divided city— Berlin, Beirut, Jerusalem; peculiar to our experience, the dichotomized nation—Germany, Korea, Vietnam; peculiar to our way of thinking, the dichotomizing mind.[5]

Paul Fussell argues that it was in the troglodyte nightmare world of the trenches of the Great War that dichotomizing was, if not born, at least legitimated and confirmed.

> What we call gross dichotomizing is a persisting imaginative habit of modern times, traceable, it would seem, to the actualities of the Great War. "We" are all here on this side; "the enemy" is over there. "We" are individuals with names; "he" is a mere collective entity. We are visible; he is invisible. We are normal, he is grotesque. . . . He is not as good as we are. . . . Nevertheless, he threatens us and must be destroyed. . . . Prolonged trench warfare, whether enacted or remembered fosters paranoid melodrama, which I take to be the primary mode in modern writing. . . . The most indispensable concept underlying the energies of modern writing is that of "the enemy" (75–76).

By the 1960s, the modernist vision no longer seemed to match the world it had helped to form. The "basic building blocks" that were the social and political formations of the day seemed no longer to hold. In 1968 there were riots in Paris. Communism with a human face was crushed in Czechoslovakia. In the United States, Robert Kennedy and Martin Luther King, Jr. were assassinated. Riots in the central cities and during the Democratic convention paralleled the crescendo of violence in the Vietnam war, where five hundred U.S. soldiers were dying each week. Some were suggesting that the real "enemy" was "us," or at least "within" us.[6]

Juxtaposed by the purity, singleness, polish, precision of modernism was mixture, plurality, unfinishedness, ornament. Postmodernism is a move toward history and all its messiness. It accepts the social as an intimate expression of the individual. Instead of Self, postmodern sees selves. Essence interests less than change, differences more than sameness; the dappled, pied, spotted, the eclectic more than the strict puritanism of the modern; the popular (even populist) rather than just the expert or the professional.

> "Purity" abets a division of labor within culture which, as a result, comes to partake of both the special professionalism of the academy and the commercial commodity production of industry (Foster 190).

In the late 1960s and early 1970s, U.S. universities and colleges began admitting large numbers of students who traditionally would have never gone to college. Because of political pressures on campus that resulted to a large extent from a student movement that gained momentum in the civil rights struggles and in the anti-Vietnam war protests, many universities put into effect a policy of open admissions. These students, who only ten years before never dreamed of going to college and for whom college was only made possible by open admissions and financial grants, all took at least one common course—composition.

Why did these new students seem so academically unprepared and what might we do to teach them to read and write effectively enough to get their degrees? From such questions Composition was born.[7] Today we are still squabbling about whether or not Composition is a discipline. What some take to be problematic about Composition—our mixedness, our diversity, our eclecticism, our interests in both the arts and sciences, our concern with both the academic and the professional, the inter- even trans-disciplinary nature of our scholarship, our multiple worldviews, our plural methods, and even our democratic interest in teaching all students who desire to read and write—are the very things that make Composition a postmodern "discipline." Composition only falls short as a discipline when modernist yardsticks are used to measure it. Composition's uniqueness is that unlike other related disciplines, which are still struggling to transform themselves from modernist to postmodern fields, it is already postmodern, by virtue of its commitments and the contexts of its recent origins. What others take to be Composition's "problem," I take to be its strength. Composition straddles the borderlines of the entrenched modernist disciplines within the modern university. We live in No Man's Land.[8]

This is all well and good, but two objections come immediately to mind. First, doesn't this approach simply substitute one "smaller" dichotomy (research/teaching) with another "larger" dichotomy (modernism/postmodernism)? And second, does this have anything to do directly with how we act in our composition classrooms?

The first objection is only valid if one accepts that postmodernism is the opposite of modernism. It isn't. A postmodernist is very aware of the dialogue begun in modernism. It is *both* connected with *and* disconnected from modernism. There need be no single, abrupt, and unbridgeable break for there to be radical sorts of differences between modernism and postmodernism. *Different,* even *very* different, does not equal *opposite.* Difference does not imply dichotomy.

Postmodernism, because it accepts plurality and mixture as "primary," can in part absorb modernism. Thus, modernism/postmodernism is a part of our intellectual history, which affects the very ways we view our world, which is immanent in many of our categories of perceiving/thinking/communicating. Postmodernism encircles much of modernism, but includes much else beside.

Charles Jencks, in his instructive little book *What Is Postmodernism,* deals with this objection early on as it relates to literary modernism/postmodernism, but also as it bears on contemporary architecture. Jencks notes:

> John Barth (1980) and Umberto Eco (1983), among many other authors, now define it [postmodernism] as a writing which may use traditional forms in ironic or displaced ways to treat perennial themes. It acknowledges the validity of modernism—the change in world view brought on by Nietzsche, Einstein, Freud et al.—but, as John Barth says, it hopes to go beyond the limited means and audience which characterize modernist fiction: "My ideal postmodernist author neither merely repudiates nor merely imitates either his twentieth-century modernist parents or his nineteenth-century premodernist grandparents. He has the first half of our century under his belt, but not on his back. Without lapsing into moral or artistic simplism, shoddy craftsmanship, Madison Avenue venality, or either false or real naivete, he nevertheless aspires to a fiction more democratic in its appeal than such late-modernist marvels (by my definition and in my judgment) as Beckett's *Stories and Texts for Nothing* or Nabakov's *Pale Fire*" (7).

This "search for a wider audience" also distinguishes composition from most other established (modernist) disciplines. As the only teachers on campus who teach all students at all levels and who, additionally, have major commitments beyond campus to outreach literacy programs for nontraditional students, and who have moved to understand and transform literacy as it is used in business and government, we are the discipline that is resisting the dichotomies of our era and modernist notions of specialization and disciplinarity. Composition, then, may well have to be accepted as a discipline to have any power in the university, but I do believe we can be a discipline with a difference.[9] We don't have to oppose or ignore the lessons of modernism to prove our postmodernity.

If we accept Composition's postmodern character and understand that Composition will sometimes be in conflict with modernist assumptions about disciplines and disciplinarity and academic work, then we should expect that what goes on in our classrooms will probably look pretty different. We can no longer act on a model of communication and teaching where there are rigid, modernist boundaries between teaching and research, between teacher and researcher, between teacher and student.[10] Instead, a postmodern approach blurs rigid boundaries, critiques the idea of a centered, static self that possesses an "essence" (an atomistic, individualistic, bounded "teacher," "student," "researcher"), abandons the concept of language (and education) as a passive, transmissive enterprise, and wonders about the all too convenient and "coincidental" fit between the model of researcher/research/teacher; teacher/subject matter/student; writer/text/reader and the "model" of producer/commodity/consumer that we in late capitalist society live.

What happens if we purposely begin to blur these boundaries? It is my goal in my classroom to collaborate with students in designing assignments that do exactly this. By blurring role and genre boundaries and working—with students—to redraw them, I hope to create opportunities for the dramatis personae to play all of these (and other) roles. By circulating various roles, I want to suggest to students that the division of labor inside and outside of the classroom is not a static, "essentialized" fact of nature but instead is a social construct that, with great effort and struggle, can be transformed. Accepting the idea that knowledge is *a process,* continually being created, negotiated, evaluated, and transformed, I try to imagine a classroom where "student," "teacher," "researcher" are roles, rather than "persons" who possess "essences," and where there is a democracy, a sharing, of such roles. To be sure, I remain a teacher and researcher, but I also am a student. And I am even more than this. I play many other roles that, in turn, define my "self" and, in the process, my significant "others."

Ethnographic writing has been the method I have extensively used to encourage the blurring of such roles and genres and the raising of such issues. Ethnography is writing about a people and their way of life.[11] It bears a strong resemblance, in this age of blurring genres, not only to what some (not all) cultural anthropologists do, but to what many "new journalists," historians, travel book writers, novelists, and compositionists do, whether all these folk are conscious of it or not. Much of Studs Terkel's work is ethnographic, as are many of the "nonfiction" essays of Joan Didion.

Ethnographic writing has allowed both my students and me to simultaneously play the roles of "researcher" and "teacher," as well as "student." The key to ethnographic writing is that the writer becomes a student of the people she studies. The people of the community in which the writer participates and observes become the experts and the teachers of the "student," but also of the class which includes the "teacher."

The ethnographic writer tries to experience and understand the way of life, the "lived experience," of a community. He tries to do this in the community's own terms, as much as possible. Yet the ethnographic writer is also trying to communicate this to the people back "home" in the class who do not know the site.

The "ethnographer" then has to be equally versatile in (1) seeing the world from the perspective of another community, (2) knowing the power but also the limits of language to express this experience, and (3) discovering ways of communicating all of this to those unfamiliar with it. Thus, the "student" in my classroom doing "ethnographic writing" has to (1) become a different sort of nonacademic "student" in the community in which she is doing fieldwork, (2) become a "researcher" who creates knowledge and becomes an expert, and (3) become a "teacher" in trying to share all of this with fellow students and the teacher back in the classroom.

Ethnographic writers in my classes spend considerable time at the site (three to five hours a week for four to six weeks) doing their fieldwork and writing it up in a continuing stream of notes and reflections, which they share with me and other students at least once a week. The members of the class choose their own sites, arrange their own schedules, observe and interview the people, and write this all up in some appropriate form at the end of the project. "Appropriate" is purposely a vague term, since the ethnographic writer has to determine the form of language that can best sum up the unique events and way of life of the people. The only stipulations are that the writer consider what form would have the "best" effect on the audience—the class—and that a lot of the language of the people at the site be recorded and included. (Suddenly, students are very interested in how to use quotations marks and quotes within quotes and how to attribute discourse!)

During the whole process, we all talk a great deal about composition and different strategies for capturing life in the written word. When the ethnographic projects draw to a close, the class reproduces and collates the ethnographic essays into a class book that becomes our textbook for the next several weeks. We closely read the essays, discuss emerging themes, and begin to recognize contradictions both in the texts and in our own lives, evoked by the discussions and the texts.

And what do I, in my university "researcher" role, have to show for all this teaching/studying/researching? I know my students better, in quite detailed ways. I know more about who they are and what is bothering them and what they value and why. Thus, my students teach me about their worlds. It seems to me that that ought to count for something. This knowledge certainly finds expression in articles I write about composition (like this one) and in papers I present at conferences.

Then, too, I am doing ethnographic writing through all of this. I record observations of and reflections on my classes and write up the institutional communities of which I am a part. Every meeting, every piece of mail, every memo, becomes "layered," opens to a reading, to interpretation, and contributes to my scholarship. The acts of my institutional life as "university professor" are also part of my "research," contributing to my understanding and my analysis of the social contexts of literacy and literacy programs. I collaborate with my students in discovering the uses of literacy in their lives and I collaborate with my colleagues in learning about the social structures that give birth to the ideas/discourses circulating through our fields—whether canon formation in literary studies or writing across/against the curriculum in Composition.

All of this flows into my dialogue with the world. In this dialogue, I sometimes reach insights that help me to change my life and my world. As a tentative postmodernist, I find that I am less and less interested in what something "is"—its "essence"—and more and more interested in its "becoming," how it can be changed into something else, how it flows into a whole range of relations. Whether we are talking about reading and writing, literature and composition, science and art, research and teaching—no matter— the action is where one of the pair changes into the other or into something else entirely. Freire calls this critical consciousness,[12] when these sorts of insights into transformation are applied in the arena of one's society and one's life and when one acts on them. It seems to me that it is precisely when one reaches this point, when one has faint glimmers of critical consciousness, that dichotomies of all sorts become less and less attractive. Dichotomies are a way of trying to hold the world still. If one believes that a changing world is far more interesting and perhaps more desirable than a static world, then dichotomies become transformed, and after a brief time erase themselves.

Notes

1. See Stephen North, *The Making of Knowledge in Composition: Portrait of an Emerging Field* (Portsmouth, NH: Boynton/Cook, 1987). I make no claims here regarding North's own position on teacher research and on the ability of practitioners to make "substantial" contributions to "scholarship." What appeals to me is North's "story" and his connection of knowledge (epistemology) with institutional power (struggles between camps within the society of Composition). I do have fundamental reservations about some aspects of North's text. I question, for example, North's reliance on Diesing's notions of "method" and "discipline," which both seem more modernist than postmodern. Still, on the whole, I feel North deserves praise for writing the book that needed to be written, but which no one else would write.

2. In this section, I am trying to suggest that "ideas" are "interrelated" to and "interconnected" with material circumstance. For the concept of relation and Relation and interrelation see B. Ollman, *Alienation* (Cambridge: Cambridge UP 1976). One of the more prominent material circumstances of this century—not unrelated to the prevalence of class society in Western imperial nations—is war. This has been a century of "total war" and even its more peaceful moments have been lived out under the sign of nuclear annihilation.

To say this is not to reduce intellectual history to material circumstances, nor is it to assert that material practices are severed from, or "causative" of, ideas. Rather, it is to argue that recurring rhythms run through the plural temporality that we name history.

3. There are many discussions of modernism/postmodernism available. The following works have informed my use of the term "(post)modernism."

Arac, J., ed. *Postmodernism and Politics.* Minneapolis: U of Minnesota P, 1986.

Bradbury, M. and J. McFarlane, eds. *Modernism:* 1890–1930. New York: Penguin, 1976.

Cowley, M. *A Second Flowering: Works and Days of the Lost Generation.* New York: Penguin, 1973.

Cowley, M. *Exile's Return: The Literary Odyssey of the 1920s.* New York: Viking, 1976.

Craige, B. J. *Reconnection: Dualism to Holism in Literary Study.* Athens, GA: U of Georgia P, 1988.

Foster, H., ed. *The Anti-Aesthetic: Essays in Postmodern Culture.* Port Townsend, WA: Bay Press, 1983.

Foster, H. *Recodings: Art, Spectacle, Cultural Politics.* Port Townsend, WA: Bay Press, 1985.

Fussell, P. *The Great War and Modern Memory.* New York: Oxford UP, 1975.

Hall, J. and B. Ulanov, eds. *Modern Culture and the Arts.* New York: McGraw Hill, 1972.

Harland, R. *Superstructuralism*. New York: Methuen, 1987.

Jameson, J. *The Prison-House of Language*. Princeton: Princeton UP, 1972.

Jencks, C. *What Is Post-modernism?* New York: Academy/St. Martin's.

Karl, F. *Modern and Modernism: The Sovereignty of the Artist—1885–1925*. New York: Atheneum, 1985.

Kuh, K. *Break-up: The Core of Modern Art*. Greenwich, CT: New York Graphic Society, 1965.

Lucie-Smith, E. *Late Modern: The Visual Arts Since 1945*. New York: Praeger, 1969.

McMullen, R. *Art, Affluence, and Alienation*. New York: Mentor Books, 1968.

Steiner, W. *The Colors of Rhetoric: Problems in the Relation Between Modern Literature and Painting*. Chicago: U of Chicago P, 1982.

Wallis, B., ed. *Art After Modernism: Rethinking Representation*. New York: New York Museum of Contemporary Art, 1984.

4. I rely on Katherine Kuh's discussion of modernism in painting as "break-up" throughout this section. However, I want to go one step further and connect this tendency to atomize with the tendency to dichotomize. Dichotomy has been a strategy used to both extend breakup and to react to it, to try to control it.

5. Some might argue that dichotomies have been around for a lot longer than just this century. Certainly this is true. We are told by scholars such as James Frazer, Joseph Campbell, Carl Jung, and Claude Lévi-Strauss that binary oppositions, if not indeed dichotomizing, are a seemingly universal trait of human thinking across time and cultures. I am not going to deny this, though I find it suspicious that these scholars and their ideas in fact come out of the modernist tradition. Might it be that the universality of binarism/dichotomies "discovered" in "primitive" cultures by these scholars already be a part of the setting in which they lived and worked?

Regardless, my point is not that dichotomies never existed before or that, during this century, dichotomies didn't serve other purposes. Rather, I am arguing for the historical specificity of certain modernist uses of dichotomy.

Some important modernist dichotomies include the following: Susanne Langer's "discursive" versus "presentational" modes; the New Critical separation of "ordinary" from "scientific" discourse, of "scientific" discourse from "aesthetic" discourse, of "structure" from "texture." In Saussure, of course, we find the father figure of dichotomies authorizing the "diachronic" versus "synchronic," "parole" versus "langue," "speech" versus "writing"—and so on to Chomsky's "competence" versus "performance," "deep" versus "surface" structures. Composition is wracked by modernist dichotomies: Rosenblatt's "efferent" versus "aesthetic" reading; Britton's "spectator" versus "participant" roles; Emig's "refexive" versus "extensive" modes; Flower's "writer-based prose" versus "reader-based prose." There is a tradition of thinking revealed by such categories, it seems to me. I find nothing quite like it in any of the texts that came before modernism. Even Aristotle's taxonomies tend to be in threes, fours, any number of categories, rather than two.

6. The nation-state as we have come to think of it in the twentieth century is still reeling from this jolt, East bloc countries no less than West. Since about 1968, the peculiarities of twentieth-century nation-states (modernist states, if you will) have been in sharp tension with transnationalism. The reasons for this are both economic—capital finds foreign labor more accessible and cheaper—and technological—satellite television and the proliferation of media of all sorts, including audio and video cassettes, transistorized and miniaturized electronic devices, computer and computer systems accessible to many new consumers—all these forces have made it less easy to clearly demarcate and close off the boundaries of any traditional nation-state.

7. I want to suggest here that Composition has arisen as a discipline in large measure because it has been open to students who otherwise would not have been allowed into university and would not have previously been considered "college material." Our students, once we decided to commit ourselves to them, have taught us.

Further, I want to add that Composition has continued to be a dynamic field in part because it has drawn on some of the very people who might have been considered "nontraditional" college students in the late sixties and early seventies. These "newcomers" to academe, persons whose parents often were not even college graduates, have received the first doctorates in composition. My intuition is that these folks make up a larger proportion of the society of Composition than do newcomers in any other established discipline. I also feel that these people bring new perspectives and account for much that is interesting in the field. I hope that that's the case, since I am one of them.

8. The best recent book that I have read about the new directions the "human sciences" (and the notions of "disciplinarity" and "method") are taking is Betty Jean Craige's *Reconnection: Dualism to Holism in Literary Study*. Craige's discussion of the direction of current literary studies parallels the case I make in this essay for Composition. Craige's study is more philosophical than this essay can be, and the moment she attends to is longer—essentially, Craige finds the roots of what I would in this essay term the modernist dilemma in our acceptance of the dualisms of Descartes and Kant, among others. While I would hesitate to accept the McLuhan-Ong hypothesis regarding the change in consciousness rendered by literacy, specifically print, I still feel that Craige's "story" is quite open to a "material" reading and complements my "story" in the same way that my story complements North's.

9. I am *not* arguing that the only reason Composition has become a discipline, or *should* be considered a discipline, is to be "acceptable" in the university, to build its own empire. We have our own intrinsic reasons for making writing the object of inquiry and for discipline building. But there are some who argue that Composition should not push to become independent, that to do so is to trade in the very trans-disciplinary, if not

anti-disciplinary, stance that makes Composition so attractive as a field of study. I would argue that no one exists outside of institutions and that to accomplish what we want requires a power base. That means representing ourself to others as a "discipline" with a difference.

10. For a discussion of the reigning dichotomies embodied in this "banking" concept of education, and of its contradictions, see P. Freire, *Pedagogy of the Oppressed* (New York: Seabury, 1970). Also see *Education for Critical Consciousness* (New York: Seabury, 1973).

11. I use the term "ethnography" with some hesitation since what I am interested in is a postmodern sort of ethnographic practice rather than modernist notions of ethnographic "research." Linda Brodkey is getting at a similar idea when she juxtaposes and critiques the dichotomous "analytic" versus "interpretive" ethnography. See Linda Brodkey, Writing Ethnographic Narrative, *Written Communication* 9 (January 1987): 25–50 and Linda Brodkey, "Modernism and the Scene(s) of Writing," *College English* 49 (April 1987): 396–418. And James Clifford, in a new book, pulls together what I consider the most important strands of ethnographic practice—boundary blurring writing, art, and politics. See James Clifford, *The Predicament of Culture: Twentieth-Century Ethnography, Literature, and Art* (Cambridge: Harvard UP, 1988).

12. In Freire, "conscientizacao."

Works Cited

Brodkey, Linda. "Writing Ethnographic Narrative." *Written Communication* 9 (January 1987): 25–50.

———. "Modernism and the Scene(s) of Writing." *College English* 49 (April 1987): 396–418.

Clifford, James. *The Predicament of Culture: Twentieth Century Ethnography Literature and Art.* Cambridge, MA: Harvard UP, 1988.

Cowley, Malcolm. *A Second Flowering: Works and Days of the Lost Generation.* New York: Penguin, 1973.

Foster, Hal. *Recodings: Art, Spectacle, Cultural Politics.* Port Townsend, WA: Bay Press, 1983.

Freire, Paulo. *Pedagogy of the Oppressed.* New York: Seabury, 1970.

———. *Education for Critical Consciousness.* New York: Seabury, 1973.

Fussell, Paul. *The Great War and Modern Memory.* New York: Oxford UP, 1975.

Jencks, Charles. *What Is Post-Modernism?* New York: Academy/St. Martin's, 1986.

Kuh, Katherine. *Break-up: The Core of Modern Art.* Greenwich, CT: New York Graphic Society, 1965.

North, Stephen. *The Making of Knowledge in Composition: Portrait of an Emerging Field.* Portsmouth, NH: Boynton/Cook, 1987.

TWELVE

The Demons of Old and New Rhetoric

DOROTHY C. BROADDUS

> Fortunately, I had enough exposure to a few critical teachers, whose examples helped distance me from worshipping monuments. . . .
>
> Ira Shor
> *Critical Teaching and Everyday Life*

> You'll learn good from the good.
>
> Plato
> *Meno*

Meeting by chance in our college bookstore, a philosopher-colleague, a mutual student, and I were having a friendly conversation about the idiosyncracies of the brilliant philosopher Immanuel Kant. Our student, Steve Larmey, stated he had read somewhere that Kant said he didn't mind being visited by women as long as they didn't claim to understand his philosophy. Without attempting to mask my anger, I replied that I try not only to understand philosophy but also to understand philosophers—I'm interested in why a person would hold such views. My colleague, Gill Ring, who always has the punch line, said, "Then Kant definitely wouldn't want you to visit him."

After several false starts at writing an essay on the arbitrary dichotomy between old and new rhetoric, I remembered this conversation and, partially because chauvinism presents a challenge for me, I decided I would write about rhetoricians instead of rhetorics. But I have another, better reason—rhetoricians have "taught" me more than rhetorics. Teaching (instructing or informing), it seems to me, is not possible without persuading, and people usually are not persuaded by mere logical arguments. According to Aristotle, people become convinced by three means—*logos, ethos, pathos. Logos* is effected through the speech itself, its "proof" or "apparent proof." *Ethos* is achieved by the "personal goodness" or credibility of the speaker. *Pathos* is achieved when the speaker reaches the emotions of the audience (*Rhetoric* 1356a).

While in Aristotle's scheme *logos* refers to words themselves, or to the logical arrangement of a certain text, or to the "logic" of a particular argument, in its larger sense it can also refer to logical structures or rational principles, or even to complete rhetorical systems. Thus, when scholars argue about rhetorical theory, their arguments usually focus on issues that fall under the rubric *logos*. To illustrate, two important books, both published in 1984, take opposing stands on using classical rhetoric in contemporary composition theory and practice. Attacking classical rhetoric, C. H. Knoblach and Lil Brannon contend that "revolutions in epistemology" have resulted in reconceptions of the "very foundations, dimensions, and aspirations of intellectual inquiry." They argue that traditional composition teaching, grounded in classical rhetoric, reflects beliefs that knowledge is "separable from as well as prior to discourse," that a "privileged class possesses, safeguards, and conveys the truth, and that writing is merely a vehicle for transmitting the known to those who don't yet know" (23–26). Knoblauch and Brannon's attack on classical rhetoric relies exclusively on their reading of the logical principles inside classical texts and the apparent incompatibility of these principles with ways people learn or construct their own *logos*.

Defending classical rhetoric, Robert Connors, Lise Ede, and Andrea Lunsford, editors of *Essays on Classical Rhetoric and Modern Discourse*, assume that an understanding of classical rhetorical theory is essential for enlightened teachers of composition. They argue that narrow and restrictive composition teaching is not the fault of classical rhetoric but instead the consequence of its being ignored, disregarded, or reduced to rigid rules in the nineteenth century (2–5). The authors of several essays in their collection defend classical rhetoric by focusing on its logical elements. For example, Frank D'Angelo argues that the analytic *topoi* parallel stages in the evolution of consciousness (50–68), and John Gage demonstrates that dialectic, enthymeme, and stasis theory were reduced from central roles in classical rhetoric to "technical formulae" in modern rhetoric

(152–169). As a matter of fact, Lunsford and Ede offer compelling arguments that distinctions typically drawn between the logical structures of classical and modern rhetoric are inaccurate (137–149).

Because composition theorists have given a great deal of attention to the logical and epistemological dimensions of classical and modern rhetorical systems, I want to focus this essay in a way that eliminates divisions, whether real or apparent, between old and new rhetoric, and I intend it to eliminate other dichotomies as well, dichotomies between professional and personal writing, and even between scholarly and imaginative writing. The locus of my discussion is *ethos*, but I will also touch on *eros*. Composition theorists rarely discuss *ethos* (and almost never discuss *eros*), except in an abstract way, since the concept refers to people rather than texts. More explicitly, *ethos* refers to *us* as we speak and write and teach, and we are understandably uncomfortable with this frame of reference. Moreover, scholars tend to perceive *ethos* as a slippery concept because it does not inhere entirely in speakers and writers. While "style" and "voice" may manifest a certain set of features by which speakers or writers can be characterized, *ethos* depends on relationship, what eighteenth-century writers called "sympathy" or "fellow-feeling." Thus, the *ethos* of a particular speaker or writer is the cumulation of his or her evocation and hearers' or readers' reactions. In other words, *ethos* is the offspring of call and response. Because this particular essay is about the "call" to me of a few rhetoricians and my responses to them, it reveals as much about me as it does about them. Thus, the essay itself was born of *ethos*.

I begin, as you might have predicted, with the ethical and erotic Plato and Socrates. To Plato, Socrates personifies excellence, yet the Socrates of the text is hard for me to love since at times he seems comical and pompous. He has a snub-nose and protruding eyes, he has a habit of not wearing shoes except on special occasions, and he flirts outrageously with handsome young men. As an indication of Socrates's apparent arrogance, we learn in the *Apology* that teaching became his divine mission when from a question someone asked the Delphic oracle he drew the conclusion that he was the wisest man in the world. Nevertheless, as soon as I become involved with Socrates the person, I forgive him for being funny looking and pompous. In order to "read" Socrates (*ethos*) as well as what Socrates says (*logos*), I train myself to something resembling double vision, keeping one eye on the progression of the argument and on Socrates's pointed questions and comments, and another eye on what Walter Pater calls the "accidents of conversation"— the digressions and surprises, which turn out to be showplaces for Socrates's wit and irony. I'll forgive anybody practically anything as long as they are witty and can maintain an ironic stance. But the most intriguing feature of Socrates is not his sense of irony but rather his demon (*daimon*), a spirit who speaks only to him, especially when he is about to act in error or to speak untruth.

While Socrates's demon doesn't carry the Jewish and Christian connotation of "evil," it does represent an assertive and often inhibiting power. For instance, in the *Phaedrus*, when Socrates concludes his first speech and is ready to leave, the demon's voice restrains him, and as a result, he then makes an honest speech that supersedes the deceitful one (242C). Throughout history, philosophers have argued about the source and the significance of Socrates's demon (see Friedlander's Chapter 2). Some scholars have argued that the voice of the demon is merely the voice of Socrates's own conscience, admonishing him for his wrongdoing. However, in the *Apology*, Socrates tells us that when he was on his way to court to defend himself, the voice remained silent. The demon's silence indicates approval to Socrates, who interprets the silence as a sign that what is happening to him is good (40 A–B). Therefore, the demon must be more than conscience. As a matter of fact, Paul Friedlander argues that for Plato "god" and "demon" are very close and in some instances merge into one (40).

Furthermore, the word *daimon*, typically defined as a subordinate god or attendant spirit, is the root for *eudaimonia*, a word usually translated as "happiness" but which to the Greeks meant "human flourishing." The close association of the two words, along with Socrates's consistently positive attitude toward his *daimon*, suggests that the demon is an affirming force that promotes happiness and well-being to those who "listen." For Plato, who was a geometer, *eudaimonia* was impossible without proper proportion or "middle ground." In the *Symposium* the prophetess Diotima stresses the importance of the "middle" by noting, for example, that right opinion lies between knowledge and ignorance. Further, in her myth of *Eros* she perceives love as a great demon who acts as intermediary between the divine and the mortal (202E). Consequently, Socrates's demon, linked on the one extreme to restraint and on the other to love, exemplifies a "medium"—an active interpretive force that, while it initially inhibits or restricts, ultimately enables Socrates to achieve clarity and truth. Attracted first perhaps by the erotic power of the demon, Socrates willingly submits to its authority. Later, however, he pushes away from it and, as in the *Phaedrus*, draws on his own resources.

Those of us who emulate Socrates, that is, we "lovers of wisdom," also have our demons. A few of us have even written about our relationships with them. In the collection *Writers on Writ-*

ing, for example, several composition theorists acknowledge the influence of masterful former teachers on their own formation as writers and thinkers. Examples of demons in this collection are Joe Comprone's teacher Sister Rita Ann and David Bartholomae's mentors Richard Poirier and William Coles, teachers who affected the writers in personal and potent ways. But Bartholomae implies that demons also can spring from the *ethos* of texts and readers. He states, "For me, nothing happens, or could happen, until I imagine myself within a discourse—a kind of textual conversation/confrontation with people whose work matters to me and whose work, then, makes my own possible" (21). Bartholomae's term "conversation/confrontation" implies that even though we listen to and even talk with our demons, the greater "lovers of wisdom" must become bold enough to draw on their own resources, like Socrates, and ultimately confront the demons.

Aristotle's demon was Plato, a demon so powerful that Aristotle didn't confront him until after Plato's death. Joining the Academy at age seventeen, and remaining there for twenty years, Aristotle eulogized Plato as the man "whom bad men have not even the right to praise, and who showed in his life and teachings how to be happy and good at the same time" (quoted in Copleston vol. 1, 266). Even though he dissented from some of Plato's teaching, criticizing, for example, his doctrine of Ideas, he assimilated or adapted other principles. Book A of the *Metaphysics,* which summarizes the philosophies of his predecessors and shows where he differs from Plato, probably represents part of Aristotle's confrontation with his demon. But even as he criticizes Plato, he refers to himself as a Platonist, an act that calls into question the popular notion that the radical differences between the two philosophers necessitates our choosing between them, in other words, deciding whether to keep Plato or Aristotle as demon.

Aristotle's early writings, which unfortunately are lost, were composed while he was studying under Plato at the Academy and were dialogues in the Platonic style. Most of his extant writings, including the *Rhetoric,* are from his later period and were written at the Lyceum as lectures for his students. In contrast, Plato wrote his dialogues for the general literate public, though apparently he also wrote out lectures, which are lost. I wonder how different our perceptions would be if we possessed Plato's lectures and Aristotle's dialogues! The Plato of his texts appeals to my romantic persona, that part of my personality that fervently believes I can change people and the world. Plato is a reformer; he reforms by perpetually challenging conventional ways of thinking. In contrast, Aristotle is an informer, a theoretician and codifier of habit, custom, tradition.

Plato's success in persuading and teaching me is largely the result of his speculative style. After all, he has Socrates, the "wisest man in the world," admit that he is perplexed, much as I am often perplexed. Thus, I love Plato because I perceive him as fellow inquirer, willing to engage with me in investigation and speculation. On the other hand, I am intimidated by Aristotle, since the Aristotle I perceive in his texts has completed his investigation, discovered truth, defined it, and classified it in several ways.

Consequently, as I look at my old copy of the *Rhetoric*, I find that I have read it exactly like William Covino says I shouldn't: "as a body of precepts and principles that can be represented schematically" (21). I have marked carefully the three modes of persuasion, the three elements of speech making, the three divisions of oratory, the five "matters on which all men deliberate," etc. I have underlined Aristotle's definitions, noting where I strongly agree by writing "yes!" or "wow!" For example, happiness as the "secure enjoyment of the maximum of pleasure" merited a "wow!" I have carefully noted his divisions, for instance, general reason as distinguished from individual reason. I have even copied onto index cards passages that are not necessarily profound but which ring so true I want them stored in my commonplace repository. Examples are "Uneducated men argue from common knowledge and draw obvious conclusions" (1395B), and "Bring yourself on the stage from the first in the right character..." (1417B). However, as I look back at my notes and underlinings, I discover that I seldom question Aristotle since the authority he establishes in the text is that of One Who Knows. As a matter of fact, early in the history of philosophy, Aristotle became the Authority demon for scholars such as Thomas Aquinas, who referred to him simply as "The Philosopher."

Aristotle was a collector of specimens and examples of all kinds—biological, ethical, literary, political. In order to write the *Politics*, he had more than a hundred and fifty constitutions described in detail, undertaking himself the description of the constitution of Athens. Because he was an amasser of knowledge, he also was a taxonomer. However, his taxonomies (unlike my taxonomy of demons) were not derived from "first principles"; that is, they are not *a priori* categories. In the *Ethics* Aristotle states that inquiry begins with what is known; then, perceiving the ambiguity of his statement, he refines it, acknowledging that things are known in two ways: absolutely known and "known to us." Members of the Lyceum, he maintains, begin with what is "known to us" (I.iv.6). In the *Metaphysics* he affirms the value of observation and experience in forming categories and theories: "Art comes into being when many observations of experience give rise to a single universal conviction about a class of similar cases" (981A). Consequently, in the *Rhetoric,* when Aristotle differentiates the three types of speeches or the three kinds of appeals, his categories have formed themselves from his experience. In other words, they are syntheses of his extensive dialectic with the "nature of things." When we criticize him for being too authoritative, we tend to overlook the breadth of his experience. As an authority, Aristotle, in the sense Jesse Jackson uses the word, is "qualified."

Nevertheless, the authority of the Aristotelian treatise became a demon writ large for academics, since the treatise, rather than the Platonic dialogue or even the Montaigne essay, remained the institutional model. As a consequence, Aristotle's authoritative style was imitated by philosophers and rhetoricians, who, though they found comfort in the imitation, had far less breadth of knowledge. One imitator, the eighteenth-century Scottish Calvinist rhetorician George Campbell, intended his *Philosophy of Rhetoric* to be a treatise that refutes not only Aristotle's logic but also David Hume's skepticism—a difficult task for any reasoner. But instead of refuting Aristotle, Campbell grounds his own logic in Aristotelian "first principles," and as a result, his rhetorical theory is tangled and sometimes lacks logical consistency (has bad *logos*). Further, Campbell's voice becomes angry at times when he discusses the evils of Catholicism and rationalism. In essence, Campbell's text is a treatise based on Aristotelian logic tinged with Calvinist theology and with moral sense and common sense philosophy. Thus, Campbell stands as a prime example of a rhetorician who did not squarely enough face his Authority demons.

I also have an Authority demon, so I understand Campbell's infirmity of purpose. James Berlin, whose voice is not nearly so didactic as Campbell's, writes histories of American rhetoric in the Aristotelian taxonomic style. In *Writing Instruction in Nineteenth-Century American Colleges,* Berlin differentiates three rhetorics—classical, eighteenth-century, and romantic—and suggests that each rhetoric supersedes the former. Classical rhetoric, he argues, which was "overthrown" in American colleges with English rule, was replaced by Hugh Blair and George Campbell's rhetorics, which Berlin associates with Scottish Common Sense Realism. Romantic rhetoric, Berlin maintains, growing from the work of Emerson, Thoreau, and other transcendentalists, found its way into composition courses late in the nineteenth century (6–12). The remainder of Berlin's book describes the features of each rhetoric, their manifestations in the nineteenth century, and their remnants in current composition theory.

As I "hear" Berlin I want to agree with him. Because they appeal to my desire for certitude, his taxonomies are seductive. And Berlin is enchanting to me in other ways as well. For example, he often uses the feminine pronoun when referring to "the scholar" or "the historian," and he does it in writing as well as speaking, thereby making his commitment permanent. Further, in his more recent book on twentieth-century composition theory, he confronts the problem of objectivity in writing history by acknowledging the "ineluctability of terministic screens" (*Rhetoric and Reality* 17). Berlin's candid remarks about his own biases, reminiscent of Socrates, are not typical of rigid Aristotle-imitators. Berlin has been one of my demons since the first time I heard him speak, even though I knew I would confront the Authority demon eventually.

On the occasion of our first meeting I was nervous and told Berlin that as Kant said of Hume, he had "awakened me from my dogmatic slumbers." I realized instantly that I was pretentiously placing myself in Kant's position. But Berlin laughed, not even condescendingly. Even though I was embarrassed at the time, now after pondering my statement, it seems true. Berlin's work represents a call to me, as Hume's did to Kant, that needs a response. And I respond by arguing that "moral sense" rather than "common sense" is the fundamental informing philosophy in the rhetorics of George Campbell and Hugh Blair. While Berlin classifies Emerson's rhetoric as romantic, I argue that Emerson took much of his rhetoric from his teacher at Harvard, Edward T. Channing. Channing's text *Lectures Read to the Seniors in Harvard College* exhibits features derived from classical theories as well as from Campbell and Blair's rhetorical theories. My response to the Authority demon may not represent a more "honest speech," but it is my "speech."

Another one of my demons, Peter Elbow, is quite different from the Authority demon. In the *Theaetetus*, Socrates calls himself a midwife and explains that a midwife's skills include "matchmaking" in order to produce the best children, knowing when a person is suffering "pains of travail," making an easy or a difficult labor, and being able to tell whether the delivery produces a real child or a "mere phantom" (148E–150 B). As I read Elbow, I discover that he practices the maieutic skills described by Socrates. Elbow even admits that as teacher he wanted to be Socrates and a "good guy" at the same time (*Embracing Contraries* 67). But Socrates *was* a good guy at times, and I perceive Elbow as similar to the "good guy" *in* Socrates. Since Elbow's pedagogy is much like Socrates's maieutic method, I call him the Midwife demon.

Elbow's metaphors for learning are physical metaphors such as eating, cooking, growing, wrestling, and in *Writing With Power* he even includes a section on nausea (173–175). He argues that learning never occurs merely in the mind as intellection; rather it is a physical, sexual, even violent act. To translate Elbow's pedagogical theory into maieutic terms, learners become pregnant with learning, bear the travail, and, with the midwife's help, deliver "children" of worth. Drawing on Piaget's concepts of assimilation and accommodation, Elbow perceives teaching and learning as cooperative efforts: the teacher must "deform" subject matter so that it fits inside the learner, and the learner must deform herself so that she fits around the subject matter. Good learning, Elbow argues, never occurs unless both parties are "maximally transformed—in a sense deformed" (*Embracing Contraries* 148). Socrates might say that here Elbow is describing the process of "matchmaking." Creating or writing or learning require a certain amount of force, and the midwife, anticipating the product of the creation and delivery processes, knows that if the parties involved are transformed only minimally, the result may be a "mere phantom." Furthermore, in order for the real child to be delivered with less difficulty, the midwife exploits the push and pull of the delivery process, as Elbow's pedagogy exploits the opposing forces of independence/dependence, creating/criticizing, doubting/believing.

Whether he is "speaking" to student writers or to teachers, Elbow never assumes the voice of authority; instead, he sounds like a kindred spirit, or even learner, who himself suffers "pains of travail," an insider who talks freely about his own experiences. Even though he brings his wide reading in other disciplines (philosophy, religion, cognitive psychology) to bear upon his pedagogy, Elbow uses theory to explain his own experience and refine his own notions. At times he is almost the "humble" Socrates, who in the *Theaetetus* protests that he has no wisdom. Elbow, however, is not barren of wisdom.

Like Berlin, Elbow distances himself from typical male ways of talking and teaching. In his discussion of the "doubting/believing game," he associates "doubting" with culturally defined male behavior: "aggressive, thrusting, combative, competitive, and initiatory" (*Writing Without Teachers* 180). In contrast, "believing," which Elbow calls the "dialectics of experience," emphasizes yielding, supporting, listening, cooperating, incorporating—typical female behavior. Elbow argues that "believing" yields truth that is better but dirtier (177–179). Indeed, a significant feature of the Midwife demon is his willingness to get messy. Unlike the stereotypical obstetrician who remains detached and formal, the midwife is engaged, involved, personal, and willing to adapt his strategies and change his own behavior. Always sensitive to the person in travail, he will coach, cajole, even demand when the learner needs it, but otherwise he maintains silence. These are the traits most valued in Elbow's pedagogy.

Confronting his own demons, Elbow acknowledges the love and hatred he had for his teachers. He writes, "I didn't just 'go along' with my teachers, I hungered to please them, I fell in love with them, I wanted to be them. Similarly, I didn't just engage in 'independent thinking' (thereby earning approving pats on the head from them); eventually I seemed driven to reject, spit out, and indeed hate those teachers and all they stood for. And then subsequently back and forth. Without the extremities of these responses, I probably would not have made teaching and learning so deep a part of me" (*Embracing Contraries* 65–66). Elbow's candid comments, which pertain to both *ethos* and *eros*, demonstrate that confrontation does not destroy demons. On the contrary, demons reappear, and when they do, we listen attentively. Thus Elbow, like Socrates, has managed to coopt his demons.

As my Midwife demon, Elbow persuades and teaches compellingly. Nevertheless, I try to objectify my enchantment with him by reminding myself that I cannot rely solely on *his* art. The inherent danger of his method, it seems to me, is the potential for the midwife to become too essential and therefore too powerful. Thus, when I work with learners, I anticipate not only the "child" we will deliver, but also the kinds of "children" they will need to create and deliver for the biologist, the Thomist philosopher, and the classicist. If they produce "mere phantoms" for other teachers, then they are relying too much on my art and not enough on their own power. Further, since I perpetually create and develop and change my own art, I need to listen to voices of other demons.

One such voice reminds me that Socrates has another persona—he was also referred to as a stingray. In the *Meno*, whose subject is whether virtue can be taught, Socrates asks Menon first to define virtue. After several tries, Menon becomes frustrated and accuses Socrates of being a stingray, stinging and numbing learners and causing them to become puzzled (30A–B). Later in the dialogue, Socrates demonstrates his skill on a young servant by "numbing" and perplexing him until he discovers what he knows. Impressed by Socrates's stingray-art, Menon concedes that the boy gained knowledge by being numbed (86A).

Besides portraying Socrates as stingray-teacher, the *Meno* touches on other issues pertinent to rhetoricians. For example, Plato uses this dialogue to advance his theory of anamnesis—the notion that learning is the recovery of latent knowledge, sometimes in the form of "right opinion," which Diotima in the *Symposium* referred to as the "middle" between knowledge and ignorance. The stingray's skills enable the learner to "fasten up" right opinion so that, like the statues of Daedelus, it becomes valuable (202E). Further, the *Meno* reveals Plato's disdain for using the dialectic for eristic purposes. Socrates maintains that clever people who "chop logic" and argue merely to win cannot help souls to remember (79C).

Ann Berthoff, my Stingray demon, is often as perplexing as Socrates is in his stingray persona because she refuses to give me simple answers or even simple means for finding answers. Unlike the Midwife demon, Berthoff doesn't attempt to beguile me as reader into thinking she's a "good guy." Admitting that her tone is sometimes "magisterial," she states she is going to "rock the boat," and she justifies it by arguing that "finding directions always entails rocking the boat" (30). Instead of coaxing or coaching, like the midwife, the stingray's potency at first lies in the force of her stings. Thus, I know immediately when I've been wrong. But the effects of the stings are long-lasting and ultimately positive because they persuade me to either fasten up or abandon preciously held opinions.

One of Berthoff's goals is to wrench power from the Authority demons who have assumed control of the definitions and methodology of learning. She perceives current teaching methods to be fundamentally corrupting to learners, so she advocates radical pedagogical reforms. As a beginning, she calls for "ritual burning" of all instructors' manuals, study guides, and felt-tip highlighters—instruments of the prefabricated or simple-minded question and answer (35). But on a more substantive level, Berthoff wants to replace the old educational psychologies with a theory of the imagination. Conceiving imagination as the "form-finding and form-creating power," Berthoff wants imagination rescued from the "creativity corner" and restored as a "speculative instrument" to the center of learning (23–29).

Thus, the dialectic for learning and teaching that Berthoff proposes is in one sense simple, but not simplistic. And since "learning" is not synonymous with "winning," the dialectic is not eristic. Unlike the midwife who exploits contraries in the learning process, Berthoff wants to eliminate them, perceiving them as arbitrary divisions. Her aim is to eradicate distinctions between scholarship/teaching, theory/practice, cognitive domain/affective domain, reading/writing, personal or creative writing/expository or "structured" writing. Defining the dialectic after I. A. Richards as "the continuing audit of meaning," the stingray-teacher practices her art by listening for and encouraging emergent "right opinion," or, to paraphrase Berthoff paraphrasing Michelangelo, for occasions where learners can be helped to liberate the form in the stone (65).

Like Socrates, Berthoff has eminent faith in learners' capacity to learn. She cites as exemplary teachers Tolstoy, Montessori, and Freire, all of whom learned to teach by teaching illiterate or "remedial" learners. In Berthoff's pedagogy, if learners don't learn, the fault lies in the false philosophies of their teachers. When learners have been taught wrongheadedly, the stingray-teacher's job becomes more difficult because she has to unteach "anticomposing" (3). Ideally, teachers' obligations to learners would consist mainly in removing obstacles to what Socrates called "remembering," that is, in enabling learners to form their meaning and interpret their interpretations. Most important, Berthoff's pedagogy, like Socrates's stings, places the onus of learning squarely on learners, forcing them to take charge of their own remembering, researching, reforming.

As my Stingray demon Berthoff's voice compels me to form and reform my own notions. For example, I am compelled to "fasten up" what I mean when I utter such commonly used terms as "process," "critical thinking," "literacy." Thus, when colleagues in other disciplines ask for easy ways to implement critical reading and writing activities in their classrooms, her voice warns me not to become entrapped in the Writing-Across-the-Curriculum version of the "Exercise Exchange"—the practice without the theory. If I emulate her stingray art, perhaps I can "give" students and colleagues the speculative instruments they need in order to find form and meaning in their own stones. The Stingray demon challenges me to say what I mean as well as to mean and practice what I say.

My demons, as you can tell, have disparate qualities, and I jealously and persistently keep all three, leaving me unsure at times which voice to heed. On some occasions I listen to the Authority, on others the Midwife, and on still others the Stingray. In addition, I have to decide when to listen and when to speak and how to interpret the demons' silence. But as lover of wisdom and lover of demons, I am getting better at making those decisions, and someday maybe I'll be good enough to be a demon myself. The genus "demon," as I have illustrated, is an honorific category to which all teachers should aspire if they don't want to remain idle babblers.

In the myth of the three metamorphoses of the spirit, Nietzche (a demon of a different color) suggests that the spirit begins its journey as a camel, a beast of burden who submits to authority in order to learn. In the second stage, the spirit becomes the lion named "I Will," but only after killing the dragon named "Thou Shalt." Finally, the spirit becomes a child (25–28). At first, I thought Nietzche's dragon was similar to Socrates's demon. But I was wrong, or perhaps Nietzche is wrong. I don't want to kill my demons as Nietzche proscribes the dragon, but even if I wanted to, I couldn't. They are far too powerful for me to annihilate. Thus when Knoblach and Brannon want to eradicate the use of classical rhetoric in composition teaching, or when William Howell claims that in the seventeenth century John Locke "demolished" the Aristotelian tradition (267), I laugh. Nietzche's dragon may be destructible, but demons are invincible.

Works Cited

Aristotle. *Aristotle's Metaphysics*. Trans. Hippocrates G. Apostle. Bloomington: Indiana UP, 1966.

———. *The Ethics of Aristotle: The Nichomachean Ethics*. Trans. J. A. K. Thomson. Baltimore: Penguin, 1962.

———. *Rhetoric*. Trans. W. Rhys Roberts. New York: Random House, 1954.

Bartholomae, David. "Against the Grain." *Writers on Writing*. Ed. Tom Waldrup. New York: Random House, 1985.

Berlin, James. *Rhetoric and Reality*. Carbondale: Southern Illinois UP, 1984.

———. *Writing Instruction in Nineteenth-Century American Colleges*. Carbondale: Southern Illinois UP, 1984.

Berthoff, Ann E. *The Making of Meaning*. Portsmouth, NH: Boynton/Cook, 1981.

Campbell, George. *The Philosophy of Rhetoric*. Ed. Lloyd F. Bitzer. Carbondale: Southern Illinois UP, 1988.

Channing, Edward T. *Lectures Read to the Seniors in Harvard College*. Ed. Dorothy I. Anderson and Waldo W. Braden. Carbondale: Southern Illinois UP, 1968.

Connors, Robert, Lisa Ede, Andra Lunsford. *Essays in Classical Rhetoric & Modern Discourse*. Carbondale, IL: SIUP, 1984.

Coppleston, Frederick S. J. *A History of Philosophy*. 9 vols. Garden City, NY: Doubleday, 1985.

Covino, William A. *The Art of Wondering*. Portsmouth, NH: Boynton/Cook, 1988.

Elbow, Peter. *Embracing Contraries*. New York: Oxford UP, 1986.

———. *Writing without Teachers*. New York: Oxford UP, 1973.

———. *Writing with Power*. New York: Oxford UP, 1981.

Friedlander, Paul. *Plato: An Introduction*. Trans. Hans Meyerhoff. Princeton: Princeton UP, 1969.

Howell, William S. *Eighteenth-Century British Logic and Rhetoric*. Princeton: Princeton UP, 1971.

Knoblauch, C. H. and Lil Brannon. *Rhetorical Traditions and the Teaching of Writing*. Portsmouth, NH: Boynton/Cook, 1984.

Nietzche, Friedrich. *Thus Spoke Zarathustra*. Trans. Walter Kaufmann. New York: Penguin, 1985.

Plato. *Great Dialogues of Plato*. Trans. W. H. D. Rouse. New York: Mentor, 1956.

———. *Phaedrus*. Trans. Walter Hamilton. New York: Penguin, 1973.

———. *Theaetetus*. Trans. Francis MacDonald Cornford. Indianapolis: Bobbs-Merrill, 1977.

White, Hayden. *Metahistory. The Historical Imagination in 19th C Europe*. Baltimore: Johns Hopkins, 1973.

Bibliography of Works That Transform Dichotomies

If you look back at the Works Cited pages of the essays in this collection, you'll notice that some entries appear again and again. Mina Shaughnessy, Louise Rosenblatt, James Britton, Peter Elbow, Ann Berthoff, and others have written compellingly within and around dichotomies, and their work has helped us move beyond confrontation and toward dialectic in our teaching and writing. Like that group of works so many of us used in our essays, the bibliography that follows includes readings that have moved our thinking farther along by challenging us to see beyond dichotomies and toward the mediating principles in ideas. Most of these books come from areas outside composition studies, and the selections are personal; it's an idiosyncratic list, meant as a suggestive rather than inclusive supplement. But the range of subject matter and of perspective chosen by the editors and some of the contributors prove that transformation is neither new nor the property of any one ideology or interest. The only principle of selection among the thinkers whose work appears here, in fact, seems to be a genuine desire for dialogue more than monologue. C. S. Peirce said, "We individually cannot reasonably hope to attain the ultimate philosophy which we pursue; we can only seek it, therefore, for the community of philosophers." In the spirit of community, then, we offer this list.

Bakhtin, Mikhail. *The Dialogic Imagination*. Austin: U of Texas P, 1981.

"As a living, socio-ideological concrete thing, as heteroglot opinion, language, for the individual consciousness, lies on the borderline between oneself and the other. The word in language is half someone else's. It becomes one's own only when the speaker populates it with his own intention."

Berthoff, Ann E., ed. *Reclaiming the Imagination.* Portsmouth, NH: Boynton/Cook, 1984.
"Studying perception and the apprehension of reality is a way to reclaim the imagination as the forming power of mind."

Booth, Wayne. *The Company We Keep: An Ethics of Fiction.* Berkeley: U of California P, 1988.
"The book now aims, first, to restore the full intellectual legitimacy of our common-sense inclination to talk about stories in ethical terms, treating the characters in them and their makers as more like people than labyrinths, enigmas, or textual puzzles to be deciphered; and second, it aims to 'relocate' ethical criticism, turning it from flat judgment for or against supposedly stable works to fluid conversation about the qualities of the company we keep—and the company that we ourselves provide."

Bruner, Jerome. *On Knowing: Essays for the Left Hand.* Cambridge, MA: Harvard UP, 1979.
"And so I have argued in one of the essays that the scientist and the poet do not live at antipodes, and I urge in another that the artificial separation of the two modes of knowing cripples the contemporary intellectual as an effective mythmaker for his times."

Burke, Kenneth. *Counterstatement.* 1931. Berkeley: U of California P, 1968.
"There is pamphleteering; there is inquiry. [The writer's] actual work will probably show an indeterminate wavering between the two positions; he himself will himself not be sure just when he is inquiring and when pamphleteering. And he may not be wholly satisfied by the thought of doing exclusively either."

Clifford, James, and George E. Marcus, eds. *Writing Culture: The Poetics and Politics of Ethnography.* Berkeley: U of California P, 1986.
"It has long been asserted that scientific anthropology is also an 'art,' that ethnographies have literary qualities. . . . A work is deemed evocative or artfully composed in addition to being factual; expressive or rhetorical functions are conceived as

decorative or merely as ways to present an objective analysis or description more effectively. Thus the facts of the matter may be kept separate, at least in principle, from their means of communication. But the literary or rhetorical dimensions of ethnography can no longer be so easily compartmentalized. They are active at every level of cultural science.

Coleridge, Samuel Taylor. *Biographia Literaria, 1815.*
"The poet, described in ideal perfection, brings the whole soul of man into activity, with the subordination of its faculties to each other, according to their relative worth and dignity. He diffuses a tone and spirit of unity, that blends, and (as it were) fuses, each into each, by that sympathetic and magical power, to which we have exclusively appropriated the name of the imagination."

Didion, Joan. *The White Album*. New York: Simon and Schuster, 1979.
"If I could believe that going to a barricade would affect man's fate in the slightest I would go to that barricade, and quite often I wish that I could, but it would be less than honest to say that I expect to happen upon such a happy ending."

Elbow, Peter. *Embracing Contraries: Explorations in Learning and Teaching*. New York: Oxford, 1986.
"It is the spirit or principle of serving contraries that I want to emphasize here, not any particular fleshing out in practice. ... For one of the main attractions of this theory is that it helps explain why people are able to be terrific teachers in such diverse ways. If someone is managing to do two things that conflict with one another, he is probably doing something mysterious; it's altogether natural if his success involves slipperiness, irony, or paradox. ... For it is one's spirit or stance that is at issue here, not the mechanics of how to organize a course in semester units or how to deal in tests, grading, or credits."

Fish, Stanley. *Self-Consuming Artifacts*. Berkeley: U of California P, 1972.
"In a dialectical experience, one moves, or is moved, from the first to the second way, which has various names, the way of the good, the way of the inner light, the way of faith; but whatever the designation, the moment of its full emergence is marked by the transformation of the visible and segmented world into an emblem of its creator's indwelling presence, and at that moment the motion of the rational consciousness is

stilled, for it has become indistinguishable from the object of its inquiry."

Freire, Paulo, and Donaldo Macedo. *Literacy: Reading the Word and the World*. South Hadley, MA: Bergin & Garvey, 1987.
"The command of reading and writing is achieved beginning with words and themes meaningful to the common experience of those becoming literate, not with words and themes linked only to the experience of the educator."

Frye, Northrop. *The Great Code: The Bible and Literature*. New York: Harcourt Brace, 1983.
"Academics, like other people, start with a personality that is afflicted by ignorance and prejudice, and try to escape from that personality, in Eliot's phrase, through absorption in impersonal scholarship. One emerges on the other side of this realizing once again that all knowledge is personal knowledge, but with some hope that the person may have been, to whatever degree, transformed in the meantime."

Geertz, Clifford. *Local Knowledge*. New York: Basic Books, 1983.
"We don't need another, new cryptography, but a new diagnostics—a science that can determine the meaning of things for the life that surrounds them, locate in the tenor of their setting the sources of their spell."

Gilbert, G. Nigel, and Michael Mulkay. *Opening Pandora's Box: A Sociological Analysis of Scientists' Discourse*. Cambridge: Cambridge UP, 1984.
"One of the central claims of this book is that sociologists' attempts to tell *the* story of a particular social setting or to formulate *the* way in which social life operates are fundamentally unsatisfactory. Such 'definitive versions' are unsatisfactory because they imply unjustifiably that the analyst can reconcile his version of events with all the multiple and divergent versions generated by the actors themselves.... There is much to be gained by opening Pandora's box in the sense of setting free the multitude of divergent and conflicting voices with which scientists speak."

Gleick, James. *Chaos*. New York: Viking, 1987.
"To some physicists chaos is a science of process rather than state, of becoming rather than being."

Hampden-Turner, Charles. *Maps of the Mind*. New York: Macmillan, 1982.
"The entire book is a plea for the revision of social science,

religion, and philosophy to stress connectedness, coherence, relationship, organicism and wholeness, as against the fragmenting, reductive and compartmentalizing forces of the prevailing orthodoxies. My belief is that industrial cultures are dangerously overdifferentiated and underintegrated. We compulsively exaggerate our differences while ignoring what we have in common. The maps here are deliberately selected and described with a view to their overall compatibility, complementarity and convergence. W. H. Auden wrote that 'we must love each other or die.' 'Love' is a trifle too ambitious perhaps, but we can understand."

Hearne, Vicki. *Adam's Task: Calling Animals by Name.* New York: Knopf, 1986.

"For some years I uneasily inhabited at least two completely different worlds of discourse, each using a group of languages that were intertranslatable—dog trainers can talk to horse trainers, and philosophers can talk to linguists, and psychologists, but dog trainers and philosophers can't make much sense of each other. (Philosophers and linguists may have sometimes thought that they found each other incomprehensible, but their quarrels were usually about the interior decoration of the house of intellect and not about fundamental structural principles.) Because I had learned to talk, more or less, in both worlds, I was intensely alert to the implications of Wittgenstein's remark, "To imagine a language is to imagine a form of life.' "

Heath, Shirley Brice. *Ways with Words: Language, Life, and Work in Communities and Classrooms.* Cambridge: Cambridge UP, 1983.

"In any case, unless the boundaries between classrooms and communities can be broken, and the flow of cultural patterns between them encouraged, the schools will continue to legitimate and produce communities of townspeople who control and limit the potential progress of other communities and who themselves remain untouched by other values and ways of life."

Langer, Susanne. *Philosophy in a New Key: A Study in the Symbolism of Reason, Rite, and Art.* Cambridge: Harvard UP, 1942.

"At best, human thought is but a tiny, grammar-bound island, in the midst of a sea of feeling expressed by "oh-oh" and sheer babble. The island has a periphery, perhaps, of mud—factual and hypothetical concepts broken down by the emotional tides into the material mode, a mixture of meaning and nonsense."

Martin, Jane Roland. *Reclaiming a Conversation: The Ideal of the Educated Woman*. New Haven: Yale UP, 1985.
"A good conversation is neither a fight nor a contest. Circular in form, cooperative in manner, and constructive in intent, it is an interchange of ideas by those who see themselves not as adversaries but as human beings come together to talk and listen and learn from one another."

Merleau-Ponty, Maurice. *The Primacy of Perception*. Ed. James M. Edie. Chicago: Northwestern UP, 1964.
"The writer's thought does not control his language from without; the writer is himself a kind of new idiom, constructing itself, inventing ways of expression, and diversifying itself according to its own meaning. Perhaps poetry is only that part of literature where this autonomy is ostentatiously displayed. All great prose is also a recreation of the signifying instrument, henceforth manipulated according to a new syntax."

Peirce, Charles S. *Chance, Love, and Logic*. Ed. Morris Cohen. New York: Barnes and Noble, 1923. Rpt. Harcourt Brace, 1968.
"A person is nothing but a symbol involving a general idea and every general idea has the unified living feeling of a person."

Plato. "Phaedrus." *Collected Dialogues*. Eds. Edith Hamilton and Huntington Cairns. Princeton: Princeton UP, 1961.
"Yes, indeed, dear Phaedrus. But far more excellent, I think, is the serious treatment of [words and topics], which employs the art of dialectic. The dialectician selects a soul of the right type, and in it he plants and sows his words founded on knowledge, words which can defend both themselves and him who planted them, words which instead of remaining barren contain a seed whence new words grow up in new characters, whereby the seed is vouchsafed immortality, and its possessor the fullest measure of blessedness that a man can attain to."

Polanyi, Michael. *Personal Knowledge: Toward a Post-Critical Philosophy*. Chicago: U of Chicago P, 1962.
"The inquiring scientist's intimations of a hidden reality are personal. They are his own beliefs, which—owing to his originality—as yet he alone holds. Yet they are not a subjective state of mind, but convictions held with universal intent. . . . It was he who decided what to believe, yet there is no arbitrariness in his decision. For he arrived at his conclusions by the utmost exercise of responsibility."

Richards, I. A. *Speculative Instruments*. New York: Harcourt, 1955.
"Through these assumptions [the work] divides and combines—dividing in order to combine, combining in order to
divide—and simultaneously."

Rosenblatt, Louise. *The Reader, the Text, the Poem*. Carbondale:
Southern Illinois UP, 1978.
"The poem, then, must be thought of as an event in time.
It is not an object or an ideal entity. It happens during a
coming-together, a compenetration, of a reader and a text.
The reader brings to the text his past experience and present
personality. Under the magnetism of the ordered symbols of
the text, he marshals his resources and crystallizes out from
the stuff of memory, thought, and feeling a new order, a new
experience, which he sees as the poem. This becomes part
of the ongoing stream of his life experience, to be reflected on
from any angle important to him as a human being."

Selzer, Richard. *Letters to a Young Doctor*. New York: Simon and
Schuster, 1982.
"Each of you who is full grown must learn to exist in two
states—Littleness and Bigness. In your littleness you descend
for hours each day through a cleft in the body into a tiny space
that is both your workshop and your temple. Your attention
in Lilliput is total and undistracted. Every artery is a river to
be forded or dammed, each organ a mountain to be skirted
or moved. At last, the work having been done, you ascend.
You blink and look about at the vast space peopled by giants
and massive furniture. Take a deep breath . . . and you are
Big. Such instantaneous hypertrophy is the process by which
a surgeon enters the outside world. Any breakdown in this
resonance between the sizes causes the surgeon to live in a
Renaissance painting where the depth perception is so bad."

Sontag, Susan. *On Photography*. New York: Farrar, Straus & Giroux,
1966.
"But the notions of image and reality are complementary.
When the notion of reality changes, so does that of the image,
and vice versa."

Summerfield, Judith, and Geoffrey Summerfield. *Texts and Contexts*.
New York: Random House, 1986.
"The pedagogical and heuristic potentialities of dialectic—
arguing both with the self and with others—as a mode of
thinking and as a way of shaping texts, these potentialities,
we propose, will never be exhausted. . . . Appropriately dis-

posed, as frames for pedagogical, learning, and textual considerations, these dialectics offer us a more useful and effective alternative to the current orthodoxies offered by the term *process*, which however flexibly offered represents an 'idealized' lock-step sequence for pre-writing, drafting, revising, rewriting, and end-product. What we seek and desire has to do with *matter*—what is being attended to—as much as it has to do with means."

Trollope, Anthony. *Autobiography*. Berkeley: U of California P, 1947.

"[The writer's] language must come from him as music comes from the rapid touch of the great performer's fingers; as words come from the mouth of the indignant orator; as letters fly from the fingers of the trained compositor; as the syllables tinkled out by little bells form themselves to the ear of the telegraphist. A man who thinks much of his words as he writes them will generally leave behind him work that smells of oil."

Tuchman, Barbara. *The March of Folly: From Troy to Vietnam*. New York: Ballantine, 1984.

"Mental standstill or stagnation—the maintenance intact by rulers and policy-makers of the ideas they started with—is fertile ground for folly. Montezuma is a fatal and tragic example. Leaders in government, on the authority of Henry Kissinger, do not learn beyond the convictions they bring with them; these are the 'intellectual capital they will consume as long as they are in office'. . . . In the first stage, mental standstill fixes the principles and boundaries governing a political problem. In the second stage, when dissonances and failing function begin to appear, the initial principles rigidify. This is the period when, if wisdom were operative, re-examination and re-thinking and a change of course are possible, but they are as rare as rubies in a backyard. Rigidifying leads to increase of investment and the need to protect egos; policy founded upon error multiplies, never retreats. The greater the investment and the more involved in it the sponsor's ego, the more unacceptable is disengagement. In the third stage, pursuit of failure enlarges the damages until it causes the fall of Troy, the defection from the Papacy, the loss of a transatlantic empire, the classic humiliation in Vietnam."

Vygotsky, Lev. *Thought and Language*. Ed. and Trans. Eugene Hanfmann and Gertrude Vakar. Cambridge: MIT P, 1962.

"Thought and language . . . are the keys to the nature of human consciousness. Words play a central part not only in the development of thought but in the historical growth of consciousness as a whole. A word is a microcosm of human consciousness."

White, Hayden. *Metahistory: The Historical Imagination in 19th Century Europe*. Baltimore: Johns Hopkins, 1973.

"The general conclusions I have drawn from my study of nineteenth century consciousness can be summarized as follows: (1) there can be no 'proper history' which is not at the same time 'philosophy of history'; (2) the possible modes of historiography are the same as the possible modes of speculative philosophy of history; (3) these modes, in turn, are in reality *formalizations* of poetic insights that analytically precede them and that sanction the particular theories used to give historical accounts the aspect of an 'explanation.' "

Notes on Contributors

PHILLIP K. ARRINGTON is an associate professor of English Language and Literature at Eastern Michigan University. He has published articles in *CCC*, *CE*, *FEN*, and *American Literature*. Currently he is studying theories of composition and research methods in composition.

KEN AUTREY is an assistant professor of English at Francis Marion College in Florence, South Carolina. He teaches writing, writes poetry, and studies the discourse of personal journals.

ANN E. BERTHOFF is author of *The Making of Meaning*, *Forming/Thinking/Writing*, and editor of *Reclaiming the Imagination*, all Boynton/Cook publications. She is completing a collection of essays on I. A. Richards and an anthology of his writings.

JOHN BRERETON is a professor at the University of Massachusetts at Boston where he teaches rhetoric and composition and directs the professional writing program.

DOROTHY C. BROADDUS has been an assistant professor in English and Director of the Learning Resources Center at St. Meinrad College in St. Meinrad, Indiana. She now teaches at Arizona State West in Phoenix.

JOSEPH J. COMPRONE directed the Ph.D. program in Rhetoric and Composition at the University of Louisville from 1976–1989. He is now Head of the Department of Humanities at Michigan Technological University.

KATHRYN T. FLANNERY is an assistant professor of English at Indiana University, where she is working with a new Ph.D. program in Language, Literature, and Literacy. A former special education and public school teacher, her research interests center questions of composition and literacy under larger questions about culture and the sociopolitical connections between literature and literacy.

WANDA MARTIN is an assistant professor of English at the University of New Mexico. She studies political rhetoric and the role of politics in teaching.

JOY RITCHIE is an assistant professor of English at the University of Nebraska-Lincoln. She has taught grades K-35 and now co-directs the Nebraska Writing Project.

KATE RONALD is an assistant professor of English at the University of Nebraska-Lincoln, where she is co-coordinator of composition. She works with teachers in the public schools and writes about connections between classical and modern rhetoric, public and private aims of discourse.

HEPHZIBAH ROSKELLY is an assistant professor of English at the University of North Carolina-Greensboro. She has taught high school and now works with teacher preparation and connections between literature and composition.

JAMES THOMAS ZEBROSKI is a professor at Syracuse University, where he teaches composition in the Writing Program and works with graduate students and other teachers of composition.